THEORIES OF VALUE AND DISTRIBUTION
SINCE ADAM SMITH

THEORIES OF VALUE AND DISTRIBUTION SINCE ADAM SMITH

IDEOLOGY AND ECONOMIC THEORY

BY

MAURICE DOBB

CAMBRIDGE
AT THE UNIVERSITY PRESS
1973

Published by the Syndics of the Cambridge University Press
Bentley House, 200 Euston Road, London NW1 2DB
American Branch: 32 East 57th Street, New York, N.Y.10022

© Cambridge University Press 1973

Library of Congress Catalogue Card Number: 72-88619

ISBN: 0 521 20100 4

Printed in Great Britain
at the University Printing House, Cambridge
(Brooke Crutchley, University Printer)

CONTENTS

NOTE OF ACKNOWLEDGEMENT

It should be obvious to all readers, especially of Chapter 3 below, how much is owed by the author to the illumination shed by Mr Piero Sraffa's interpretation of Ricardo, in his superb edition of *The Works and Correspondence of David Ricardo*, of twenty-odd years ago – not to mention Mr Sraffa's later work that is summarised (no doubt inadequately) in Chapter 9. For reading and critically commenting upon some aspects of Chapter 1 the author is further indebted to Mr Maurice Cornforth and to Mrs Krishna Bharadwaj, and for this as well as helpfully scrutinising certain sections towards the end of the book to Dr D. M. Nuti; also to Mr John Eatwell for introducing me to some yet unpublished ideas about general equilibrium theory. The usual disclaimer should be added absolving all these from any responsibility for errors and opinions expressed herein.

April 1972   M.D.

INTRODUCTORY: ON IDEOLOGY

I

Around the question of the so-called 'ideological' element in economic theory (as of social theory in general) there has been in recent times increasing debate. In entering this debate at this stage it would be tedious to start by embarking on a genealogy and a quest for unique and precise definition of the term. On this let it suffice for the moment to say that, while the concept bears a close relationship to the Hegelian 'false consciousness' that serves to obstruct man's vision of himself and of his conditions of existence, it is not to be taken as synonymous therewith, still less as referring exclusively to the delusive element in thought (as some have indeed used it). Its central reference, undoubtedly, is to the historically-relative character of ideas, whether this be regarded as no more than an element or aspect of them or as characterising them in their entirety. But such historical relativity may embrace both insight and partiality,* and this perhaps from the very nature of the situation, in a way that defies any complete analytical separation. It will be this reference, at any rate, that we shall have principally in mind in what follows. Perhaps it is unnecessary to add, further, that when the word, 'ideology', is used, this must necessarily refer to a whole *system* of thought, or coordinated set of beliefs and ideas, which form a framework, or higher-level group of related concepts, for more specific and particular notions, analyses, applications and conclusions. As such it will generally be related to certain activities and policies, but not necessarily in any simple and obvious or direct manner; and to

---

* *Cf.* Oskar Lange, *Political Economy*, Eng. ed. (Warsaw and London, 1963) Vol. 1, pp. 327–30. In a 'Note on ideology and tendencies in economic research', *International Social Sciences Journal* (UNESCO), Vol. xvi, No. 4, 1964, p. 525, Oskar Lange wrote: "Ideological influences do not always lead to the apologetic degeneration of social science. Under certain conditions they may be a stimulus of true objective research."

those who conduct discussion at the higher (or more general) level the relation may not always be fully conscious, still less explicit. At its most general an ideology constitutes or implies a philosophical standpoint, in our present context a social philosophy, provided that this is not given too formal or methodological a connotation.

In the field of political economy or economic theory, the rôle of ideology (and by implication its definition) has been treated in various ways. First, it has been contrasted with the scientific core of the subject, by implication being regarded as the inter-mixture or accretion of ethical postulates and so-called 'value judgements'. Thus it is an alien element in what should be designed as an objective and 'positive' enquiry, which although inevitably encroaching upon most people's thinking about practical affairs, deserves to be purged by more rigorous analysis and precise definition. Thus the proposition that on a competitive market factors of production are priced according to their marginal or incremental productivity is sometimes contrasted with the statement that people *ought* to be rewarded according to their contributions to production, and the latter abjured as an unscientific intrusion; or again theories about how income-distribution is in fact determined are contrasted with postulates about what income-distribution ideally should be. Sometimes, while this contrast between an ideological and scientific element in a theory or doctrine is preserved, the boundaries of the former are more widely drawn to include other classes of statement than purely ethical ones: we find them, for example, called 'metaphysical' statements,* which

---

* Thus Professor Joan Robinson has answered the question, "what are the criteria of an ethical proposition as opposed to a scientific one?" by saying: "if an ideo-logical proposition is treated in a logical manner, it either dissolves into a completely meaningless noise or turns out to be a circular argument". These she seems virtually to identify with "metaphysical" propositions, which are admittedly "not without content" and although "they do not belong to the realm of science yet they are necessary to it" and, in social sciences at least, have "played an important, perhaps an indispensable, role". "Whether or not ideology can be eliminated from the world of thought in the social sciences, it is certainly indispensable in the world of action in social life." The classical notion of 'value' is here classed as "one of the great metaphysical ideas in economics" (Joan Robinson, *Economic Philosophy* (London, 1964) pp. 7–9, 29 *seq.*). *Cf.* also the

have no proper place in a scientific theory since they are incapable of being tested or disproved; nevertheless they perform a function in persuading people to adopt certain attitudes and to undertake certain activities.

Joseph Schumpeter, who among modern economists has made what is, perhaps, the fullest and most serious contribution to the discussion, has adopted a rather different – one could perhaps say less *simpliste* – attitude to this question.* What he has justly singled out and aptly called 'vision' – vision, *i.e.* of the complex shape of reality and of the nature of the problems confronting mankind in any given historical situation – is inevitably ideological. Thus ideology "enters on the very ground floor, into the pre-analytical cognitive act" and with the necessary start of theory "with material provided by our vision of things"; "this vision [being] ideological almost by definition", since "it embodies the picture of things as we see them".† The reason adduced for this seems to be less the historically-conditioned perspective of the observer, inevitably limited as this must be by time and place and position in society, than emotional commitment prompting men to draw pleasing pictures of themselves and of their kind – the fact that "the way in which we see things can hardly be distinguished from the way in which we wish to see them" (although it is added that "the more honest and naive our vision is, the more dangerous is it to the eventual emergence of anything for which general validity can be claimed"). Hence he concludes that, while "Political Economy" and "Economic Thought" generally‡ must almost

dismissal of the whole classical (especially Ricardian) notion of 'real value' as being "metaphysical" in Gunnar Myrdal, *The Political Element in the Development of Economic Theory*, trans. P. Streeten (London, 1953) pp. 62–5. For comment on this, see, on the other hand, R. L. Meek, *Economics and Ideology and other Essays* (London, 1967) pp. 210–15.

* Schumpeter incidentally starts by denying that ideology is to be equated with 'value judgements': "an economist's value judgements often *reveal* his ideology but they *are not* his ideology" (*History of Economic Analysis* (New York and London, 1954) p. 37).

† *Ibid.*, pp. 41–2.

‡ Political Economy is defined as "certain unifying (normative) principles such as the principles of economic liberalism, of socialism, and so on", leading to the advocacy of "a comprehensive set of economic policies"; Economic Thought as

inevitably be ideologically conditioned, "economic analysis" proper can be treated as independent and objective – a hard core of formal techniques and instruments that are governed by supra-historical standards and rules to be discussed and assessed independently, and about which a separate history can be composed to answer unambiguously such questions as whether and "in what sense there has been 'scientific progress' between Mill and Samuelson".*

This Schumpeterian view, qualified and hedged about with numerous reservations as it is, is clearly connected with the more crude and forthright 'box of tools' view of economic analysis as being (in its modern form at least) purely instrumental, concerned with techniques capable of application to a wide variety of purposes and situations. As such it has no interest in normative judgements; and it is unconcerned with the specific purposes to which it is put – whether to clarify the problems of a profit-making monopoly or those of the planners of a socialist economy. This conception of the pure economist's rôle has, naturally, been furthered by the vogue of mathematical methods and forms of statements in economics, to the point even of purifying the subject of notions, elements or relations incapable of being quantified and expressed in an equational system.

Of this attempt to separate economic technique from its product it is, surely, appropriate to say simply this. *Either* the 'analysis' of which Schumpeter speaks is a purely formal structure without any relation to economic problems or sets of questions to which it is being designed as an answer (or aid to answering) – in which case it does not constitute a set of propositions or statements with any economic content – *or* else it is a logical system designed as the vehicle of certain statements *about* economic phenomena or activities. If it is, indeed, the former it cannot be identified with the history of economic

"the sum total of all the opinions and desires concerning economic subjects, especially concerning public policy . . . that, at any given time and place, float in the public mind" (*ibid.*, p. 38).

* *Ibid.*, pp. 38–9. In a like vein Professor J. J. Spengler has confidently stated that "whatever be the effects of ideology, they tend to diminish in importance as economics matures and achieves scientific autonomy" (in R. V. Eagley (ed.) *Events, Ideology and Economic Theory* (Detroit, 1968) p. 175).

theories such as those we review below; since these theories, as we shall see, are very much concerned with economic state- ment, if at a fairly general level. If it is the latter of our stated alternatives, it surely can*not* be separated from the answers to questions that it frames, and hence from the actual (or supposed) shape of the economic *problems* with which it is designed to deal – and this however 'rarified' or abstract the structure of statement happens to be. In this case it is impossible to claim for it 'independence' of the economic content and meaning of the propositions which *are* (on Schumpeter's own admission) ideologically conditioned, and hence impossible to regard it as supra-ideological. Theoretical analysis and generalisation invariably build upon classification, in the sense of using what has first been classified as its material units or counters; and what is classification but a drawing of boundaries between discrete objects, which are in turn derived from the structural pattern one senses (or deems to have discovered) in the real world? Schumpeter himself makes this clear in his very defini- tion of 'Vision' – "the thing that comes first . . .in every scientific venture": as he emphasises, "before embarking upon analytic work of any kind we must first single out the set of phenomena we wish to investigate, and acquire 'intuitively' a preliminary notion of how they hang together or, in other words, of what appear from our standpoint to be their fundamental properties".*

To say this is not to deny that a separate study could be made of economic theory in its analytical aspect alone and even a history be written of this aspect *per se*, viewed as the perfecting of a technical apparatus (as one could write the history of any other technique).† But what is dubious is whether if this were

---

* Schumpeter, *History of Economic Analysis*, pp. 561-2.
† Presumably this would be concerned with such questions as to the time and occasion when the differential calculus was first employed as a vehicle of economic statement, with discussion perhaps of its appropriateness for certain uses and its inappropriateness for others; and similarly with the use of 'difference equations' as distinct from differential, or of matrix algebra; perhaps also the concept of elasticity and the geometry of certain types of curve and the types of theory to which they are relevant. But it has to be remembered that implicit in techniques may be certain axioms which conceal a certain philosophical approach (*cf*. the footnote on page 7).

done one could regard it as a study of some separable and definable section of the subject itself: *i.e.* as a set of propositions or statements which the analytical apparatus has been designed to carry. This would seem to be an altogether different matter. Admittedly it may be hard to divide one's talk about the analysis as an instrument, and one's assessment of its rôle, from the particular use to which this analysis is put. But there surely *is* a difference, and a crucial one, between discussion of the syntax of sentences and of the content of particular statements that are cast in any given syntactic form. What is highly questionable is whether in economics, or in any branch of social science, if one pays attention to the economic *content* of a theory as distinct from its analytical framework, any part of the theory can preserve the independence and neutrality claimed (and with some reason) for the formal analysis itself.* Such content must consist of some kind of statement about the shape and functioning of actual economic processes, however particularised or however generalised the statement claims to be. This must, surely, be the case unless reference is being made to some entirely imaginary land of Cathay. Here the simile of a picture or map seems applicable, and no longer that of a tool or instrument. Into its formation Schumpeter's 'vision' must essentially enter; the statement which theory enshrines, *qua* 'picture' or 'map', being entirely dependent upon and relative to such 'vision',† and the latter, as Schumpeter himself so wisely

---

* There is, however, the view that has been expressed, *e.g.* by Professor F. A. Hayek, that the propositions of economic theory have a universal and necessary character akin to that of "synthetic *a priori* propositions"; the objects that form the subject matter of social sciences being "not physical facts" but wholes "constituted" from "familiar categories of our own minds". Since economic principles or laws are not empirical rules, then they presumably have, according to this view, both independence and neutrality, alike in content and in form. *Cf.* citation and comment on this view in the present writer's *Studies in the Development of Capitalism* (London, 1946) p. 27, n. 2. Perhaps it was something like this which Marshall had in mind when he spoke (in connection with the theoretical basis of Free Trade) of "economic truths as certain as those of geometry" (*Official Papers* by Alfred Marshall (London, 1926) p. 388).

† One would suppose, indeed, that this was the implication of Schumpeter's statement that we have quoted, to the effect that ideology "enters on the very ground floor, into the preanalytic cognitive act", to which is added: "Analytic work begins with material provided by our vision of things, and this vision is ideologic almost by definition" (*History of Economic Analysis*, p. 42).

stresses, being always relative to a particular time and social place in the process of history. No examination of economic theory, still less historical examination of *systems* of theories, seems to be justified in denying or ignoring this relativity. A mathematical 'model' can be (and should be, *inter alia*) examined in its purely formal aspect, as a consistent structure. At the same time, *qua* economic theory, its very structure is relevant to the statement it is making about reality – to its diagnostic quality. In choosing one structure in preference to another, the model-builder is not only providing a scaffolding or framework within which human thought can operate, but is laying emphasis upon certain factors and relationships and excluding others or casting them into the shadows;* and in doing so he can be judged to be distorting or illuminating reality, and thus affording an unsound or a sound basis for interpretation and prediction – more likely perhaps he is illuminating some corners or facet of reality, or certain situations that recur, at the same time as he is obscuring, or totally concealing, others. This is not to say, of course, that any such distortion or partiality is part of the conscious intention of the model-builder, who may indeed have chosen its shape for purely formal reasons, because he regarded it as intellectually ingenious or aesthetically pleasing. But in the degree that he is influenced by its economic implications – in the degree, that is, to which he is trying to be an economist – its shape and projection will be influenced by his vision of the economic process, and by whatever socio-historical conditions shape and limit his mental picture of social reality.

If, however, some economic statements, at any rate those at the most general level, are capable of expression in purely mathematical form, it might seem as though the 'picture' of economic reality they embody must be of too abstract a character to be affected by 'ideological' influences in any marked degree and even less to carry in themselves any particular bias or partiality. Hence the content of the statement as

* Even the choice of technique may not be without material implication (*e.g.* continuity).

well as its form could here be qualified as 'ideologically neutral' and 'supra-historical', in sufficiently high degree at least for any historically-relative element in its make-up not to matter and to be justifiably ignored. It has often been said that a system of simultaneous equations carries *per se* no causal implication. All that such a system does is to provide a description of a situation as a set of interrelations: a situation composed of a cluster of internally related elements and treated as being isolated, comparatively speaking, from what lies outside it, at least to the extent of not interacting with the latter. But it does no more than this.

As such, however, a description of this kind does not amount to an *explanation*, in the sense of depicting the situation as an economic process that works in a certain way and is capable of being acted upon and influenced.* For this purpose the equational system must be made to tell us something *more*; and this 'something more' almost inevitably has a causal form, whether as complex mutual interaction of a set of variables or as the simpler type of uni-directional causal linkage.† This is quite commonly done, in fact, even with what lay claim to be purely formal systems depicting a *catena* of interrelations and no more; an *order* of determination being implied as soon as some of the variables are treated as exogenously determined from outside

---

* In this context let us not forget the statement of Wittgenstein: "In life ... we use mathematical propositions *only* in order to infer from propositions which do not belong to mathematics to others which equally do not belong to mathematics" (*Tractatus logico-philosophicus* (London, 1922) p. 169).

† It has been stated that "the formulation of causal relations in terms of functional interdependence is precisely the aim of the more advanced sciences which have got beyond the imprecise concepts of cause and effect" (T. W. Hutchison, *The Significance and Basic Postulates of Economic Theory* (London, 1938) p. 71). On the other hand, Mario Bunge has said that "the disclosure of interactions need not always *exhaust* the problems of determination unless an extreme symmetry is at stake", and that, for example, "the usual interpretation of quantum mechanics does not sweep out causes and effects, but rather the rigid causal nexus among them" (so-called "quantum indeterminacy" being "a consequence of the idealistic hypothesis inherent in modern positivism"). It is added that "a causal interpretation of a mathematical form ... does not belong to the mathematical symbols but to the system of relations linking the signs with the physical, chemical, biological ... entities in question. Sometimes such an interpretation is not made explicitly but is taken for granted" (Mario Bunge, *Causality* (Cambridge, Mass., 1959) pp. 14, 76–7, 164).

the system, or else treated as constants, and hence specified as *data* (implicitly or explicitly) and the others as being dependent on the internal relations of the system or as the 'unknowns' awaiting a solution.* This is certainly true of the Walrasian system of general equilibrium, despite assertions (or at least implications) sometimes made to the contrary. Walras himself, as we shall later see, did not refrain from speaking of "forces [which] are the primary cause and conditions of the variation of prices" or of the prices of the productive services of factors as being "determined in the market for products".† In the case of those dynamic 'models' that have played so large a rôle in modern theories of growth, the system of interrelation-

---

* *Cf.* F. Zeuthen, *Economic Theory and Method* (London, 1955) p. 23: "If we have a special economic science, it is because there exists a particularly intensive connection within the circle of phenomena which are generally termed economic, so that in a great part of the work of investigation these can with advantage be considered as mutually interdependent variables, whereas a series of other phenomena . . . are to a lesser extent influenced by the economic phenomena and therefore with a very good approximation may be taken as data." *Cf.* also Professor Gautam Mathur who has been rightly concerned to emphasise the incorrectness of asserting "that in an equilibrium system there are no causal relations, because such a situation is described by a set of simultaneous equations." This is an incorrect interpretation because "every equation depicting an economic relation has got one or two direction signs, which we neglect in print, but which must not be lost sight of when we analyse the solution of simultaneous equations" (*Planning for Steady Growth* (Oxford, 1965) p. 70).

† L. Walras, *Elements of Pure Economics*, ed. W. Jaffé (London, 1954) pp. 146–8, 422. R. Bentzel and B. Hansen ('On Recursiveness and Interdependency in Economic Models', *Review of Economic Studies*, Vol. XXII, 1954–5, pp. 153 *seq.*) have argued that the apparent "interdependency" (merely) of a Walrasian system "only arises because the system is a static equilibrium system" and "a static equilibrium system only expresses the *conditions* for an unspecified dynamic system to be in equilibrium, *i.e.* to repeat itself". Such a system "is a derived model . . . Static equilibrium assumptions can at most be *special* hypotheses and can never be accepted as a general argument for interdependency" (pp. 160–1). *Cf.* also J. L. Simon, 'The Concept of Causality in Economics', *Kyklos*, Vol. XXIII, 1970, *Fasc.* 2, pp. 226–44, who says incidentally that "in economics, a statement that is deduced from, compatible with, and logically connected into the general framework of systematic economics, is much more likely to be considered causal than is a statement that stands alone without logical connections to the body of economic theory. This is because the theoretical connection provides support for belief that the side conditions necessary for the statement to hold true are not restrictive ones and that the likelihood of 'spurious correlations' is not great" (p. 241). Analogously P. W. Bridgeman in *The Logic of Modern Physics* (New York, 1928) speaks of "the causality concept" as being "a relative one, in that it involves the whole system in which the events take place" and as applying "to sub-groups of events separated out from the aggregate of all events" (pp. 83, 91).

ships is so interpreted as to depict the interaction between variables as of a particular kind and having a certain direction; this being of considerable significance for the stability or instability of the equilibrium to which the system tends. The particular interpretation that gives the theory its essential character and its practical implications comes from introducing additional hypotheses (sometimes by imputing particular values to particular variables) that were no part of the schema in its pure form. Moreover, the mere definition of what is the proper sphere of relevant interrelations (and hence the boundaries of a theoretical system) can be crucial, as we shall see: crucial in distinguishing different ways of locating the determining influences.

Associated with the notion of economic theory as a purely formal structure, *qua* theory of general equilibrium, is that of the 'reconciling' rôle of such generalised economic analysis with respect to rival and opposed (and less general) theories that formerly agitated rival schools. This is a view of which a good deal has been heard recently, at least in certain circles, and is evidently germane to any critical examination of the history of economic thought. One example of it is the attempts made soon after the appearance of Keynes's *General Theory* to display the different emphasis and conclusions of Keynesian and pre-Keynesian doctrine as depending upon different values or 'shapes' implicitly assumed for certain parameters or generalised functional relationships (and in some cases implicit assumptions of independence). Thus the General Theory of the *General Theory* should represent the contending doctrines as special cases of the more comprehensive, and 'true', form of statement. What 'reconciliation', however, seems to have amounted to in this case was little more than the statement that one kind of mechanism characterised one type of situation and another kind of mechanism was appropriate to a different situation (*e.g.* where some special 'boost' factor sufficed to maintain full employment and/or full-capacity working). Perhaps a more pertinent example is the suggestion that has recently been heard (following renewed interest in the classical approach) to the effect that there is no real opposition between what had traditionally been rival theories of value of Ricardo and Marx, on the one hand, and of Jevons and the Austrian school, on the other: in any equational system of general equilibrium (*e.g.* of Walrasian type) both quantities of labour expenditures and consumers' substitution-ratios (or marginal utilities) will need to be included, and with appropriate interpretation emphasis can be thrown upon the determinative influence of either the one or the other.* Increasing formalisation of the subject is thus identified with increasing neutralisation, so far as the intrusion of ideological influence is concerned, and is accordingly held to exemplify the scientific progress in the subject that Schumpeter sought to find in historical examination of the march of economic analysis *per se*. If this progress in analytical techniques involved some restriction on the boundaries of the subject as compared with those more generously drawn by the classical pioneers, this was something to be applauded and not deplored: at most it was to be regarded as a cost well compensated for by the resulting gain in scientific rigour.

All that can be shortly said, I think, about such an allegedly 'neutral' corpus is that when carefully formulated and analysed it will be found to be extremely thin in factual content: *i.e.* its apparent neutrality is because it contains very little in the way of factual statement about economic situations or processes and their behaviour – so little, perhaps, as to evoke serious doubt as to whether it is entitled to rank as an economic theory at all in the sense of a theory that *explains* social action and behaviour.

---

* *Cf.* the statement of Leif Johansen, 'Marxism and Mathematical Economics' in *Monthly Review* (New York) January 1963, p. 508: "For goods which can be reproduced on any scale . . . it is very easy to demonstrate that a complete model still leaves prices determined by the labour theory of value even if one accepts a marginal utility theory of consumers' behaviour"; and his elaboration of this point in a paper, 'Some Observations on Labour Theory of Value and Marginal Utilities', *Economics of Planning*, Vol. 3, No. 2, September 1963, pp. 89 *seq.* (where the passage from the *Monthly Review* is cited). The implication here is that *both* quantities of labour *and* marginal utilities enter into the equations defining equilibrium. But it is to be noted that Professor Johansen emphasises the distinction that, while prices are related to labour-expenditures (being proportional thereto when compositions of capital are equal), "the marginal utility functions interact with the prices . . . only in determining the *quantities* to be produced and consumed of the different commodities".

To qualify as the latter it must be so framed as to show how certain results or events are *determined*; and a system of equilibrium defined in terms of a set of equivalences or identities may well amount to no more than a series of tautologies.*

To question the status of an apparently 'neutral' corpus of theory of this type is not equivalent to denying the existence of certain high-level generalisations that apply to a variety of economic situations, including even situations pertaining to different institutional systems. Marxist writers, for example, have always granted that there are general statements, even 'laws', that apply to all modes of production or socio-economic systems, or at any rate to all systems embodying a common characteristic such as commodity-production for sale in a market, and hence some form of division of labour and exchange.† Again, to take an example from modern 'growth models' (*e.g.* the von Neumann model), there are certain interrelationships between quantities in economic growth that will apply to any economic system, given only a minimum of common assumptions as to prices and price-flexibility, technical possibilities and supply-elasticities. But it does not follow at all that these consist merely of analytical statements about an (undefined) equilibrium of interrelated variables: if so, as we have seen, their significance for practice would be distinctly trivial, and even as a framework for more concrete statement they could probably be ignored without much loss of illumination. Restriction of this kind certainly does not apply to the type of general statement to which we have been referring, about exchange-

---

* As, for example, Dr L. Pasinetti has shown profit-theories of the Irving Fisher type (in terms of 'a rate of return on capital') to be (in *Economic Journal*, Vol. XXIX, No. 315, September 1969, pp. 508 *seq.*, and especially pp. 511, 525, 529).

† Oskar Lange, for example, in his *Political Economy*, Vol. I (Warsaw, 1963), after distinguishing "technical and balance laws of production" from "laws of human behaviour" and "laws of interplay of human actions", and emphasising that the first of these have "the widest application in history", speaks of "common economic laws" applying to "different social formations" in addition to "specific economic laws of a given social formation" (*ibid.*, pp. 58–68); citing in this connection Engels's postscript to Vol. III of *Das Kapital*, where it is stated that, since "commodity exchange appears in the period before written history", "the law of value reigned supreme for a period of time lasting from five to seven thousand years". Also *cf.* Marx's letter to Kugelmann of 11 July 1868.

situations or structural relations in growth, which do not refrain from speaking in causal terms about factors affecting equilibrium price-ratios or conditioning influences upon the process of growth.

It should be emphasised once again, perhaps, to avoid any possibility of misunderstanding, that there can be no question of denying a place in economic theory to statements of complex mutual or reciprocal interdependence, in addition to the more familiar statements of simple and direct causation of the type of "if A, then B follows" or "A is a necessary and sufficient condition for the occurrence of B". The point is (as we have stressed already) that these, in so far as they define the nature of the interdependence, speak about the shape and pattern of actual situations and processes, thus depending, in some degree at least, upon 'vision' of the latter and are by no means purely formal or *a priori*. Curiously enough, what we have said applies to much of the pure analysis lying at the base of 'optimising' theory (with its affiliations with normative economics, as we shall see in a moment) as well as to statements of general equilibrium of the Walrasian type.

For example, take any statement that certain variables are interrelated, such as the simple statement that the level of present output, the growth-rate of output and the quantity of labour-inputs in the system are interdependent. It is true that this statement implies no *direction* of dependence, which is entirely reciprocal. But as soon as the assumption is introduced (*e.g.* by postulation or knowledge of what the general situation or 'setting' of the problem is like) that any two of the quantities in our example are to be taken as *given*, in the sense of being treated as independent (or exogenously determined) variables, it will follow of course that the other is *ipso facto* determined (*i.e.* it becomes the dependent variable). Thus, if the labour force is taken as a given factor at any one date, as a feature of the demographic situation (together with the policy-imperative of its being fully employed), then for any given level of present final output there will be a certain rate of growth that is the maximum possible; so that if in addition a certain level of present output is taken as necessary (as an historical *datum* or because of the need for a certain minimum level of real wages or consumption), then the maximum feasible growth-rate is determined as resultant. If, adding a fourth variable to the situation in the shape of a choice between alternative methods of production (or techniques), a given growth-rate is postulated as the (feasible) policy-objective of a planned economy, then it follows that there is a certain optimum choice of methods of production in the sense of one that will maximise the level of output (and hence of consumption) consistently with maintaining the intended objective (or alternatively maximise the growth-rate that is possible with any given level of present consumption). Thus a transition from a mere statement of mutual dependence to an optimising theorem requires, on the one hand, the postulation of some normative objective (the 'objective function') and, on the other hand, of some constraint (or constraints) as an accepted feature of actual situations, such as given economic resources available to production (since without a limit on the latter there would be no point in economising on their use, and hence no economic problem to be solved).

The essential point here is that this transition is made (or is started at least) as soon as one fills in the picture with any additional features of an actual situation. By doing so certain direction-pointers in the dependence are immediately implied. What is more, this 'filling in of the picture' may be done almost unconsciously, and hence be inexplicit because the human mind is apt to think of situations in wholes, even when it has the intention of abstracting certain features only from them and treating these in isolation. Then it is that the differences in depiction of a total situation dependent on differences of 'vision' and perspective can become crucial.

We have been speaking of economic theory as describing the structure and functioning of an exchange society, stressing particularly as it does the manner of interdependence of difference prices and markets. This, needless to say, is an essential basis for policy, in telling it what it can and cannot do, and by what instruments it may pursue this or that objective. But theories of equilibrium *per se* afford little guidance as to *what* objective policy should pursue among the range of possible alternatives; and alternatives evidently exist despite the determinism implied by economists' postulation of 'economic laws'. This concern with policy-ends, and the means available to further them, represents the *normative* tradition in economics, which positivists have tended to eschew as an alien element and an intrusion into economic theory *qua* scientific discipline, concerned (it is said) with positive statement about what *is* and not with what *ought* to be. Nonetheless it has commanded increasing respect and attention in recent decades, no doubt in response to the growing pressure of problems concerned with consciously devised State intervention in the economic sphere, and to-day increasingly with economic planning of the economy as a whole. Indeed in the actual development of theory, the 'positive' and the 'normative' elements have proved hard to separate and have increasingly tended to fuse. Progress in this direction has, moreover, been registered in the sphere of highly formalised techniques of analysis.* This has taken the form of using the methods of handling so-called 'extremal problems' to prescribe the conditions for maximising whatever economic quantity is taken as 'the objective function'. Towards choice of the latter the maximising technique *per se* is, of course, neutral; but its economic interpretation and empirical implications will be crucially affected thereby. Here, in the choice and use of maximand, there is clearly abundant room for those ideological influences of which we have spoken to enter, and to do so decisively.

* An Hungarian writer, referring to the von Neumann model ("not an optimisation model but one of equilibrium") and the Leontief model (which "again is of a descriptive-causal structure"), states that "as a matter of fact, the individual members of this group of models may – independently of their original structure – be equally interpreted as descriptive-causal equilibrium or teleological optimisation models. Between these aspects there is no contradiction whatever." In linear programming the connection is explicit in "the interrelation between the program of optimum activity and the shadow prices belonging to it", as the primal and dual solutions of the problem (A. Bródy, 'The Dual Concept of the Economy in Marx's Capital', *Acta Oeconomica* (Budapest) *Tom* 2, *Fasc.* 4, 1967, p. 311).

II

In the actual history of economic thought as a whole, there is plenty of evidence of the historical conditioning of economic theory, treated as a more or less integrated system at any one time, as we shall try to show in the sequel. Since it is essentially an applied science, closely related to judgements and assessments of actual systems and policies, this is scarcely surprising: it might be more surprising, indeed, if no trace of such social conditioning were to be found. This is, moreover, true even of economic thought at its most abstract, and of the most formalised systems, which on examination turn out to speak with surprising directness about economic reality, and have exerted considerable influence (if at one remove) upon actual policy. This raises the question as to how and why this should be so: as to the manner and modes of this social and historical conditioning of abstract thought.

One would not wish to deny that the kind of subjective factor to which Schumpeter alludes (emotional feelings, wishes, beliefs) is part of the explanation, and that, since economists are subject to the usual weaknesses of the flesh and of the human spirit, it is to be found in many if not most cases as an important ingredient colouring the vision of particular thinkers. What can, I think, be denied is that this is the only or the principal mode of conditioning. One could, indeed, speak of it as the least interesting way in which social relations condition thought. More fundamental, yet perhaps harder to identify in particular cases, is the extent to which thinking is shaped by the *problems* that are thrown up from a particular social context.* This context is itself a complex mixture and interaction of accepted ideas and systems of thought (which more probably than not consist

* *Cf.* Gunnar Myrdal: "Rarely, if ever, has the development of economics by its own force blazed the way to new perspectives. The cue to the continual reorientation of our work has normally come from the sphere of politics." (*Asian Drama* (London, 1968) Vol. I, p. 9.) "Social scientists are in an unusual position in that the objectives of their studies and their own activities are within the same context. For these studies are themselves socially conditioned activities ... [Economists] have continually tried to lift their investigation out of the social context into a supposedly 'objective' realm ... This attempt makes economists naively innocent of their own social determinants" (*ibid.*, Vol. III, App. 3, p. 1941).

partly of metaphysical elements and untested hypotheses and largely exert an innately conservative bias) and the problems presented by current events and practical situations. Thus do accepted generalisation and current practice continually confront one another. But in this confrontation it would be wrong to conceive of something termed 'practice', independently and animistically conceived, as formulating problems for thought to contemplate as passive observer. There is always a subjective element in the march of knowledge, not only in the sense that action and experiment play a crucial rôle, but that these are preceded and shaped by the formation of concepts. Current problems are something created as much by thought-inspired human action *upon* an existent situation as by the given objective (but changing) situation itself; and in this sense can be said to represent continually, in varying degree, a contradiction between the two. Problems arising in this way then form the starting-point of new thinking, the formation of new concepts and of new theories; and to this extent the latter are always relative to a particular historical context. These changing concepts and ideas represent in part a commentary upon or interpretation of – a 'reflection' if one cares to use so passive a simile – the objective situation from the particular perspective in which it is seen. But since inherited ideas and concepts, operating as a refracting medium, affect this perspective and the resulting vision of the situation, new ideas are always at the same time a critique of old ideas which form the heritage of thinking; hence these new ideas are necessarily shaped in part by the antithetical relation in which they stand to the old as well as being empirical statements about actuality. It is for this reason that debate as to whether ideas have a genealogy of their own or on the contrary always 'reflect' current objective reality is apt to be so unsatisfactory and frustrating. What is here commonly neglected, however, is that in so far as ideas are being confronted with problems, and problems are formulated (whether implicitly or explicitly, and if not directly at least indirectly) with reference to potential *activity*, the process of critique and development can hardly fail to be influenced by the social *milieu* (or reference-point within the complex of social relations) of the individual or 'school' by whom the formulation is made. Social or economic action, at least, can only be conceived with some subject, whether institution, person, social group, class or organisation, in mind; and for problems to have an operational interpretation, it would seem that they must have some implied reference of this kind.

This inherited framework within which (or in reaction against which) real problems are formulated, and against the background of which, if not literally in terms of it, theoretical debate occurs, necessarily includes presumptions and general statements which are a mixture of the analytical and the synthetic. These, forming a "conceptual web" (as it has been called) or set of conceptual categories or "boxes" in terms of which our thinking operates,* are crucial both to the way in which problems are framed and to the methods and instruments devised for yielding answers to them. In the formation of general notions of this kind it is scarcely possible for reasoning by analogy to be altogether excluded. It is, indeed, hard to see how anything that claims to be a general picture of society, and hence to be relevant to society treated as a whole and to changing its entire framework (as distinct from depicting particular bits and pieces or facets of it), can fail to include propositions, explicitly or implicitly, that go beyond what Professor Popper might admit as 'synthetic' and 'scientific'. These represent a view (necessarily an imperfect one, but not necessarily lacking in some true insight) of what society as a whole is like and how it functions, into the formation of which subjective or *a priori* elements of all kinds must inevitably enter. These elements are

---

* *Cf.* T. S. Kuhn, *The Structure of Scientific Revolutions* (*International Encyclopaedia of Unified Science* (Chicago) Vol. II, No. 2, 1962), pp. 5, 148. This author has used the term "paradigm" for such a group or cluster of general notions, or "ways of seeing the world"; and in reference to the natural sciences speaks of its acquisition as being, indeed, "a sign of maturity in the development of any given scientific field" (*ibid.*, p. 11). These paradigms "gain their status because they are more successful than their competitors in solving a few problems that the group of practitioners have come to recognise as acute"; at the same time "normal-scientific research is directed to the articulation of those phenomena and theories that the paradigm already supplies" (*ibid.*, pp. 23–4). *Cf.* also the same author's *The Copernican Revolution* (Harvard, 1957) especially pp. 3–4, 261–3.

not timeless; nor can they be simply judged by any absolute standards. But this does not mean that they cannot be rationally debated and that there are no criteria by which they can be criticised and assessed, at least in terms of more realistic and less. They have to be judged as approximations (only); and there may be good reason for holding one approximation to be closer than another at the same time as holding that there is a socio-historical explanation for the appearance of a particular approximation at a particular time (in which sense the latter is 'historically relative').*

In speaking of such conceptual frameworks two things need, perhaps, to be emphasised, even though the whole subject be admittedly controversial. Far from being superfluous, *some* general framework of this kind, it would seem, can scarcely be dispensed with by the most thorough-going empiricist, and less so, at any rate, in the social sciences than in cosmology. It is needed if only as the basis for suggesting and selecting questions for further enquiry, and hence for guiding future research and for bringing order into a mass of empirical observations that without more general concepts and hypotheses, depicting some pattern of interrelationships, would appear as uncoordinated and inexplicable. Unlike more particular statements, such a conceptual framework is not easily verified or disproved. Indeed, what would seem to be relevant here is not so much whether it is stated or not in a potentially 'testable' or 'falsifiable' form (the Popper-criterion), but rather the degree of *generality* of statement, which is what renders it remote from the actual possibility of empirical disproof.† It is the latter which

* *Cf.* more generally on this D. Bohm, *Causality and Chance in Modern Physics* (London, 1957) pp. 164–70. "We cannot actually come to know all reciprocal relationships in any finite time, however long. Nevertheless, the more we learn about them, the more we will know about what matter in the process of becoming is, since its totality is defined by nothing more than the totality of all such relationships . . . The essential character of scientific research is that it moves towards the absolute by studying the relative, in its inexhaustible multiplicity and diversity" (*ibid.*, p. 170).

† Professor Popper has himself pointed out that falsifiability is "a matter of degree", with metaphysical statements having "a zero degree of falsifiability". Even the latter "may have helped . . . to bring order into man's picture of the world, and in some cases have led to successful prediction" (Karl R. Popper, *The Logic of Scientific Discovery* (London, 1959) pp. 112, 116, 278).

renders it specially prone to the intrusion of ideological influence. Once such influences have entered they are commonly not easy to detect, let alone to combat and dislodge. Here not only logical but also psychological reasons will enhance the appeal of a general concept – or in another case contribute to its rejection: not only a sense of logical consistency but also of its 'appropriateness' in a larger sense. It has been said, indeed, that "observation is never *absolutely* incompatible with a conceptual scheme";* and rival framework-schemes (like the Ptolemaic or Copernican in cosmology) may continue to coexist for some time, each with its rival band of disciples and apologists.† In the social sciences controversy between rival general theories is apt to be notoriously inconclusive and drawn out; its conclusion, when this comes, often owing as much to change of intellectual fashion or of current assumption as to the strict logic of argument.

To speak of the more direct impact of situations on economic theory: it is fairly obvious – so obvious as to seem perhaps too simple an example – that no developed theory of money is conceivable until a money economy of some kind has come into being; just as most of the modern difficulties about monetary theory, and controversy over its proper interpretation (*e.g.* as regards the influence of money-supply upon the rest of the economy and the efficacy of certain actions by central banks), are dependent upon the modern growth of money-substitutes, credit-instruments and other means of payment. A general equilibrium 'model' of an economy is at least unlikely to be forthcoming until the growth of market relations and of economic mobility has reached the level of development that they had begun to do in mid-nineteenth century England: without

* T. S. Kuhn, *The Copernican Revolution* (Harvard, 1957) p. 75.
† *Cf. ibid.*, p. 39: "The history of science is cluttered with the relics of conceptual schemes that were once fervently believed and that have since been replaced by incompatible theories. There is no way of proving that a conceptual scheme is final. But, rash or not, this commitment to a conceptual scheme is a common phenomenon in the sciences, and it seems an indispensable one, because it endows conceptual schemes with one new and all-important function. Conceptual schemes are comprehensive; their consequences are not limited to what is already known . . . The theory will transcend the known, becoming first and foremost a powerful tool for predicting and exploring the unknown. It will affect the future of science as well as its past."

it the very notion of interdependence of all prices could hardly be seized upon by the mind.* At least some degree of development of these conditions seems necessary before the notion of a general level of wages or of profits such as we find in Adam Smith could be formulated. Similarly it required a certain level of mechanical technique in industry for the special problems associated with fixed capital to be recognised and to receive attention (and although Ricardo added a special chapter on Machinery to his third edition, this came as something of an afterthought; and his general treatment of profit was to lay him open to Marx's criticism that he failed to appreciate the rôle of what the latter called 'constant capital'). The very content of terms, most notably profit on capital, may change, and in their change reflect changing relationships and institutions.† Something similar is no doubt true more generally of the relationships and connections which thinkers hold to be relevant and significant. While the possibility of unemployment as a chronic product of 'deficiency of effective demand' had been voiced for long in "the underworld of heretics", it is a remarkable, and surely significant, fact that not until the impact of the world economic crisis of 1929–31 did this previously neglected idea stand a chance of claiming academic recognition. Until then Say's Law held almost undisputed sway over accepted economic opinion: striking evidence, surely, of how strongly prejudice, tradition and wishful thinking, embodied in an abstraction, can blind human vision even to the obvious. How much less chance of penetrating academic

---

* It could be said, perhaps, that this notion was already latent, at least, in Smith and Ricardo; but if so it did not take the form as yet of Walrasian interdependence and mutual determination, but rather of the influence of some prices upon others. Although the germ of input–output notions was present (as is now recognised) in Quesnay's *Tableau*, the notion of interdependence was here no more than embryonic and operated purely through exchange between agriculture and manufactures. Moreover, this embryonic notion, significantly enough, seems to have made little or no impact on economic thought (save through its influence on Marx) for a century or more.

† *Cf.* G. L. S. Tucker, *Progress and Profits in British Economic Thought 1650–1850* (Cambridge, 1960) p. 74: "A particular discussion may appear at first sight to persist more or less continuously over a long period of time; whereas in fact, beneath the mere verbal similarities, there may have emerged new meanings which alter the whole nature of the point in question."

orthodoxy in a bourgeois society had the Marxian notion of income on capital as fruit of exploitation, and of the profit–wage relationship as one of antagonism and not of partnership. It is almost self-evident that the question could hardly be posed at all until, with the creation of a proletariat, a free market for wage-labour on modern lines had appeared; and even then, viewed from a ruling-class perspective, what caught the attention and appeared as significant was the freedom rather than the dispossession.

Whatever one might be led to expect *a priori*, the history of political economy from its inception makes abundantly clear how closely (and even consciously) the formation of economic theory was linked with the formation and advocacy of policy. Although the doctrines of the classical school were very abstract, especially in the form given to them by Ricardo (whom Bagehot called "the true founder of abstract Political Economy"), they were related very closely to practical issues of their day, indeed surprisingly closely as we shall see. Moreover, to appreciate this connection, and to view their theories in the light of actual policy-questions for which they were seeking an answer, is often an essential key to understanding the intention and emphasis of their theories. Thus the very structure of Adam Smith's *Wealth of Nations* is shaped and moulded by his preoccupation with Mercantilist policies and their supporting theories. It is well known that Malthus propounded his *Essay on Population* as an answer to his father's optimistic (and at the time radical) Godwinian views about the possibilities of material progress and a future egalitarian society of human happiness.* Ricardo's first public appearance as an economist, formulating a theory of money and the foreign exchanges, was in the rôle of critic of the Bank of England's policy during the Bullion Controversy, and the germ of his theories of value and distribution emerged in a topical pamphlet of February 1815† directed towards the

---

* *Cf.* J. M. Keynes, *Essays in Biography* (ed. London, 1961) p. 98, quoting the authority of Bishop Otter (Malthus's friend and editor of the posthumous second edition of Malthus's *Principles*); and *cf.* Memoir of Robert Malthus in 1836 ed. of Malthus's *Principles*, pp. xxxviii–xxxix.

† *An Essay on The Influence of a low Price of Corn on the Profits of Stock; shewing the Inexpediency of Restrictions on Importation* (London, 1815); reprinted in Vol. IV of the Sraffa ed. of *Works and Correspondence of David Ricardo* (Cambridge, 1951) pp. 1–41.

debate of that same month in the House of Commons on the new Corn Law and towards establishing the theoretical case for free import of corn. John Stuart Mill expounded in his *Principles* of 1848 doctrines (with special emphasis on their "social application") which have to be seen against the background of his previous championing of 'philosophic radicalism' in the 1820s with the *Westminster Review*; and if he viewed his *System of Logic* as largely concerned to set an empirical view of knowledge against "the German 'a priori' view of human knowledge" as being "the great intellectual support of false doctrines and bad institutions",* something like this was even more true of his approach to Political Economy. Writers like Senior and Mountifort Longfield, floating on the tide of an early reaction against Ricardianism, were evidently (and Longfield quite explicitly†) preoccupied with the perverse claims of trade unions and with affording some justification for Profit in answer to incipient socialist criticism. Indeed, so far as classical Political Economy is concerned, Edwin Cannan has made the following comment: "Among all the delusions which prevail as to the history of English political economy there is none greater than the belief that the economics of the Ricardian school and period was of an almost wholly abstract and unpractical character." Of nineteenth-century economists generally he says: "With them, in the great majority of cases, practical aims were paramount ... (and) the close connection between the economics and the politics of the Ricardian period ... provides a key to many riddles."‡

But in the matter of focus upon actual problems are there not

* *Cf.* his *Autobiography* (London, 1873) p. 225.
† Longfield in the Preface to his Dublin lectures of 1833 emphasises his concern to show "how impossible it is to *regulate wages generally* either by combination of workmen or by legislative enactment", and his final lecture concludes that "the laws according to which wealth is created, distributed and consumed, have been framed by the Great Author of our being, with the same regard to our happiness which is manifested by the laws that govern the material world". (Perhaps he spoke here *qua* Judge rather than *qua* economist?)
‡ *History of the Theories of Production and Distribution in English Political Economy from 1796–1848*, 2nd ed. (London, 1903) pp. 383–4. Particularising, Cannan says (p. 391) that "for the basis of an argument against the Corn Laws, it would have been difficult to invent anything more effective than the Ricardian theory of distribution"; and that, as regards Malthus in bringing out the first edition of his *Essay on Population*, "he was inspired ... to produce acquiescence, if not

differences of degree, indeed of kind, sufficient to preclude any general label being attached to theories of any particular period defining their social *tendenz*? Some thinkers, it is clear, have greater awareness of particular contemporary problems than others, whether by reason of their contacts or experience, or because concern with policy-prescriptions suits their inclinations and their particular cast of mind. Others, again, whether less or equally well aware of the contemporary scene and its minutiae, may feel more concern for synthesis of ideas and for 'high-level generalisation' – for the formal elegance of newly-fashioned systems and theorems, with little concern for corollaries and prescriptions that can be extracted from them. As we have already suggested, such a contrast – or perhaps, rather, difference of emphasis and focus – does not necessarily depend on the degree of abstraction of the theories in question. While in one sense it is true that theorems which aim at 'high-level generalisation' must from their nature make abstraction of the multiplicity of detailed particulars, it by no means follows that those which have an intimate relation with and bearing upon practice tend necessarily to be less abstract in form. The reason may possibly be because their very feat of concentration upon certain lineaments and facets of the total scene (with a view to lending them operational relevance) may itself involve a feat of selection and abstraction from other aspects, and hence the setting of reality in a special (and in some sense and degree 'unreal') perspective. Ricardo, and perhaps also Walras, seem to illustrate this so far as economic theory is concerned. There is not much sign of the increasing formalism of economic theory in recent decades having reduced the intrusion of ideological issues into economic discussion (*e.g.* about the stability or instability of growth-models).*

contentment, with the existing order of things, and prevent the adoption of hasty experiments" like the French Revolution (p. 384). J. K. Ingram attributed the high reputation of Ricardo in his time partly at least to "a sense of the support his system gave to the manufacturers and other capitalists in their growing antagonism to the old aristocracy of landowners" (*A History of Political Economy*, 2nd ed. (London, 1907) p. 136).

* This despite what Oskar Lange termed the recent "professionalisation of economic science" (*Political Economy* (Warsaw and London, 1963) Vol. i, pp. 314–15) which he seemed to think "pushes economic thought beyond the bounds of the views and interests of the social milieu from which it arose" – at least does so to a certain extent.

In this matter of focus, and hence in the mode of selection and abstraction, there has been a fundamental difference that is so crucial to the way in which problems are viewed and interpreted as to give it cardinal importance in the classification and assessment of theories. One method of approach is to abstract from the specific characteristics of a particular system of institutions (or 'mode of production' in the Marxian style), and to concentrate attention on characteristics that are common to all, or at least several, distinct systems, and which are to this extent supra-historical. A theory fashioned in this way out of what is 'universal', if presented as anything more than pro-legomenon,* carries the implication that in the causal interpret-ation of events these elements are in some sense primary, and that what is peculiar to the special institutional complex is secondary. In other words, the form and angle of generalisation, according to what it selects for emphasis and what it casts into shadow, cannot be without influence, not only upon human attitudes and beliefs, and hence upon social activity (*e.g.* whether 'social engineering' is attempted or radical institu-tional change), but upon the intellectual diagnosis of particular social and economic problems. It cannot refrain from being ideological *in this sense*. *Per contra*, an approach that starts from the historically-changing character of the subject-matter of the social sciences and focusses attention upon what is historically contingent in the contemporary situation that is analysed will carry contrary implications. Either approach may fail, of course, to reveal itself as productive of entirely convincing or fruitful interpretation; in this way – probably the only way in which theorems in the social sciences can be tested – being rejected by the test of experience. What is more likely to happen,

---

* It might seem that any general socio-historical theory must be of this kind, including the Marxian, since this attempts to generalise about different historical societies and their movement. This may well be true. But in doing so, these theories may or may not concentrate attention upon peculiarities that are of specific importance for the specific functioning of any particular society; the Marxian being distinguished by its emphasis precisely upon the specific influence of the 'social relations' of production defining any particular mode of production (and exchange). In this sense it is itself a way of presenting not only the common elements but also the *differentia*.

for a time at least, is that the two rival types of interpretation will coexist and their implications for action and experience conflict, possibly without the true nature of their different visions of reality being brought plainly to view (since it is quite possible, indeed not uncommon, for some crucial assumption of a theorem to remain implicit and ignored until exposed by intensive polemical discussion and criticism). Even when this difference of vision is clearly established and perceived, the rival viewpoints may find sincerely convinced champions because they severally fit the perspective from which different social classes view the social complex of interacting relationships and change. Accordingly they continue side by side as rival schools.

The obvious example of the contrast that we have been describing (to which we shall presently return) is the divergent emphasis of that type of theory, embracing most of the purely 'exchange' or market theories, which casts the economic problem in terms of 'natural' or universal factors* and theories which by stressing social relations of production and/or income-distribution have given prominence to 'institutional' factors and displayed economic problems in a mainly 'institutional' shape. Needless to say, Marx's analysis of *Capital*, with "a critical analysis of capitalist production" as the sub-title of its initial volume, belongs to this second type. We shall see that even earlier John Stuart Mill was sufficiently alive to the significance of this kind of contrast as to make plain, as against his predecessors, that in his view, while "laws of Production" were natural and universal, those of Distribution *per contra* were "partly of human institution, since the manner in which wealth is distributed in any given society, depends on the statutes or usages therein prevalent"† : in this sense they were historically relative and rooted in specific property-institutions. With the generation that followed Mill, and its focus upon a demand-theory of exchange-relationships and a derivation of income-distribution (*via* factor-prices) from these exchange-

---

* *Cf.* J. B. Clark, *The Distribution of Wealth* (New York, 1899) p. 37: "The law itself [of distribution] is universal, and hence 'natural'."
† J. S. Mill, *Principles of Political Economy* (London, 1848) Vol. I, p. 26.

relationships, the emphasis was surely tilted back again – back to a portrayal of the economic problem in its essentials as shaped and moulded by universal and supra-historical conditions of any exchange society, whatever its particular social relations, class structure and property-institutions might be. Thus one's view of the nature of historical change – its structure, sequence and causal mechanism – will colour one's view of the permitted limits and permissible forms of generalisation, if the resulting abstract projections and theorems are to have relevance to actual problems and to feasible policy.

As an analogous but rather different kind of example of this we could consider the contrasting emphasis that there has always been among theorists between those who see new revelation as coming from the construction of theoretical models at the highest level of abstraction and those who are sufficiently impressed with concrete multiplicity and difference as to deny to such abstract generalisation anything but an obscurantist rôle. A recent example of the latter is to be found in the study of poverty and underdevelopment in South Asia by Professor Gunnar Myrdal, who in stressing the institutional peculiarities of the economies he is investigating dismisses the usual economists' categories as unreal and inapplicable, singling out for criticism especially the semi-mathematical growth-models that have been so much in vogue in discussions of development and planning since the Second World War.* Such a question of

* Professor Myrdal writes, *e.g.*: "Economic models have come to stereotype this whole way of thinking, which we have called the Western or modern approach, and in turn have strongly influenced the plans and the discussion of planning for development in the S. Asian countries ... This type of model-thinking has systematically biased the planner's view of reality in a way that suits the convenience and vested interests of conservatives and radicals alike ... To observe that models are *selective, abstract and logically complete, and quantifiable*, is to expose their limitations: they are not comprehensive but partial; they can be difficult to quantify ... It also facilitates the neglect of relevance and realism, and ambiguities enter by reason of the various possible interpretations of the logically formulated premises. When the models are 'applied', their selective and therefore arbitrary nature is usually forgotten ... Generally, the application to the underdeveloped countries of S. Asia of concepts that may be appropriate to developed countries leads to what philosophers call 'category mistakes' – ascribing to one category attributes appropriate to another ... It may be safer to do without a model than to use a biased and faulty one" (*Asian Drama* (London, 1968) Vol. III, pp. 1942, 1944, 1962).

relevance and applicability is far from easy to determine, if it can be determined by any simple and direct criterion at all. In the very long term the issue could presumably be put to the test by counting the number of corollaries or prescriptions of the rival schools that seemed to have 'worked' in practice, and awarding the accolade to the one showing the highest score. In the meantime decision between them can hardly fail to be influenced by the particular uses and policy-prescriptions that the two schools happen to have advanced as implications of their respective theories or viewpoints, and by one's attitudes towards these. One may, for instance, regard the policy-prescriptions in question as plausible (or implausible) on other grounds, and the fact that they seem also to follow from some general theorem one may regard as reinforcement of one's initial supposition. Judgements on this account – working back pragmatically from policy-prescriptions to supporting general concepts – must almost inevitably be influenced by 'ideological' considerations and leanings. There seems to be plenty of experience to show that in fact they are.

With such differences in type of generalisation is connected (even if this be not immediately apparent) the difficult question as to how, if it is right to speak of social theories having an ideological character, one is to distinguish and to classify this ideological rôle. Needless to say, in polemical literature the usage of such labels as 'apologetic' to describe this or that school of writers and theories according to social provenance and *tendenz* has been far from clear or consistent. It is well-known that Marx spoke of the school of classical political economy (a term which he himself originated) as the 'bourgeois school'. But in saying this he by no means intended to dismiss their doctrines as entirely negative and deluded by 'false consciousness': indeed he singled out for praise the positive advance which their thought represented and the scientific insight which they showed into the nature of economic society (even if within "the limits beyond which" their thought "could not pass").* Even of the post-1830 period, of which he spoke as

---

* *Cf.* Marx's Preface to the Second Edition of Volume I of *Capital*, Moore and Aveling ed. (London, 1886) pp. xxi–xxiii. Here it is that he speaks of Political

that of "vulgar-economy", he was careful to discriminate and by no means treated all economists as "hired prize-fighters" or as a "homogeneous reactionary mass" (saying of John Stuart Mill and those like him, for example, that "it would be very wrong to class them with the herd of vulgar economic apologists").* Coming closer to the present day, is *The General Theory* of J. Maynard Keynes to be regarded as a critique of (then existing) capitalism, or as an "apologetic theory of monopoly capitalism", as some Marxist writers of the time regarded it;† and if the latter, how are its claims to be compared with those of some of Schumpeter's work in affording a dynamic justification of monopoly that has proved so very influential? Again, there is the kind of problem posed, even more recently, by the suggestion of a Soviet economist (writing on the centenary of *Das Kapital*) that a distinction can be drawn between political economy proper (in the classical and Marxian sense) and generalised applied economics, which in taking the socio-institutional basis of society for granted can produce theoretical models about the mechanical structure and functioning of that economy which have objective validity, and hence by implication are to be distinguished from 'bourgeois apologetics' (much of modern macro-economic theory, especially growth-models, being cited in illustration).‡ It would certainly seem as

Economy "remain[ing] a science only so long as the class-struggle is latent or manifests itself only in isolated and sporadic phenomena" and of Ricardo as the "last great representative" of the classical school; also of the period between 1820 and 1830 as being "notable in England for scientific activity in the domain of Political Economy". It was the period after 1830 (when "the class struggle practically as well as theoretically took on more and more outspoken and threatening forms") which he treated as "sound[ing] the knell of scientific bourgeois economy" and introducing "in place of genuine scientific research, the bad conscience and evil intent of apologetic". Earlier he had described Ricardo (in the *Grundrisse*) as being "the economist *par excellence* of production" (which for Marx was fairly high praise); and in the *Theorien über den Mehrwert* he was to speak of "the scientific importance, the great historical value of Ricardo's theory", despite its defects (*Theorien*, ed. Kautsky (Berlin, 1923) Vol. II, pp. 4–5; Eng. trans. by G. A. Bonner and Emile Burns, *Theories of Surplus Value: Selections* (London, 1951) pp. 203–4).

* *Capital*, Vol. I (Moore and Aveling ed.) p. 623n.

† *Cf. inter alia*, the Soviet textbook on *Political Economy*, Eng. ed. (London, 1957) pp. 393–4; and a somewhat less crude expression of this standpoint, *Fundamentals of Marxism–Leninism*, ed. O. Kuusínen, Eng. trans. (London, 1961) pp. 338–9.

‡ V. Afanaseyev, *Voprosi Ekonomiki*, No. 7, 1967, pp. 14 *seq.*

though an ideological rôle of a theory in affording some kind of justification of the existing system, and hence in assuaging criticism and fending off revolt (or in the opposite case affording a condemnation of the *status quo*) can be distinguished from a theoretical analysis that does no more than afford certain policy-corollaries (*e.g.* as regards budgetary policy) for governments meeting particular contingencies ('social engineering' in some limited *ad hoc* context). At the same time the line does not seem at all easy to draw between both these types of theory and an apparently objective study of the general conditions of market equilibrium (static or dynamic) of which the Walrasian system affords a good example.

This example might seem to suggest that the answer depends on whether the latter type of theory lays itself open to normative interpretation, and whether certain normative conclusions are explicitly derived, as was in fact the case with the Walrasian system once there was attached to it the theorem about maximising utility under conditions of free competition. That this is one way in which formal analysis can have, and has had, apologetic implications cannot be denied. But is it the *only* way? If so, it might seem that the formal analysis *per se* could be acquitted of the result, and the apologetic function be attributed to normative intrusion; the fact that one type of analysis lent itself more than another to such treatment (*e.g.* by casting utility in a key rôle) being 'accidental' so far as the analysis *per se* was concerned. To adopt this view, however, would be to neglect what was emphasised earlier; namely that theoretical analysis, at any rate in a social theory like economics, inevitably has a causal story to tell. Different types of causal story may have very different implications for what it is *possible* to do and to achieve by way of policy and social action; thus it is relevant, indeed crucial, for establishing what alternatives are viable – whether, indeed, there is *any* viable alternative to the existing socio-economic framework – and this entirely within the bounds of 'positive' and *non*-normative discourse. One may instance the simple contrast between Keynesian and pre-Keynesian treatment of the determinants of the level of income and of employment, which essentially turned on the former depicting the order of causal determination as being that of investment $\rightarrow$ saving (*via* the multiplier-effect on income of a change in investment);* whereas pre-Keynesian theory had treated investment as being determined and limited by saving *via* the influence of the latter on the rate of interest. On the quite crucial implications of this theoretical shift for policy (in particular, as regards practicable techniques and instruments for combatting unemployment and influencing the level of activity) one need scarcely enlarge. Even so, one could say that this kind of shift of causal sequence (within what Marx would have termed the 'sphere of circulation') did not change *fundamentally* the conceptual picture of how a capitalist system functioned. More crucial for this is the contrast between theories that approach the determination of prices, or the relations of exchange, through and by means of conditions of production (costs, input-coefficients and the like) and those that approach it primarily from the side of demand.

Undoubtedly this latter has been the principal and distinguishing contrast between the two main and rival systems of economic thought in the nineteenth century and since; and it is a distinction that is concealed by purely formal attempts to 'reconcile' them, or alternatively to interpret the differences between them in exclusively formal terms. Moreover, the contrast goes deeper than at first sight would appear because, as we shall see, it involves a difference in the 'frontiers' of the subject, or in the factors and influences included within the circle of relevant influences or determining factors. For the classical economists, and especially for Marx, the study of Political Economy and the analysis of exchange-value necessarily *started* from those socio-economic conditions that shaped the class relations of society. Adam Smith considered it important to distinguish the "early and rude state of society which precedes both the accumulation of stock and the appropriation

* *Cf.* the fuller statement of the causal pattern implied by Keynes's *General Theory* in Mathur, *Steady Growth*, p. 71. Also A. Tustin, *The Mechanism of Economic Systems* (London, 1958) pp. 4, 7 *seq.*, on "a sequence of dependence" in the Keynesian system.

of land" from class society after "stock has accumulated in the hands of particular persons"; while Ricardo saw "the laws which regulate" distribution as "the principal problem in Political Economy" since these explained the principles according to which "the product of the earth is divided among three classes of the community, namely the proprietor of the land, the owner of the stock or capital necessary for its cultivation, and the labourers by whose industry it is cultivated".* One could say that for them Political Economy was a theory of distribution *before* it was a theory of exchange-value: certainly Ricardo, as we shall see, devised his theory of profit *before* he perfected his theory of value as foundation and framework of the former. More deliberately and explicitly Marx always emphasised the distinction between the essential processes and relations in human society and the realm of appearances; identifying exchange, or commodity-money circulation, with the latter, and social relations of production with the former. Concentration of attention upon exchange *per se*, isolated from its socio-historical setting, was the source of 'false consciousness' and delusive theorising. He said in his polemic against Proudhon: "In principle there is not exchange of products, but exchange of labours which compete in production. It is on the mode of exchange of productive forces that the mode of exchange of products depends."† The same idea recurs in his reference to "fetishism of commodities" in *Das Kapital*: "A definite social relation between men assumes in their eyes the fantastic form of a relation between things";‡ and again in his *Theorien über den Mehrwert* (speaking of post-Ricardian *vulgärökonomie*): "the existence of the revenue, as it appears on the surface, is separated from its inner relations and from all connections. Thus land becomes the source of rent, capital the source of profit, and labour the source of wages."§ The boundaries of the

---

* Adam Smith, *An Inquiry into the Nature and Causes of the Wealth of Nations*, 4th ed., complete in one volume (London, 1826) Book I, Ch. VI, p. 51; D. Ricardo, *On the Principles of Political Economy and Taxation*, Preface; *Works and Correspondence of Ricardo*, Sraffa ed. (Cambridge, 1951) Vol. I, p. 5.

† *Misère de la Philosophie* (1847 ed.) p. 61.

‡ *Capital*, Vol. I (trans. Moore and Aveling, London, 1886) p. 43.

§ *Theorien über den Mehrwert*, ed. Karl Kautsky (Berlin, 1923) Vol. III, pp. 521-2.

subject as he drew them were accordingly not arbitrary: they were regarded, consistently with his interpretation of historical development, as necessary for embracing all the factors necessary to any explanation that was to be both complete and substantial.

By contrast with this approach the methodology ushered in by the 'Jevonian revolution' and given more systematic formulation by Menger and the 'Austrian school' sought to derive an explanation of exchange-value from the attitudes of individual consumers towards commodities as use-values catering for the satisfaction of individual wants. The significance of this is not simply (as has commonly been the focus of attention) that emphasis is laid at the opposite end of a chain of interdependent events or processes, but consists rather of two crucial consequences of this approach. First, it treated individuals, their structure of wants and the choices and substitutions resulting therefrom, as the ultimate and independent data of the economic problem: these were the ultimate atoms of the exchange process and of market-behaviour, beyond which analysis did not go (*e.g.* it did not, indeed could not, concern itself with the social conditioning or social interdependence of individuals' desires and behaviour-reactions). Secondly, it derived a theory of distribution as incidental to the pricing-process – as the pricing of 'original factors' or productive services according to the rôle they played in the creation of commodities which at first or second remove were of utility to ultimate consumers. In Menger's conception, as we shall see later, there was a simple hierarchy of 'goods of first order' and 'goods of higher order'; the values of the latter being dependent on the former in a simple manner according to their rôle in the unidirectional process whereby goods or services of 'higher order' were productively transformed into final consumers' goods and use-values. This, and not the use of the formal device of marginal increments, was the crux of the new trend of the last quarter of the nineteenth century (a reason why the designation of 'marginalism' to describe the latter is misplaced).

Anticipating discussion in later chapters: it is perhaps

deserving of incidental mention that this inclusion of a theory of distribution *within* the theory of the pricing-process, as a constituent set of the larger set of market processes viewed as an interrelated whole, is question-begging in an important respect. A structure of market demands can only be derived from consumers' desires, preferences or behaviour-reactions on the assumption of consumers being equipped with a given money-income.* Hence an initial distribution of income between individuals is implicit in the general pricing-process, in the sense that it must be included as one of the determinants of the structure of demand from which all prices (including prices of productive factors) are derived; the whole pricing process being relative to this postulated distribution. A theory of distribution, in other words, if it is conceived as a theory of derived prices of productive services or factors, cannot be independent of initial income-distribution as essential premise.†

The important, but much-too-seldom noticed, consequence of this contrast between the classical approach and the modern follows directly from what has been said: namely, that in the former income-distribution is treated as being the result of social institutions (*e.g.* property-ownership) and social relations, whereas in the latter it is determined by the conditions of exchange. In the one case it is determined from outside and in the other case from inside the process of market prices (Marx would have expressed the former by saying that social conditions and class forces were more fundamental than relations of

---

* In Walras's formulation, for example, of "*rareté*" as "the cause of exchange value" this appears as the initial "quantity possessed" of the commodities that are objects of exchange. (He points out, in *Leçon* 14, that prices remain unchanged when redistribution of quantities among holders occurs if (but only if) "the value of the sum of the quantities possessed by each of these parties [to the exchange] remains the same".) Appeal is made (not at all convincingly, one must add) to "the law of large numbers" for supposing that this condition will generally be fulfilled when transactions occur in a competitive market.

† To take a quite simple example: suppose a two-commodity economy, with x a relatively cheap (compared to its utility) necessity and y a relatively dear luxury consumed only by those with high incomes. The fact that the demand for x comes from low-income groups (and conversely the demand for y from those with high incomes) will tend, *ceteris paribus*, to keep the price of x low (and of y high) and likewise the price of whichever factor (e.g. labour) is most intensively used in its production.

exchange).* Classically, income-distribution (*e.g.* the wage–profit ratio) was a *pre*-condition of the formation of relative prices. *Per contra*, in post-Jevonian and Austrian theory income-distribution is derived as part of the general pricing process – as a constituent set of equations in the total equational system of market equilibrium (although not without circularity, as we have seen, to the extent that an initial distribution of income has to be assumed for the translation of consumers' wants or preferences into terms of market demand). Thus income-distribution is made to appear as something independent of property institutions and of social relations: as something supra-institutional and supra-historical so far, at least, as income-distribution between *factors* is concerned. We shall see later that this is the substance and essence of the critique of the theory of marginal productivity in modern discussion (the polemic against the so-called 'neo-classical' school); although the discussion itself has been mainly concerned with formal matters (of consistency and the like). As one writer has recently put it: "The theory of production relations was meant to be independent of the institutions of society; that is, relations between men were treated as irrelevant for an explanation of distribution. It was Marx's insight that this separation is invalid, even in the world of pure logic, and the significance of this distinction for the case of more than one capital good has been emphasised by the modern critics of the neo-classical parables."†

III

What conclusion, then, in summary do we seem to have reached? In brief, it is that the distinction that Schumpeter tried to draw between Economics as pure analysis and as Vision of the economic process into which ideological slant and colouring

---

* It is true that Marx treated wages (and hence, given productivity, surplus-value) as being governed by the general law of value: *i.e.* by the 'value of labour power'. But his very definition of 'value of labour power', and hence the rate of surplus value, depended on socio-historical assumptions, while any deviation of the current price of labour-power from its value depended on the balance of class forces (*e.g.* strength of trade unions). See Chapter 6.

† Professor G. C. Harcourt, 'Some Cambridge Controversies in the Theory of Capital', *Journal of Economic Literature*, Vol. VII, No. 3, June 1969, p. 395.

inevitably enter cannot be sustained, unless the former is restricted to the formal framework, simply, of economic statement, and not to economic theory as substantial statement about the real relations of economic society; since into the formulation of the latter, and into the very act of judgement of its degree of realism, historical intuition, social perspective and vision cannot fail to enter. For this reason it is possible to characterise and to classify economic theories, even the most abstract, according to the manner in which they depict the structure and roots of economic society, and according to the significance of so depicting it for historical judgement and contemporary social practice. Indeed, to do so is an essential part of intellectual interpretation of the theories in question and of their place in the history of ideas; and without such appreciation something crucial is lacking in our understanding of particular theories, treated in isolation and viewed exclusively in terms of their internal logical structure – and *a fortiori* in our understanding of the development of economic thought. In this sense historical assessment of theory and of its unfolding is essential to any full appreciation of theory itself, if this is taken to mean the relation (and implications) of formal structures to reality as well as analysis of formal structures *per se*. While the latter may properly be treated as a technical achievement pure and simple, the former, which is crucially concerned with relevance – whether a theory has point or is pointless – and general viability as a *social* theory, cannot be so treated.

Historical assessment and interpretation of economic doctrine has commonly consisted of enquiring into the actual problems that particular doctrines were designed to illuminate. This is, of course, an element in interpretation, perhaps an essential starting point; affording at any rate a suggestive clue. But it has to be recognised as no more than a starting point; and in some cases there may be no visible sign that concrete formulation of a problem preceded theoretical invention in the mind of an intellectual innovator. Historical interpretation, in other words, needs to be conceived more widely than this, and in a sense less literally. In this connection it is wise to bear in mind that the unfolding and development of thought must be conceived neither, on the one hand, as a largely discontinuous series of answers (or frameworks for answers) to problems that are different in each successive generation from those of the preceding one, nor, on the other hand, as a straight-line elaboration of a basic set of concepts by successive adaptation of these to problems emerging from contact with the real world. New concepts and formal structures are as much prompted by the desire to answer the inadequacies of (and hence to contradict or 'negate') their predecessors, so far as the latters' relevance and realism are concerned, as to provide answers in any simple and immediate sense to contemporary problems, even if the latter (*e.g.* corn prices in 1815 or unemployment in the 1930s) give the impulse (or reinforce it) to reconsider the adequacy of the traditional conceptual structure. Quite commonly questioning of the old will start by disclosing previously latent assumptions underlying the old formalism or its conventional corollaries – assumptions, perhaps, about the total situation on which it depends, or about the independence (or alternatively the specific contingency) of some factor or factors in it, or yet again as to the value of certain parameters that turn out on examination to be crucial to the *modus operandi* of the model. As a sequel to this, attempts will probably be made, not merely to remove and replace these particular assumptions, but to construct a radically different picture of the total situation and to explore the implications of so doing; and this even if a taste for paradox in the innovator does not add zest to his search for cases where new theorems show relationships or yield corollaries that are precisely opposite to the old.

This may be, indeed, only another way of saying what has already been said: that new concepts and theorems have to be envisaged simultaneously as being fashioned in response to (and hence patterned upon) older ones – as critical assessment of their adequacy to fulfil the rôle for which they have been cast – and as a reflection of changing human experience and of the problems and conflicts involved in human social activity that is itself motivated by the use of abstract notions applied to human beings in general, to their artifacts and to 'things'.

2

ADAM SMITH

I

The underlying preoccupation of the early economists of the age of Adam Smith was the notion of individual self-interest as the economic driving-force. From this was fashioned the general conception of an economic *system* propelled by a momentum of its own, and its motions shaped by specific economic laws that it was the unique contribution of classical political economy to disclose and establish. In Hegel's well-known phrase, "out of the actions of men comes something different from what they have consciously willed and intended". The idea of the potentially creative force of individual self-interest harks back to the "private vices public virtues" of Mandeville's *Fable of the Bees* (despite Adam Smith's dismissal of this as "wholly pernicious"*); it is of course the substantial kernel within the metaphysical husk of Smith's "unseen hand"; and to this even the *Theory of Moral Sentiments* was germane as being concerned with exploring human motivation, which was the core of the self-acting bourgeois order.† This demonstration of a mechanism within the affairs of men, with which un-comprehending meddling of sovereign or statesmen was incompatible, was the crucial innovation in human thinking about society, essentially replacing older thinking couched in terms of 'natural right', and not continuing it as has sometimes

---

* The reason adduced was that it "seems to take away altogether the distinction between vice and virtue" (*Theory of Moral Sentiments*, 11th ed. (Edinburgh, 1808) Vol. II, p. 290).

† Wesley Mitchell said apparently that "any person's system of economics must be based upon his conception of human nature, tacit or expressed, so long as his system of economic theory consists of reasoning about what people will do". He then went on to speak of Bentham's "potent influence upon the development of economic theory" as being "due to the fact that he formulated far more explicitly and clearly than anybody else the conception of human nature which prevailed among his contemporaries" (Wesley C. Mitchell, *Lecture Notes on Types of Economic Theory* (New York, 1949) I, pp. 90–1).

been alleged.* As Lord Robbins has said, although Smith "so frequently uses the terminology of *Naturrecht*", his "arguments are so consistently utilitarian in character".† What was strikingly new in Smith's "principle of Natural Liberty", which he enunciated as early as 1749, was the empirical assertion that (as Schumpeter paraphrased it) "free interaction of individuals produces not chaos but an orderly pattern that is logically determined"‡ – a pattern which, accordingly, could be elucidated in rational terms. It is true that much reference was made at the time to the 'natural order', and that this was endowed with an inherited esteem withheld from artificial man-made contrivances. But the real content of this so-called natural order was (in Dugald Stewart's words in his Memoir of Adam Smith) "allowing every man, as long as he observes the rules of justice, to pursue his own interest in his own way, and to bring both his own industry and his capital into the freest competition with those of his fellow citizens."§ It was, moreover, specially characteristic of the whole school that preoccupation with economic policy was uppermost in their minds. This preoccupation preceded and shaped their ideas about the economic order quite as much as it followed in the wake of these ideas and as corollary to them.

In similar vein the Physiocrats, the French school of eighteenth-century *économistes*, were preoccupied with transforming the traditional policies of governments with respect to

* *E.g.* by Gunnar Myrdal in *The Political Element in the Development of Economic Theory* (London, 1953) value was "usually identified with the 'just' or 'right' price, the *justum pretium*", and the theory of natural law "was the starting point both of the labour theory of value and of the doctrine of economic liberalism" (pp. 60, 71). Elsewhere he defines "the essence of this philosophy" of natural law as "a direct identification of teleology and causality" (*Value in Social Theory*, ed. by Paul Streeten (London, 1958) p. 206). Schumpeter speaks of Benthamite utilitarianism as "nothing but another natural-law system" (*History of Economic Analysis*, p. 132).

† *The Theory of Economic Policy in English Classical Political Economy* (London, 1952) p. 48.

‡ *History of Economic Analysis*, p. 185.

§ *Biographical Memoirs*, ed. by Sir William Hamilton (Edinburgh, 1858) p. 60. J. K. Ingram said of Smith's "system of natural liberty" that "this theory is, of course, not explicitly presented by Smith as a foundation of his economic doctrines, but it is really the secret substratum on which they rest" (*History of Political Economy* (London, 1907) p. 91).

trade and taxation;* and to this end they fashioned the concept of an "economic order". In a sense they did this more 'objectively' than Smith and the English school, since they were less concerned with human nature and motivation and directed their attention towards the structure or pattern of commercial relations – towards a physiology of economic society – with procedures and rules of its own to which governmental policy must be adapted if not subordinated.† To quote Professor Meek: "The Physiocrats assumed that the system of market exchange which it was their main purpose to analyse was subject to certain objective economic laws, which operated independently of the will of man and which were discoverable by the light of reason. These laws governed the shape and movement of the economic order, and therefore . . . the shape and movement of the social order as a whole."‡ What was peculiar to their approach was that they had seen the crucial point of framing the question as to the source and explanation of a *produit net* or surplus, and made an answer to this the pivot of their system. They postulated (as an empirical observation presumably) that production in agriculture alone was capable of yielding a *produit net* or surplus. The presumptive evidence for this was that a whole class of landowners in fact lived upon this in the form of rent of land; the implication being that in this way, and in this pursuit *par excellence*, Nature showed her bounty to the hand of man. "Surplus-value appears as a *gift of nature*" (Marx).§ In other lines of human economic activity man-made productive inputs (to use modern terminology) could replace themselves but in general could do no more: in

---

* This is clear from the discussion between Mirabeau and Quesnay which converted the former to Physiocracy, even if the point immediately at issue was population-policy (*cf.* R. L. Meek, *The Economics of Physiocracy* (London, 1962) pp. 16–18).

† *Cf.* Quesnay's *Philosophie Rurale*: "If the moralists and philosophers do not base their sciences on the economic order, on agriculture, their speculations will be useless and illusory. They will be doctors who perceive only symptoms and ignore the disease. Those who depict for us the morals of the age without going back to causes are only speculators and not philosophers" (*cit. ibid.*, p. 69).

‡ *Ibid.*, p. 19.

§ *Theories of Surplus-Value*, Part I, trans. Emile Burns (Moscow, n.d.) p. 51.

this sense they were *stérile* and not *productif.** From this followed, rather obviously, the famous *l'impôt unique*. If agricultural activity was source of the surplus on which both State and aristocracy alike depended, it followed that everything restrictive of such activity was to be condemned as socially harmful, such as restrictions on trade and taxation burdensome to farmers and traders, sapping the sources of those *avances foncières, primitives* and *annuelles* upon which the extent of this productive activity depended. This was, in turn, the crux of their analysis of the circular flow of exchange (it would probably to-day be termed a '*model*') embodied in Quesnay's famous *Tableau Économique*. ("Cantillon and Quesnay had this conception of the general interdependence of all sectors and all elements of the economic process in which – so Dupont actually put it – nothing stands alone and all things hang together."†) To this was added, rather than logically connected with, a parallel notion to that which we have seen characterised English writers of the eighteenth century: that individual interests, when free to operate, served the public good, and this by the "magic" of competition, which in "well-ordered society" ensures "that each man works for others, while believing that he is working for himself". For this, however, appeal was made, not to any logical demonstration that this must be so, but to "principles of economic harmony" bestowed upon the world by divine benevolence.‡

Regarding the 'debt' which Smith is sometimes said to have owed to the French School, with which he came into contact during his tour of France and Switzerland in 1764–6, the true picture would seem to be one of parallel and independent generation of ideas rather than dependence upon a single original source. We now know that many of the characteristic notions developed by Smith in the *Wealth of Nations* were present in embryo, at least, in his early lectures prior to 1764.

---

* Since they lacked a theory of value, no distinction between physical and value productivity was introduced (as Schumpeter observes, *History of Economic Analysis*, p. 238).
† *Ibid.*, p. 242.
‡ *Cf.* Meek, *Economics of Physiocracy*, p. 70.

This was the case, for example, not only with the idea of the division of labour as being limited by the extent of trade, but also that of the beneficial rôle of individual self-interest as expressed in his telling aphorism that "it is not from the benevolence of the butcher, the brewer or the baker that we expect our dinner, but from their regard to their own interest. We address ourselves, not to their humanity, but to their self-love, and never talk to them of our own necessities but of their advantages."* What Smith may well have derived from his French visit (in addition to reinforcement of his belief in economic liberty) is the notion of capital as involving an 'advance' in time – in advance, that is, of production or at least of its completion: a notion which implicitly contained all the essentials of capital theory as subsequently developed, so far as this has treated the crux of the problem of capital and its investment as revolving on time. At any rate, the notion of capital as consisting essentially of wage-advances to labourers ran through classical Political Economy in England.† Even here, however, Adam Smith seems to have had something of the same idea in his early lectures when he said that "every trade requires a stock of food and clothes and lodging to carry it on" and that "the number of people that are employed must be in proportion to it".‡ While expressly dissenting from the key principle of the Physiocratic system that agriculture was alone creative of *produit net*, he conceded the point of it so far as to accept the idea of the 'two surpluses' in agriculture. "Farmers and country labourers, indeed, over and above the stock which maintains and employs them, reproduce annually a neat produce, a free rent to the landlord. As a marriage which affords three children

---

* *Wealth of Nations*, complete in one volume (London, 1826) p. 21.

† This notion entailed his (and his successors of the Classical School) conceiving much less than modern economists of capital as a factor of production separate from but on a par with labour; and when Ricardo, for example, spoke of the diminishing productivity of successive amounts of capital employed on the land, this was not something which he distinguished (as does modern marginal productivity theory) from the productivity of successive amounts of *labour* employed on the land.

‡ *Lectures on Justice, Police, Revenue and Arms by Adam Smith, reported by a Student in 1763*, ed. Edwin Cannan (Oxford, 1896) p. 181.

is certainly more productive than one which affords only two, so the labour of farmers and country labourers is certainly more productive than that of merchants, artificers and manufacturers."* Perhaps connected with this was Smith's view that we shall consider later about the relation of the landowners' interest to the general social interest.

II

The 'natural laws' of this self-regulating economic order was the dominating concern of classical political economy to enunciate. Whereas by Quesnay this had been conceived of in terms of a flow or exchange-circuit fertilising the realm, by Smith it was viewed in terms of market forces establishing certain 'natural values' by dint of the operation of competition upon supplies and upon demand. Such 'natural values' then became a term of comparison, or norm, with which all 'artificial prices', established by interferences and obstacles in the shape of legal regulations, "exclusive privileges of corporations, statutes of apprenticeship" and monopolies, could be contrasted and exposed. 'Market price', on the other hand, dependent on particular and *ad hoc* configuration of supply and demand at any given time and place ("regulated by the quantity which is actually brought to market and the demand of those . . . who may be called the effectual demanders") tended, when conditions of freedom allowed, towards the 'natural' level in the course of time, but in a changing or imperfectly free world was never coincident therewith. "The natural price . . . is, as it were, the central price, to which the prices of all commodities are continually gravitating."† Already in the early lectures this conception was fully in mind: "whatever police tends to raise the market price above the natural, tends to diminish public opulence"; "all monopolies and exclusive privileges of corporations, for whatever good ends they were at first instituted, have the same bad effect" as "taxes upon exportation and importation" which "also hinder commerce".‡ It

---

* *Wealth of Nations*, p. 634.   † *Ibid.*, p. 61.
‡ *Lectures . . . by Adam Smith*, ed. Cannan, pp. 178, 236.

is by far the best policy to "leave things to their natural course". Of so general a statement as this no proof was afforded. Nonetheless it is not a metaphysical statement, nor was the notion of 'natural value' *per se* (that the equilibrium it defined was hypothetical does not make it metaphysical), even if some metaphysical aura attached to it by reason of the terminology, which no doubt gave it much greater rhetorical impact for a contemporary audience (as well as subsequent ones) – an audience that was steeped in metaphysical notions about *ius naturalis*.

When it came to more precise definition of this natural value and its determination, Adam Smith had remarkably little to say beyond the statement that this was the equilibrium price that competition would in due course yield through the operations of supply and demand – towards which "the prices of all commodities are continually gravitating". A commodity's "natural price" is defined as being equal to the sum of the "natural rates of wages, profit and rent", which are in turn defined as the "ordinary or average rate" of wages, profit or rent prevailing in "the general circumstances of the society" at the time: in other words, as determined by the general conditions of supply and demand for labour, stock and land, which govern respectively the three "component Parts of the Price of Commodities", into which "in every society the price of every commodity finally resolves itself into some one or other, or all of those three parts". It is then shown how when "the quantity brought to market should at any time fall short of the effectual demand", or conversely, "some of the component parts of its price must rise above their natural rate", or alternatively fall below it, and how this will influence the supply forthcoming in the ensuing period in such a way as to adapt it to the level of demand. Thus the justification of competition, with its tendency amid frequent and sometimes large fluctuations to equate market price with natural price, was that "the whole quantity of industry annually employed in order to bring any commodity to market, naturally suits itself in this manner to the effectual demand".*

* *Wealth of Nations*, pp. 53, 58–65.

At the outset, it is true, there is a hint of a labour theory of natural value, both in the discussion of "real and nominal price" (of which more will be said in a moment) and at the opening of Chapter VI of Book I, 'Of the component Parts of the Price of Commodities'. But this is quickly shown to apply only to "that early and rude state of society which precedes both the accumulation of stock and the appropriation of land". Then indeed will "the proportion between the quantities of labour necessary for acquiring different objects . . . be the only circumstance which can afford any rule for exchanging them for one another . . . In this state of things, the whole produce of labour belongs to the labourer; and the quantity of labour commonly employed in acquiring or producing any commodity is the only circumstance which can regulate the quantity of labour which it ought commonly to purchase, command or exchange for."* But "as soon as stock has accumulated in the hands of particular persons, some of them will naturally employ it in setting to work industrious people, whom they will supply with materials and subsistence, in order to make a profit by the sale of their work, or by what their labour adds to the value of the materials". In such circumstances, "the value which the workmen add to the materials resolves itself in this case into two parts", wages and profits. "In this state of things, the whole produce does not always belong to the labourer. He must in most cases share it with the owner of the stock which employs him." It follows that "in the price of commodities . . . the profits of stock constitute a component part altogether different from the wages of labour, and regulated by quite different principles". Moreover the ratio of these two components may vary considerably in different lines of production.†

As has been frequently observed, there is here a hint of a 'deduction' theory of profit; both profit and rent being treated by implication as deductions from what is 'naturally' or 'originally' the product of labour.‡ What is no more than a

---

* *Ibid.*, p. 51.   † *Ibid.*, pp. 52, 53.

‡ It is noteworthy that Marx treated this as being a concept of surplus value, at least in embryo – and Ricardo's theory even more so: as a "theory of surplus-value which of course exists in his work, although he does not define surplus-

hint in the case of profit becomes rather more explicit when he comes to the third component, rent of land, with the remark that "landlords, like all other men, love to reap where they never sowed, and demand a rent even for its natural produce". (To this is added: "The wood of the forest, the grass of the field, and all the natural fruits of the earth, which, when land was in common, cost the labourer only the trouble of gathering them"; whereas now he must "pay for the licence to gather them; and must give up to the landlord a portion of what his labour either collects or produces".)* If such a 'deduction' theory were, indeed, intended, it could plausibly be interpreted within the framework of some theory of 'natural right'. This would certainly be consistent with the general setting within which Adam Smith placed it. But it could equally well be interpreted in a comparative-historical sense as an incipient theory of exploitation, viewed as a social relationship, in a sense analogous to that of Marx.†

Thus we have in Smith a theory of price that can be characterised (in Mr Sraffa's description of it)‡ as an 'Adding-up Theory' – a summation (merely) of three primary components of price. It has alternatively been described as a simple Cost of Production Theory; in which guise it has been handed down through the nineteenth century and become known in textbooks of the subject. Smith drew from it a corollary which can be seen on examination to be questionable testimony to this

value as distinct from its particular forms, profit, rent, interest". He incidentally praises Adam Smith (his "great merit") for his historical sense in seeing (much better than Ricardo) that "with the accumulation of capital and the appearance of property in land ... something new occurs" (*Theories of Surplus Value*, Part I, tr. E. Burns (Moscow, n.d.) pp. 83–6, Part II, trans. Renate Simpson (Moscow, 1968; London, 1969) p. 169).

* *Wealth of Nations*, p. 53.

† It was in this sense that Bortkievicz later spoke of a "deduction" theory of profit, preferring this designation to that of "exploitation". We have just seen that Marx treated Smith's theory in this sense as a theory of surplus-value, although without the attribution of it to the historical emergence of labour-power itself as a commodity.

‡ General Introduction to Vol. 1 of *Works and Correspondence of David Ricardo*, ed. P. Sraffa (Cambridge, 1951) p. xxxv. Marx spoke of Smith's mode of determining natural value "by adding together the natural prices of wages, profit and rent" (*Theories of Surplus-Value*, Part I, p. 95).

adding-up-cum-supply-and-demand theory as an adequate explanation of value. The corollary, to which some considerable importance was attached, was to the effect that a tax on necessities, or more particularly on food, would have a more fundamental effect than other taxes, since by raising the level of (money) wages it would eventually raise the prices of all commodities. Thus "the money-price of corn regulates that of all other home-made commodities".* The implication that when corn rises, everything rises, immediately provokes the question: 'rises in terms of *what*?' This question was to be asked, as we shall see, by Ricardo, and was to form the spring-board of Ricardo's criticism of Adam Smith's treatment of value.

The first occasion, however, when Smith seems to relate exchange-value to labour is in the fifth chapter of Book I in connection with what he calls "the real measure" of exchange-able value, "or wherein consists the real price of all commodities", as the chapter-heading has it. Since misconception has not been uncommon, there is need to emphasise that in this chapter he is concerned, not with the cause or 'rule' (*i.e.* principle) of value, but with the standard of measurement in terms of which the values of commodities and changes in them can be properly estimated. Although these two things were closely connected in the thought of the time, the latter in par-ticular being regarded as a key to the former (as we shall see again with Ricardo), they are distinct and separable questions, and it was the second and not the first that was here Adam Smith's immediate concern. After remarking that the exchange-able value of a commodity is "more frequently estimated by the quantity of money, than by the quantity either of labour or of any other commodity which can be had in exchange for it", he proceeds to point out that money is itself variable (witness the great Tudor inflation) according to variations in the amount of labour that gold and silver cost to mine. "As a measure of quantity, such as the natural foot, fathom, or handful, which is continually varying in its own quantity, can never be an

* *Wealth of Nations*, p. 470.

accurate measure of the quantity of other things, so a commodity which is itself continually varying in its own value can never be an accurate measure of the value of other commodities." Having rejected money, he falls back on labour as the only possible standard; and the reason he gives for doing so is of some interest. It is that "equal quantities of labour, at all times and places, may be said to be of equal value to the labourer. In his ordinary state of health, strength and spirits; in the ordinary degree of his skill and dexterity, he must always lay down the same portion of his ease, liberty and his happiness ... Labour alone, therefore, never varying in its own value, is alone the ultimate and real standard by which the value of all commodities can at all times and places be estimated and compared. It is their real price; money is their nominal price only."* Perhaps one could translate this into Marshallian terminology and say that it was equivalent to claiming that labour was the ultimate real cost involved in economic activity and was accordingly the only satisfactory standard in terms of which the changing values of all commodities, including the precious metals as the money-commodity, could be measured.

In the paragraph from which this passage is quoted Adam Smith seems to hold the distinction quite clearly between the amount of labour which the production of a commodity costs and the price at which that labour will exchange in the market (or what Marx, as we shall see, was to term the value or price of labour-power). He says that "the price which he [the labourer] pays must always be the same, whatever may be the quantity of goods which he receives in return for it. Of these, indeed, it may sometimes purchase a greater and sometimes a smaller quantity; but it is their value which varies, not that of the labour which purchases them. At all times and places that is dear which it is difficult to come at, or which it costs much labour to acquire; and that cheap which is to be had easily, or with very little labour." Again, in the very next paragraph he says: "But though equal quantities of labour are always of equal value to the labourer, yet to the person who employs him

* *Ibid.*, p. 37.

they appear sometimes to be of greater and sometimes of smaller value. He purchases them sometimes with a greater and sometimes with a smaller quantity of goods, and to him the price of labour seems to vary like that of all other things ... In reality, however, it is the goods which are cheap in the one case and dear in the other."*

Yet surprisingly one finds him speaking elsewhere in the same chapter of "the quantity of labour which it [a commodity] enables him to purchase or command" as being the "real measure of exchangeable value of all commodities": this is stated, indeed, in the opening paragraph of that chapter.† This was to form the basis of Ricardo's criticism that he, apparently, confused the *price* of labour (in the sense of the wages paid) with the *quantity* of labour required to produce a given product, and that he accordingly fluctuated between a labour-commanded standard and labour-embodied. (Said Ricardo of Smith, "who so accurately defined the original source of exchangeable value", that he "has himself erected another standard measure of value ... not the quantity of labour bestowed on the production of an object, but the quantity which it can command in the market: as if these were two equivalent expressions".)‡

One could, indeed, regard this notion of labour-commanded in the context of a standard or measure as being parallel to the notion of wages as a cause of value, in the sense of "a component part of a price", which we have seen that Smith adopted as basis of his corollary about the governing rôle of corn (*qua* wage-good) in the formation of the prices of all other commodities. Evidently the two contrasted *measures* that were to be keenly debated between Ricardo and Malthus will yield identical results if (but only if) wages remain *constant* as a *proportion* of total value produced (which means that wage-changes over time are tied to changes in productivity of labour).§ On

* *Ibid.*, pp. 37–8.　　　　† *Ibid.*, p. 35.
‡ *Works and Correspondence of David Ricardo*, ed. P. Sraffa, Vol. I, pp. 13–14.
§ To take a simplified example: suppose that at a certain date a bushel of corn takes 3 units of labour to produce and a century later only 2 units. Measured in terms of labour embodied, corn would fall over the century by one-third. Suppose that wages at the earlier date consisted of $\frac{1}{4}$ bushel per unit of labour. Then it would follow that three-quarters of the total product must go as wages,

the other hand, in the context of a causal *rule* or principle for
the formation of price or exchange-value, a wages-theory and
an embodied-labour theory will be equivalent (ignoring rent)
if (but *only* if) the proportion of labour to capital, and hence
the ratio of wages to profit, is *uniform* in all lines of production.

It cannot be said that Adam Smith made much use of this
conception of a measure of value in terms of labour, in either
of the senses to which he alludes. Since it is directly related to
the question of the proportionate division of the product, one
could have expected it, perhaps, to lead into some discussion of
this subject, in the form of a more extensive disquisition upon
the subject of distribution. This, however, properly speaking
we do not find. What we do find as a sequel to the enquiry into
the Component Parts of the Price of Commodities is two related
propositions concerning the tendency of two of these components
(wages and profits) towards uniformity as between different
employments and industries, and the determination of the
general level of each by conditions of supply and demand for
labour and for capital respectively. The "circumstances which
naturally determine" the rate of wages and the rate of profits,
as well as their differences "in the different employments of
labour and stock", form the subject-matter of the ensuing
chapters (viii, ix and x), followed by a separate treatment of
the Rent of Land. It is in the first of these chapters that, in
addition to the well-known remarks about "improvement in
the circumstances of the lower ranks of the people" being an
advantage ("no society can surely be flourishing and happy, of
which the far greater part of the members are poor and miser-

---

leaving one quarter available for profit (ignoring rent); in terms of labour-
commanded one bushel would have equalled 4 units. If the corn-wage had
remained unchanged (*i.e.* at ¼ bushel per unit), then at the later date only half
the product would go in wages and a half be left over as profit; and in terms of
labour-commanded as the measure corn would have remained unchanged. For
corn to have fallen by one-third in terms of labour-commanded *as well as* in
terms of labour-embodied corn-wages would have had to rise over the period
from ¼ to ⅜ of a bushel, *i.e.* by a half, or by as much as productivity had risen
(from which it would follow that the proportionate division of the product into
wages and profit had remained constant).

able"),* and about masters having superiority in bargaining power and being "always and everywhere in a sort of tacit, but constant and uniform, combination, not to raise the wages of labour above their actual rate",† there is the clearest general statement about the dependence of wages mainly upon the rate of *change* in the demand for labour; this being in turn dependent upon the rate of accumulation of capital or stock. "The demand for those who live by wages . . . necessarily increases with the increase of the revenue and stock of every country, and cannot increase without it . . . It is not the actual greatness of national wealth, but its continual increase, which occasions a rise in the wages of labour. It is not, accordingly, in the richest countries, but in the most thriving, or in those which are growing rich the fastest, that the wages of labour are highest."‡ And again: "It deserves to be remarked that it is in the progressive state when the society is advancing . . . rather than when it has acquired its full complement of riches, that the condition of the labouring poor . . . seems to be the happiest and the most comfortable. It is hard in the stationary, and miserable in the declining state. The progressive state is in reality the cheerful and the hearty state to all the different orders of the society. The stationary is dull, the declining melancholy."§ This emphasis on the rate of change, rather than on the *level* of demand, is joined with, indeed follows from, a view of population as tending always to catch up with any growth of demand and of wages ("if this demand is continually increasing, the reward of labour must necessarily encourage in such a manner the marriage and multiplication of labourers"), until "excessive multiplication" of hands shall outpace this demand at the first sign of slackening of its increase, and thus "force back its [labour's] price to that proper rate which the circumstances of the society required". "In this manner", it is concluded, "the demand for men, like that for any other commodity, necessarily

---

* *Wealth of Nations*, p. 80. In addition it is argued (contrary to a common seventeenth- and eighteenth-century view) that plenty and good wages are favourable to industry and productivity: "where wages are high we shall find the workmen more active, diligent and expeditious, than when they are low" (p. 83).
† *Ibid.*, p. 69.　　　‡ *Ibid.*, p. 71.　　　§ *Ibid.*, p. 83.

regulates the production of men; quickens it when it goes on too slowly, and stops it when it advances too fast."*

As for profit, this is also affected by "the increasing or declining state of the wealth of the society", but in an opposite manner. "The increase of stock, which raises wages, tends to lower profit. When the stocks of many rich merchants are turned into the same trade, their mutual competition naturally tends to lower profit; and when there is a like increase of stock in all the different trades carried on in the same society, the same competition must produce the same effect in them all."† The result may be a fall in the price of many commodities, even if rising wages have the effect of raising the price of others. This Smithian reason for a falling rate of profit in the course of progress was, again, a subject for later criticism from Ricardo, who evidently regarded it as a striking example of the inadequacy of supply-and-demand explanations upon which Smith (and in his footsteps Malthus in particular), so largely relied. In the form in which it stood, at any rate, the conclusion relied on a questionable generalisation of what tends to happen in a single trade to the macro-level of all trades.

As regards *differences* of wages and profits in different employments (differences, *i.e.* that are consistent with 'natural price' and not deviations therefrom), his treatment amounts to the well-known theory of equal net advantages. Chapter x opens with the clear and unambiguous statement that "at least in a society . . . where there was perfect liberty, and where every man was perfectly free to chose what occupation he thought proper, and to change it . . . the whole of the advantages and disadvantages of the different employments of labour and stock must, in the same neighbourhood, be either perfectly equal, or continually tending to equality". Manifestly, "if in the same neighbourhood there was any employment evidently either more or less advantageous than the rest, so many people would crowd into it in the one case, and so many people would desert it in the other, that its advantages would soon return to the level of other employments".‡ The result would be that wages

* *Ibid.*, pp. 81–2.   † *Ibid.*, p. 89.   ‡ *Ibid.*, p. 99.

and profits would continually tend to be *un*equal by just so much as would offset the *differences* in the balance of advantages and disadvantages *other* than the pecuniary gain. Five "principal circumstances" were then listed as responsible for such departures of money earnings from uniformity: the "agreeableness or disagreeableness of the employments themselves", the ease or difficulty of learning the trade, constancy or inconstancy of employment, the degree of responsibility attached to the calling in question and the degree of uncertainty of success. As the second part of the chapter underlines, however, "the policy of Europe, by not leaving things at perfect liberty, occasions other inequalities of much greater importance"; and by implication such policy is condemned.

When it comes to the third component part of price, a curious inconsistency confronts us. Rent appears as a component in a different sense from the other two: so different, indeed, as to throw doubt on its ability to perform the rôle assigned to it as part-explanation or cause of price.* "Rent, it is to be observed, therefore, enters into the composition of the price of commodities in a different way from wages and profit. High or low wages and profit are the causes of high or low prices; high or low rent is the effect of it."† To which it is added that "the rent of land . . . is naturally a monopoly price. It is not at all proportioned to what the landlord may have laid out upon the improvement of the land, or to what he can afford to take; but to what the farmer can afford to give."

It is in no more than three pages at the conclusion of this chapter,‡ after a lengthy historical digression on money and prices, that one finds the only treatment of that aspect of

---

* *Cf.* Marx's reference to "this inconsistency" in *Theories of Surplus Value*, Part 2 (London, 1969) Ch. XIII, p. 321. Ricardo had of course noticed its incompatibility with an explanation of price in terms of a summation of three 'components'.

† *Wealth of Nations*, p. 144.

‡ *Ibid.*, pp. 244–7. Cannan's comment is that "Adam Smith's theory of distribution . . . is inserted . . . as a mere appendage or corollary of his doctrine of prices" (*History of Theories of Production and Distribution*, 2nd ed. (London, 1903) p. 186).

distribution to which Ricardo was to attach such great importance: namely the relation between the revenues (or incomes)
of "the three great, original, and constituent orders of every
civilised society", and of these severally to "the general interest
of the society". This relation, like that between the individual
interest and the general, is one of general harmony and not of
conflict so far as landlords and labourers are concerned. Since
rent of land rises with "every increase in the real wealth of the
society", the interest of landlords ("the first of those three
great orders") "is strictly and inseparably connected with the
general interest of society". So is the interest of wage-earners
"as strictly connected with the interest of the society as that of
the first", since wages "are never so high as when the demand
for labour is continually rising". Thus the interest of wage-
earners as well as of landlords was identified with the progress
of capital accumulation.

The exception, distinctly curious at first sight, is the interest
of "merchants and master manufacturers", who live on profit.
Of this third order it is observed that "the rate of profit does
not, like rent and wages, rise with the prosperity, and fall with
the declension of the society. On the contrary, it is naturally
low in rich, and high in poor countries, and it is always highest
in the countries which are going fastest to ruin. The interest of
this third order, therefore, has not the same connexion with the
general interest of the society as that of the other two." Be it
noted, however, that the ground for condemnation of, or at
least of warning against, this third social class or order is their
tendency to sponsor measures for the limitation of competition;
since "to widen the market and to narrow the competition, is
always the interest of the dealers . . . an order of men, whose
interest is never exactly the same with that of the public, who
have generally an interest to deceive and even to oppress the
public, and who accordingly have, upon many occasions, both
deceived and oppressed it".* Later in the book, when speaking
of protective duties, he refers to "the mean rapacity, the
monopolising spirit of merchants and manufacturers, who

* *Wealth of Nations*, pp. 246–7.

neither are, nor ought to be the rulers of mankind . . . their interest is . . . directly opposite to that of the great body of the people".*

These are hard words, and they have often been held to demonstrate that Smith cannot be regarded as giving "theoretical expression to the essential interests of the business class"† or been in any sense a spokesman for industrial capitalism. This indeed they do in any simple and direct sense of the word 'spokesman'. The historical context of the *Wealth of Nations* was certainly more complex than a phrase of this kind implies. In the first place, in the kind of judgement we have quoted he evidently had in mind the whole network of restrictive regulations embodied in the Mercantile System, representing in his view individual and sectional mercantile interest and constituting an obstruction to the general process of capital accumulation and industrial expansion. It was not inconsistent to champion the emerging system (or even by implication the class of industrial capitalists who were simultaneously its pioneers and its ultimate beneficiaries) against the sectional interest of "merchants and master manufacturers", where these were obstructive to the larger end. Secondly, it has to be remembered that Smith was writing at the very dawn, if not on the eve, of the Industrial Revolution, full forty years before Ricardo. He wrote at a time when 'manufacturers' were mainly identified with the half-merchant, half-*entrepreneur* 'putters-out' of the domestic handicraft system (or at most of what Marx was to term 'manufacture' in contradistinction to 'machinofacture'). He wrote, moreover, in a century when some of the most notable progress in capitalist investment and new productive methods was made in agriculture rather than in industry. His doctrine can be properly understood only as reflection of a period of transition, whose problems essentially consisted in clearing the ground for industrial investment and expansion, which he identified with the sweeping away of

---

* *Ibid.*, pp. 456–7.
† The description is that of Sir Erich Roll in *A History of Economic Thought*, 1st ed. (London, 1937) p. 152; *cf.* Robbins, *English Classical Political Economy*, pp. 20–2.

obstructive and sectionally-protective regulation in the interest of quickened competition and widening markets.

It may be incidentally noted that this treatment of distribution, in terms of the effect of progress upon class revenues, was new to the *Wealth of Nations* and apparently had no parallel in the early lectures. It may be (as Cannan suggested) that he was here influenced by his contact with the Physiocrats, especially by the *Tableau* of Quesnay. In the *Lectures* there were no more than a few scattered remarks, such as that "The division of opulence is not according to the work . . . Thus he who as it were bears the burden of society has the fewest advantages."*

III

Adam Smith's principal target for criticism, as is well-known, was the doctrine (or "system of political economy") of the Mercantile School. The basic principle of that school or system, as he interpreted it, consisted of a fallacious identification of wealth with money and the supposition that "to heap up gold and silver in any country to be the readiest way to enrich it". This false doctrine he saw as the main obstacle to an extension of the advantages of Natural Liberty to the sphere of foreign, as well as domestic, trade, bringing in its train all the advantages of competition and cheapness and the progressive extension of the division of labour with the great improvement in productive powers thereby engendered. In so far as this involves the theory of foreign trade, it goes beyond the self-imposed boundaries of this present study. But one is tempted here to make one general comment. This is that so far as the theoretical core of his assault on Mercantilist doctrine is concerned, it is summed up in the theory of the distribution of the precious metals in the course of trade, and that this in its essentials it would seem likely that he derived from David Hume. Already in 1752 in a volume of essays called *Political Discourses* the latter, writing 'Of

---

* *Lectures by Adam Smith*, ed. E. Cannan, 2nd ed. (London, 1903) p. 163. Edwin Cannan comments: "It is plain that Smith acquired the idea of the necessity of a scheme of distribution from the physiocrats, and that he tacked his own scheme . . . on to his already existing theory of prices" (Editor's Introduction, *ibid.*, p. xxxi).

the Balance of Trade', had included a telling passage about the connection between flows of specie in and out of a country and the balance of its imports and exports. This passage runs as follows:

> Suppose four parts of all the money in Britain to be annihilated in one night, and the nation reduced to the same condition, with regard to specie, as in the reigns of the Harrys and Edwards, what would be the consequence? Must not the price of all labour and commodities sink in proportion, and everything be sold as cheap as they were in those ages? What could then dispute with us in any foreign market, or pretend to navigate, or to sell manufactures at the same price which to us would afford such profit? In how little time therefore must this bring back all the money which we have lost, and raise us to the level of all neighbouring nations; where, after we have arrived, we immediately lose the advantage of the cheapness of labour and commodities, and the further flowing in of money be stopped by our fulness and repletion.

After setting out the converse case ("Again; suppose all the money in Britain were multiply'd fourfold in a night"), he concludes:

> Now it is evident that the same causes which would correct these exorbitant inequalities, were they to happen miraculously, must prevent their happening in the ordinary course of nature, and must, for ever, in all neighbouring nations, preserve money nearly proportionable to the art and industry of each nation. All water, wherever it communicates, remains always at the same level. Ask naturalists the reason; they tell you that, were it to be raised in any one place, the superior gravity of that part not being properly balanced, must depress it, till it meets a counterpoise; and that the same cause which redresses the inequality when it happens, must forever prevent it.*

---

* *Political Discourses* (Edinburgh, 1752) pp. 82–4, in *David Hume, Writings on Economics*, ed. E. Rotwein (London, 1955) pp. 62–4.

This is no doubt the passage to which Adam Smith seems to have referred in his early lectures, when he said that Mr Hume "proves very ingeniously that money must always bear a certain proportion to the quantity of commodities in every country; that whenever money is accumulated beyond the proportion of commodities in any country, the price of goods will necessarily rise; that this country will be undersold at the foreign market, and consequently the money must depart into other nations".*

The *Wealth of Nations* in the chapter devoted to the 'Principle of the commercial, or mercantile system' (Chapter I of Book IV) contains the following eulogy of foreign trade: "It gives a value to their superfluities, by exchanging them for something else, which may satisfy a part of their wants, and increase their enjoyments. By means of it the narrowness of the home market does not hinder the division of labour in any particular branch of art or manufacture from being carried to the highest perfection. By opening a more extensive market for whatever part of the produce of their labour may exceed the home consumption, it encourages them to improve its productive powers, and to augment its annual produce to the utmost, and thereby to increase the real revenue and wealth of the society. These great and important services foreign trade is continually occupied in performing, to all the different countries between which it is carried on. They all derive great benefit from it." To which there is added, in order to turn the edge against the export-surplus myth: "To import the gold and silver which may be wanted, into the countries which have no mines, is, no doubt, a part of the business of foreign commerce. It is, however, a most insignificant part of it. A country which carried on foreign trade merely upon this account could scarce have occasion to freight a ship in a century."†

It should not pass without notice, however, that before the Conclusion of his critique of Mercantilism is reached the attack has become generalised beyond considerations of foreign trade and distribution of the precious metals. In this Chapter (VIII of

---

* *Lectures by Adam Smith*, ed. Cannan, p. 197.
† *Wealth of Nations*, p. 411.

Book iv) the much-quoted sentence has quite a modern ring – and application: "Consumption is the sole end and purpose of all production; and the interest of the producer ought to be attended to, only so far as may be necessary for promoting that of the consumer." *Per contra*, it is added, "in the mercantile system, the interest of the consumer is almost constantly sacrificed to that of the producer; and it seems to consider production, and not consumption, as the ultimate end and object of all industry and commerce".* This essentially was the *Wealth of Nations*'s 'message' to the emerging world of competition.

There remain two final questions to which, it seems, some attention, at least, should be paid, if any treatment of Adam Smith is not to be incomplete: his notion and use of the distinction between 'productive' and 'unproductive' labour and the closely related definition of Net Revenue by contrast with Gross Revenue.

In dealing with productive labour Smith was initially concerned to reject the Physiocratic contention that labour in industry was *stérile*, or unproductive. The designation 'unproductive' he wished to reserve for 'menial servants' and retainers (whether of aristocratic households or of government) who supplied their services directly to their lord or master. These services were paid for by the latter out of 'revenue' in a transaction that was to be classified as 'consumption' and not 'production': for one thing, they were not followed or complemented by any further sale to realise a profit. "The labour of menial servants [unlike artificers and manufacturers] does not continue the existence of the fund which maintains and employs them. Their maintenance and employment is altogether at the expense of their masters, and the work which they perform is not of a nature to repay that expense. That work consists in services which perish generally in the very instant of their performance, and does not fix or realise itself in some such vendible commodity. It is upon this account that ... I have classed artificers, manufacturers and merchants,

* *Ibid.*, p. 620.

among the productive labourers, and menial servants among the barren or unproductive."*

But in explaining wherein the difference between "artificers and manufacturers and merchants", on the one hand, and "menial servants" consisted, Adam Smith is far from clear. Here he introduces two distinct, if largely overlapping, definitions, involving (as Marx pointed out) certain contradictions between them, or at least displaying no clear boundary between the productive and the unproductive.

First, there was the notion of productive labour as being that labour which, not only replaced the direct expenses of production, including its own wages, but in addition yielded a profit or a surplus over and above these expenses (or, in modern terminology, in excess of the value of all the inputs). This was essentially the same as the Physiocratic notion; and Marx was to call it "the correct definition".†

Secondly, there was the notion implicit in the passage we have just quoted of productive labour as being embodied in a "vendible commodity", having an exchange-value of its own and hence capable of being resold: this by contrast with "services which perish generally in the very instant of their performance". It is on this sense that attention has mostly been concentrated in subsequent comment and discussion up to this day (including discussion about such categories in the socialist countries). This meaning already creeps in at the first mention of productive and unproductive labour, in connection with the Accumulation of Capital in Chapter iii of Book ii, if only as an

---

* *Ibid.*, p. 635. *Cf.* Malthus's interpretation (and endorsement) of Smith's 'productive labour' as "labour which realises itself either in the production or increased value of . . . material objects" (*Principles of Political Economy* (London, 1820) p. 30).

† *Theories of Surplus-Value*, Part I, trans. Emile Burns (Moscow, n.d.) p. 148: "Productive labour, in its meaning for capitalist production, is wage-labour which, exchanged against the variable part of capital . . . reproduces not only this part of capital (or the value of its own labour-power), but in addition produces surplus-value for the capitalist . . . Only that labour is productive which produces a value greater than its own". *Cf.* also *Capital*, Vol. I (Moore and Aveling ed.) p. 517: "Capitalist production, is not merely the production of commodities, it is essentially the production of surplus value . . . That labourer alone is productive, who produces surplus-value for the capitalist and thus works for the self-expansion of capital."

ambiguity of interpretation. The opening sentence of this chapter says that "there is one sort of labour which adds to the value of the subject upon which it is bestowed: there is another which has no such effect. The former, as it produces a value, may be called productive ... The labour of a menial servant, on the contrary, adds to the value of nothing."* After a statement to the effect that "a man grows rich by employing a multitude of manufacturers: he grows poor, by maintaining a multitude of menial servants", this opening paragraph of the chapter closes, again, with references to labour being fixed in "some particular subject or vendible commodity" by contrast with "services [which] generally perish in the very instant of their performance, and seldom leave any trace of value behind them". It can reasonably be supposed that Adam Smith saw no conflict between the two definitions because he did not suppose it to be possible for there to be a profit or surplus-value *unless* the labour in question produced a vendible commodity. Over a large area, no doubt, the two notions amount to the same thing. But, as Marx again observed, actors, musicians, dancing masters, cooks and prostitutes may all create a surplus or profit for an employer if they happen to be employed by "an entrepreneur of theatres, concerts, brothels, etc.".† Again, "a writer is a productive labourer not in so far as he produces ideas, but in so far as he enriches a publisher". The crux of the matter, Marx claims, is a "social relation of production", and not "the particular speciality of the labour" or "the particular use-value in which this special labour is incorporated"; we need "a definition of labour which is derived not from its content or its result, but from its particular social form".‡

* *Wealth of Nations*, p. 311.
† *Theories of Surplus Value*, Part I, pp. 160–4. He adds: "The cook in the hotel produces a commodity for the person who as a capitalist has bought her labour – the hotel proprietor; the consumer of mutton chops has to pay for her labour, and this labour replaces for the hotel proprietor (apart from profit) the fund out of which he continues to pay the cook. On the other hand if I buy the labour of a cook for her to cook meat etc. for me ... then her labour is unproductive, in spite of the fact that this labour fixes itself in a material product and could just as well (in its result) be a vendible commodity, as it is in fact for the hotel proprietor" (*ibid.*, p. 161).
‡ *Ibid.*, pp. 153, 154, 156. In *Capital* Marx says: "That labourer alone is productive who produces surplus-value for the capitalist, and thus works for the self-

To come to Adam Smith's distinction between Gross and Net Revenue: it is clear that he again had in mind the Physiocratic notion of *produit net* as a surplus arising from economic activity. But the definition that emerges is of something different. As defined in Chapter II of Book II Net Revenue appears initially to have the accepted 'modern' (*i.e.* national income) meaning: namely, the gross product or revenue ("the whole annual produce of the land and labour" of a country) *minus* the capital used-up in producing that product, or "the expenses of maintaining, first their fixed and secondly, their circulating capital".* That it is intentionally different from surplus of the Physiocratic *genre* is not mentioned; although the interpretation of "maintaining circulating capital" intact proceeds to be qualified by saying that "the circulating capital of a society is in this respect, different from that of an individual". Despite some obscurity surrounding this interpretation (in a chapter mainly devoted to an excursion into banking and paper money) it is made clear that the intention is to include in "the neat revenue" what the inhabitants of a country spend upon "their subsistence" as well as upon their "conveniences and amusements": it is the whole of what is placed "in their stock reserved for immediate consumption", "without encroaching upon their capital".

One way of putting the question of possible differences of interpretation is to ask whether maintaining circulating capital intact is to be taken to mean, on a global (or national) scale, maintaining intact merely stocks of raw material and goods-in-process or as including *also* in circulating capital some kind of national subsistence-fund or wages-fund. Does a stock of finished wage-goods sufficient for the employed labour-force during a given cycle of production have to be deducted before

---

expansion of capital . . . The production of surplus-value has at all times been made, by classical political economists, the distinguishing characteristic of the productive labourer" (*Capital*, Vol. I (trans. Moore and Aveling) p. 517).

* *Wealth of Nations*, p. 267. It has to be remembered, incidentally, that, in common with most classical writers, he made the tacit assumption of an annual cycle of production (like the harvest cycle) with a single turnover of circulating capital during the production period (*cf.* P. Sraffa, *Production of Commodities by Means of Commodities* (Cambridge, 1960) pp. 3, 10).

the surplus is calculated, as well as stocks of raw materials and unfinished production? In a number of passages Adam Smith seems to deny that the former type of deduction is contemplated. One could take the simple agricultural case, which both Smith and the Physiocrats no doubt had in mind, with a homogeneous product corn, serving also as capital, and an annual harvest-cycle; and have, in microcosm, this kind of simplified example:

Capital consists of 20 units of corn,

divided into: { 10 seed corn
{ 10 subsistence wages.

Gross Product (*i.e.* the annual harvest) is 40 units.

The question could then be put: does the *Net* Product consist of (*a*) the farmer's profit after replacing the 20 units of capital required to provide seed *and* subsistence wages for the coming year (namely a surplus of 20), or of (*b*) the farmer's profit together with the wages of his labourers (namely 30 units, which is the difference between the gross harvest and the fund of seed-corn needed for planting in the coming year)? According to the first interpretation, Adam Smith's definition in terms of keeping circulating capital intact, if this is taken to include both wages and seed-corn, would appear to lead to the same result as the Physiocratic notion. But this result could be regarded as accidental.* Only the second interpretation is really consistent with making 'net revenue' identical with the potential consumption fund of *both* capitalists *and* wage-earners, as is Adam Smith's declared intention. To this extent Smithian 'net revenue' is a different concept from Physiocratic *produit net* and from Marxian 'surplus-value'.

We shall see that Ricardo took it unambiguously in the first sense of surplus: *i.e.* as Profit (also Rent) *after* paying Wages;

---

* Adam Smith seems to have been aware that, as regards wages at least, circulating capital in an exchange society would mainly be held in the form of money; and in one place he says: "Money, therefore, is the only part of the circulating capital of a society, of which the maintenance can occasion any diminution in their neat revenue" (*Wealth of Nations*, p. 269).

and he incidentally criticised Adam Smith because he "constantly magnifies the advantages which a country derives from a large gross, rather than a large net income".*

* *Works and Correspondence of Ricardo*, ed. Sraffa, Vol. I, pp. 347, 348, 422. The definition is qualified in a footnote on p. 348 (and its intention further clarified) to the extent that more is contained in wages "than the absolutely necessary expenses of production": "in that case a part of the net produce of the country is received by the labourer".

3

DAVID RICARDO

I

In his distinguished work on *Philosophic Radicalism* Halévy draws attention to the regret expressed by James Mill in the course of an article in *The Edinburgh Review* for October 1808 at "the great difficulty with which the salutary doctrines of political economy are propagated in this country"; adding that between 1776 and 1817 "not a single complete treatise on political economy appeared in England. Adam Smith remained the only authority, and he was little heeded."* Mill's views on doctrinal propagation may have been ambitious or he may have written in a pessimistic mood. But there was certainly nothing during this period approaching a "complete treatise" on the subject. (Even if Bentham's *Manual*† of 1793–5 had come out, and been longer than it is, it would not have qualified since it was about policy and not theory.) This is not to say that there was not considerable activity and alertness in matters affecting political economy, especially in respect to pamphleteering on particular questions. To the latter class can be said to belong William Spence's *Britain Independent of Commerce* of 1808, and James Mill's answer to it in *Commerce Defended* of the same year; the latter being chiefly memorable for its sponsoring of 'Say's Law', as first propounded in J.-B. Say's *Traité d'Économie Politique* of five years before. The year 1798, moreover, had seen Malthus's *Essay on Population*; while in the first decade of the new century articles on questions of political economy were not uncommon in *The Edinburgh Review* and were a topic of discussion among the *cognoscenti*.‡ Discussion of monetary policy

* Elie Halévy, *The Growth of Philosophic Radicalism*, trans. Mary Morris (London, 1928) pp. 264–5. Mill's article was entitled 'Money and Exchange'.
† *Cf. Jeremy Bentham's Economic Writings*, ed. W. Stark (London, 1952) Vol. I, pp. 223–73.
‡ These "early articles" from 1802 onward had "afforded often an agreeable subject for half an hour's chat, when business did not engage us" at the Stock

and of war-time depreciation at the time of the Bullion Controversy was the occasion of Ricardo's first public appearance in economic discussion; while the Parliamentary debates on the Corn Law of February 1815 were to provoke a veritable efflorescence of pamphleteering within that same month, in the course of which the theory of rent was perfected, and so far as Ricardo was concerned the essentials of his theory of profit and of its tendency to fall in the course of progress in capital accumulation were worked out. The period of which Marx was to speak as being "notable for scientific activity in the domain of Political Economy" and a time when "splendid tournaments were held",* was close at hand.

What can, indeed, be said, is that until 1817, the year of Ricardo's *Principles*, there was nothing that could be called a single theoretical system of political economy, even as a preliminary sketch. A characteristic of the *Wealth of Nations* was its unsystematic character so far as theory was concerned. Some have even regarded this perhaps as among its leading virtues: that it was able to illuminate so much because it was concerned so largely with history and with particular situations and did not strain after conceptual unity. Brilliant *aperçus*, elegantly fashioned *pieces* of theory, most persuasive commentary and judgement upon particular policies and systems of thought like the 'mercantile' and the 'agricultural' it certainly contained. But we have seen that it lacked a theory of distribution, properly speaking, and that what there was of a theory of price or of value (in the form of the adding of the three components) was logically incomplete – the distinction between natural and market price and his principle of equal net advantages, his sterling contributions in this sphere, standing apart on their own. With Ricardo, however, we meet something rather different: an integrated theory of value, of profit and of rents; its aspects or elements having something of the neatness and

Exchange for Ricardo and his friend Hutches Trower (Letter of Ricardo to Trower of 26 Jan. 1818 in *Works and Correspondence of David Ricardo*, ed. P. Sraffa, Vol. vii, p. 246, and *cf.* Vol. vi, p. xxiii).

* In the Author's Preface to the Second Edition (24 Jan. 1872), *Capital*, Vol. i (trans. Moore and Aveling) p. xxii.

precision of a mathematical demonstration, to which a major policy-corollary was most persuasively attached.

It is well-known that between 1809 and 1811 Ricardo's interest in economic questions was mainly engaged in matters of money and prices and their connection with movements in the foreign exchange-rate. His views on these matters were formed in the course of criticism of the policy of the Bank of England during the war: the Bank being accused of responsibility for excessive issue of bank notes, to which was attributed the current premium on gold (in terms of notes) and the fall in the exchange-value of the pound in Hamburg, Amsterdam and other continental financial centres. This criticism was voiced in the first instance in an anonymous article in the *Morning Chronicle* in August 1809 (followed by two letters in September and November), and then developed in a pamphlet entitled 'The High Price of Bullion, a Proof of the Depreciation of Bank Notes' in 1810. After the publication of the Report of the Bullion Committee he wrote three further letters to the *Morning Chronicle* (in September 1810) in support of its findings (which "cannot fail to carry conviction to every unprejudiced mind").* In the course of this discussion about the sterling-price of gold bullion, the essentials of the Quantity Theory of Money and of what later came to be called the Purchasing Power Parity Theory of the foreign exchanges were enunciated.

It is from the publication of the highly topical pamphlet of February 1815, *An Essay on the Influence of a Low Price of Corn on the Profits of Stock, showing the inexpediency of restrictions on importation*, that the essential elements of his theory of value and distribution really date. This pamphlet, we have seen, appeared in the same month as other pamphlets on the same topic by Malthus, West (the authorship given on the title-page was simply 'A Fellow of University College, Oxford') and Col. Robert Torrens. The *Principles of Political Economy and Taxation* of two years later was a development and elaboration of the elemental ideas presented in the *Essay* in the course of a topical and highly practical argument.

* *Works and Correspondence*, ed. Sraffa, Vol. III, pp. 15–153.

The *Essay* of 1815 starts with an enunciation of the famous theory of differential rent which has come to be known as the 'Ricardian Theory of Rent'. Actually Ricardo acknowledges his indebtedness for this theory to Malthus's pamphlet of three weeks before, *An Inquiry into Rent*; and, as Mr Sraffa has pointed out,* what seems to have happened is that Ricardo realised that the theory as expounded by Malthus neatly complemented his own theory of profits. He had previously been familiar with the notion of diminishing returns in the sense of diminishing productivity of labour at the margin as agricultural production is extended (or intensified). Indeed, it was on this that not only the price of corn relatively to manufactures but also profit (of the farmer and also of the manufacturer and trader) depended. Ricardo, accordingly, can be said to have had the essential framework for a theory of rent, but had not yet actually fitted into it the notion of rent as a surplus, with the manner of its determination, until he had read Malthus's pamphlet. The pamphlet by West, published eleven days before, which enunciated substantially the same theory of rent based on diminishing productivity at the margin of cultivation, had not been read by Ricardo at the time of writing the *Essay*.†

It may be noted that in expounding this view of rent as the surplus produce of infra-marginal land (or alternatively of infra-marginal applications of labour) where productivity was greater than at the margin, Ricardo had quite clearly in view the notion of an intensive as well as an extensive margin. At any rate this was quite evident by the time of the *Principles*, where he speaks in general terms of rent as "always the difference between the produce obtained by the employment of two equal quantities of capital and labour"‡ and as dependent upon "inequality in the produce obtained from successive portions of capital employed on the same or on new

---

* In his Note on 'Essay on Profits' in *Works and Correspondence of Ricardo*, Vol. IV, pp. 6–8.

† *Ibid.*, Vol. I, p. 71 *passim. Cf.* M. Blaug, *Ricardian Economics* (New Haven, 1958) pp. 12–13.

‡ *Ibid.*, Vol. I, p. 71 *passim. Cf.* Blaug, *Ricardian Economics*, pp. 12–13.

land".* In whichever manner it was explained – whether its increase was attributed to increased application of labour and capital to an *existing* and given quantity of land or to an extension of cultivation to new land of inferior quality – the idea that it was "a creation of value, as I understand that word, but not a creation of wealth" and that its rise was "always the effect of the increasing wealth of the country, and of the difficulty of providing food for its augmented population"† remained unaffected; and when J.-B. Say objected that there was no such thing as 'no-rent land', he could retort that this did not matter since there were always no-rent units of capital and labour at the *intensive* margin of all land.‡

His theory of profits was in many ways more crucial for the main structure of his doctrine. This, it is of some importance to appreciate, was formed even before the *Essay* and was enunciated, prior to his theory of value, in purely product terms. Mr Sraffa has again pointed out that it may well have been enunciated in a preliminary draft of a year previously which has not survived but is described in a letter as "papers on the profits of Capital" which he appears to have shown to Malthus and to Hutches Trower.§ This was essentially a surplus theory, more clearly and explicitly than in the case of Adam Smith's 'deduction' theory. It was to the effect that Profits depended upon the difference between the product of labour at the margin of cultivation and the subsistence of that labour; both being expressed in Corn. Profit was accordingly expressed as a simple product-ratio to Wages: a ratio which fell as the margin was extended and the product of a day's labour declined. As

---

* *Ibid.*, p. 83. He also says (p. 80) that "it is not necessary that land should be thrown out of cultivation, in order to reduce rent: to produce this effect, it is sufficient that successive portions of capital are employed on the same land with different results, and that the portion which gives the least result should be withdrawn". On Torrens's view that rent did not even require diminishing returns for its existence (merely scarcity), *cf.* Lionel Robbins, *Robert Torrens and the Evolution of Classical Economics* (London, 1958) pp. 42–3.

† *Works and Correspondence of Ricardo*, Vol. I, pp. 399, 77.

‡ *Ibid.*, pp. 412–13n. Schumpeter speaks of "superficial readers" as thinking that the theory requires the existence of 'no rent land' (*History of Economic Analysis*, p. 675n).

§ Introduction to Vol. I of *Works and Correspondence of Ricardo*, p. xxi.

appears from a letter of June 1814, his theory was summed-up in the proposition that "the rate of profits and of interest must depend on the proportion of production to the consumption necessary to such production".* In the *Essay on Profits* of 1815 he says that "the general profits of stock depend wholly on the profits of the last portion of capital employed on the land". De Quincey was later to express it, that "he [Ricardo] it was who first made it possible to deduce wages from rent – and therefore to deduce profits from wages . . . in one brief formula, it might be said of profits – *they are the leavings of wages*".†

With this Corn Theory of Profit (as it may be called) was coupled initially the notion that profits in agriculture determined general profits. There could not be two different profit-rates in manufacture and agriculture consistently with the 'law' of (or tendency towards) a uniform profit-rate. Since the ratio of profit to wages in agriculture was given by the conditions of production there (and being a product-ratio was invariant to any change in the price of corn), it followed that the brunt of adaptation must fall on the prices of manufactures, until as a result of these price-movements the same rate of profit was being earned in manufactures as in agriculture. The only way in which the rate of profit in agriculture (representing the relation between corn-output and corn-input as seed and wages) could be altered was by a shift in the margin of cultivation. Hence when a critic argued (as did Malthus in his correspondence with Ricardo in 1814–15) that an expansion of trade, especially of foreign trade, could raise the general rate of profit, the onus rested on him to show *how* it could shift agricultural profits by shifting the margin.

Implicit in Ricardo's conception was, of course, the assumption that wages were given in terms of corn – a subsistence, or

---

* *Ibid.*, p. xxxii; Vol. VI, p. 108. *Cf.* also the later reference in the *Principles* cited on page 74.

† T. de Quincey, *The Logic of Political Economy* (Edinburgh and London, 1844) pp. 203, 204. This he contrasted sharply with "the old superannuated doctrine" (*i.e.* of Smith). (The context makes clear that, when he referred to deducing wages from rent, he had in mind the change in money wages (or the 'value of wages') consequent on changes in the margin and in the value of corn, and that in referring to rent he here meant the *theory* of rent as a whole.)

at least (in Marshallian terminology) a supply-price, theory of independently given corn-wages.* It is clear that Ricardo treated the demand for corn at any given date, and hence the position of the agricultural margin, as determined by the size of the labouring population (with presumably a fairly inelastic demand for necessaries).† In deference to Malthus's arguments Ricardo later modified somewhat his early view that agricultural profits determine general profits absolutely: he did so to the extent, at least, of allowing for the fact that the labourers did not only consume corn, but consumed some manufactured goods also. Despite this, however, he held to the crucial pivot of his main position, that general profits could not diverge from the ratio of corn produced to the corn-wages involved in its production at the agricultural margin, even if there were circumstances in which in the course of adjustment the position of this margin might undergo some alteration. With this qualification, accordingly, he still held profits to be determined by the relation between product and wages at the margin of agriculture.

When he had fitted together this theory of profit with the theory of rent as being governed by differences in the productivity of labour successively applied to the land, or to lands of different quality, he came very close to concluding (although this was not said explicitly) that profit and rent were two species of Physiocratic *produit net*. At any rate they were viewed as being antagonistic in the sense that increase in rent was at the *expense* of profit and represented a *transfer* merely of net revenue. As it was expressed in the *Essay*: "Rent then is in all cases a portion of the profits previously obtained on the land. It is never a new creation of revenue, but always a part of a revenue already created." He then proceeded to put the

* In his Chapter On Wages there is the famous reference to the fact that "the natural price of labour, estimated even in food and necessaries . . . varies at different times in the same country, and very materially differs in different countries" according to "the habits and customs of the people" (to which he added in Edition 2 a reference to a passage to the same effect in Torrens's *Essay on the External Corn Trade*): *Works and Correspondence of Ricardo*, ed. Sraffa, Vol. I, pp. 96–7.

† *Cf.* Blaug, *Ricardian Economics*, pp. 22–3.

essence of his theory into these two key sentences: "Profits of stock fall only, because land equally well adapted to produce food cannot be procured; and the degree of the fall of profits, and the rise of rents, depends wholly on the increased expense of production. If, therefore, in the progress of countries in wealth and population, new portions of fertile land could be added to such countries, with every increase of capital, profits would never fall, nor rents rise."* The completed picture was that as a result of diminishing productivity of labour at the margin as cultivation was extended, profits tended to fall as capital accumulated and population grew with it. Thereby was provided the missing explanation in Adam Smith's theory of a tendency to falling profit (which we have seen that he had attributed, in terms of supply and demand, to greater competition). Simultaneously rents rose; thus transferring what had previously been profits for the farmer (or manufacturer) into the pockets of the landowner.†

Having thereby established in general terms the antagonism of interest between landed property and industrial capital ("the interest of the landlord is always opposed to the interest of every other class in the community"),‡ he went on to exemplify this with more particular criticism of the existing import duties on corn. These duties inevitably raised rents by raising the demand

* *Works and Correspondence of Ricardo*, ed. Sraffa, Vol. iv, p. 18.

† Ricardo was careful to qualify such statements with "in the absence of improvements". There were those who argued that, viewed dynamically, the effect of improvements would more than counteract any such tendency. But Edwin Cannan would seem to have been probably right in maintaining that "there is no doubt whatever that Ricardo, like West and Malthus, believed that the returns to agricultural industry do actually diminish in the course of history in spite of all improvements" (*History of the Theories of Production and Distribution*, 2nd ed. (London, 1903) p. 166).

‡ *Works and Correspondence of Ricardo*, ed. Sraffa, Vol. iv, p. 21. Later, in the first edition of his *Principles* (London, 1817) p. 66n, he pointed his argument against the position of Adam Smith as follows: "In dwelling on the reproduction of rent as so great an advantage to society, Dr. Smith does not reflect that rent is the effect of high price, and that what the landlord gains in this way, he gains at the expense of the community at large. There is no absolute gain to the society by the reproduction of rent; it is only one class profiting at the expense of another class" (*Works and Correspondence*, Vol. I, p. 77n). Schumpeter dismissed Ricardo's theory of rent as "neither necessary nor sufficient for an attack upon the landed interest" (*History of Economic Analysis*, p. 675n). This is curious: does he refer thereby to its formal structure or to its substantial content?

for, and the cost and price of, home-produced corn; at the same time they had the further inevitable consequence of lowering profit (in face of a given level of corn-wages). Conversely, a repeal of these duties, to allow entry of low-priced foreign corn, would raise profit and thereby promote capital accumulation. The obstacle to so advantageous a course was the landowners' interest in maintaining rents. The pamphlet ends with a capital debating point. Agricultural improvements as well as corn-imports lower the cost of growing corn and hence tend to lower both corn-prices and rents. Those who object to the latter should in consistency prohibit also the former. "If the interests of the landlord be of sufficient consequence, to determine us not to avail ourselves of all the benefits which would follow from importing corn at a cheap price, they should also influence us in rejecting all improvements in agriculture, and in the implements of husbandry; for it is as certain that corn is rendered cheap, rents are lowered, and the ability of the landlord to pay taxes, is for a time, at least, as much impaired by such improvements, as by the importation of corn. To be consistent then, let us by the same act arrest improvement, and prohibit importation."*

II

It would seem to have been in the course of generalising his primitive 'agricultural' theory of profit that Ricardo saw the need to base his theory on a developed theory of value. So long as everything was expressed in corn, both product and capital, and hence the surplus, could be expressed in the same physical unit. But as soon as he was obliged to defend (against Malthus, for example) the view that profits elsewhere were governed by the rate of surplus product in agriculture, he had to introduce a theory of value to show how the prices of those *other* commodities moved (if at all) when the cost in labour of corn increased. Malthus had answered Ricardo with the contention that

* *Works and Correspondence*, Vol. IV, p. 41. Malthus was later to challenge this contention that improvements lowered rent. But in the main Ricardo stuck to his point, although granting that *in the long-run* landlords might be benefited in so far as improvements made possible an increase of population, and increased population eventually raised the demand for corn and raised rents.

general profits could be as much affected by high prices of manufactures due to a strong demand for them, such as a flourishing export-demand, as by "the natural powers of the last land taken into cultivation". In his own *Principles* (Chapter v, Section IV) he had said that "profits depend upon the prices of commodities, and upon the cause which determines these prices, namely the supply compared with the demand"; while Ricardo's "theory of profits depends entirely upon the circumstance of the mass of commodities remaining at the same price, while money continues of the same value, whatever may be the variation in the price of labour ... We can infer nothing [he concludes] respecting the rate of profits from a rise of money wages, if commodities, instead of remaining of the same price, are very variously affected, some rising, some falling, and a very small number indeed remaining stationary."*

In using the Labour Theory of Value for this purpose, Ricardo in effect was substituting Labour for Corn as the quantity in terms of which product, wages and surplus were alike expressed. Profit was now conceived as the surplus, or residual difference, between the amount of labour required to produce subsistence for the labour-force and the total labour-force: in the language of the *Principles*, as depending upon the "proportion of the annual labour of the country ... directed to the support of the labourers".† As such it was a more general version (general because resting on less restrictive assumptions) of the dictum we have already quoted about profit depending upon "the ratio of production to the consumption necessary to that production", with both total production and necessary consumption now measured in terms of the labour needed to produce them. As soon as it was thus stated in terms of value, the proposition that profits fall because of a falling productivity of labour in terms of corn becomes translated into: profits fall

---

* T. R. Malthus, *Principles of Political Economy considered with a view to their practical application* (London, 1820) pp. 326–7, 334. *Cf.* also the letter of Malthus to Ricardo of 23 Nov. 1814: "the question is whether agriculture always takes the lead in the determination? and I should certainly say that it did not" (*Works and Correspondence of Ricardo*, ed. Sraffa, Vol. VI, p. 153).

† *Works and Correspondence of Ricardo*, ed. Sraffa, Vol. I, p. 49.

because of the rising value of corn, and hence of wages, relatively to other products.

In the argument of the *Essay*, indeed, we already meet this theory of value in embryo, even if the essentials of the theory of profit, as of rent, were still enunciated in the more primitive 'agricultural' form. Thus in stating that, owing to diminishing returns on land as corn-production is extended, profits must fall as rents rise, he says:

> The exchangeable value of all commodities rises as the difficulty of their production increases. If then new difficulties occur in the production of corn, from more labour being necessary, whilst no more labour is required to produce gold, silver, linen etc., the exchangeable value of corn will necessarily rise, as compared with those things . . . The sole effect then of the progress of wealth on prices, independently of all improvements, either in agriculture or manufactures, appears to be to raise the prices of raw produce and of labour, leaving all other commodities at their ordinary prices, and to lower general profits in consequence of the general rise of wages.*

Not uncommonly the intention of a doctrine is best seen when it is placed in direct antithesis to what it is designed to contradict. In this connection a footnote that closely follows the above passage is illuminating: one could say, indeed, that it is crucial for understanding the significance for Ricardo of his theory of value. In this footnote he writes: "It has been thought that the price of corn regulates the prices of all other things. This appears to me to be a mistake. If the price of corn is affected by the rise or fall of the precious metals themselves, then indeed will the price of commodities be also affected, but they vary because the value of money varies not because the value of corn is altered. Commodities I think cannot materially rise or fall, whilst money and commodities continue in the same proportions, or rather whilst the cost of production of both estimated in corn continues the same."†

* *Ibid.*, Vol. IV, pp. 19–20.   † *Ibid.*, p. 21.

The theory to which he is here alluding, that corn prices govern other prices (because when corn rises, money-wages have to rise to keep corn-wages constant, and this raises other prices)' was Adam Smith's theory. What Ricardo was opposing in particular with his Labour Theory of Value was manifestly Adam Smith's *Wages* Theory of Value (or what we alluded to earlier as the Adding-up Theory);* which treated the value of commodities as being governed *inter alia* by the amount of *wages* that their production cost (together with the addition of appropriate amounts of the other two "component parts of price"). In the words of the opening section of his Chapter On Value in the second and third editions of Ricardo's *Principles*: "The value of a commodity, or the quantity of any other commodity for which it will exchange, depends on the relative quantity of labour which is necessary for its production, and not on the greater or less compensation which is paid for that labour."

It is clear on reflection that the Adam Smith theory un-qualified leads to an absurd conclusion: that the values of everything can rise simultaneously whenever one of the "components" rises for any reason, whether this be due to a rise in cost of subsistence, as in the present case, or more generally to the working of supply and demand. This raises the question: in terms of *what* do all values rise? If in terms of money, then this is equivalent to depreciation of money ("to say that commodities are raised in price, is the same thing as to say that money is lowered in relative value; for it is by commodities that the relative value of gold is estimated"). But with a commodity-money standard, such depreciation can only occur if either the cost of producing the money-commodity itself falls or the cost of the generality of commodities *other* than the money-commodity rises. As to the possible effect on the latter of a rise of wages, Ricardo replies that if gold were mined *within* the country in question, the effect on gold would be no different from the effect on other commodities and their relative values would remain unchanged. In the case where gold was mined

* See Chapter 2.

abroad and imported: "If then all commodities rose in price, gold could not come from abroad to purchase these dear commodities, but it would go from home to be employed with advantage in purchasing the comparatively cheaper foreign commodities. It appears then that the rise of wages will not raise the prices of commodities, whether the metal from which money is made be produced at home or in a foreign country."*

His refutation of Smith's theory can, therefore, be seen to have turned on his bringing money itself within the circle of commodities, and in doing so postulating that the price of any commodity or group of commodities can only rise if more labour is required to produce it relatively to the amount of labour required to produce an ounce of gold. This proposition (concerning the "invariability of the value of the precious metals") he spoke of in a letter to James Mill as "the sheet anchor upon which all my propositions are built".†

When it came to the writing of the Chapter On Value in the *Principles*, Ricardo accordingly started by developing his own theoretical argument in opposition to Smith's theory. First, he criticised Adam Smith for his confusion between quantity of labour and labour commanded as measure of value. Secondly, he developed the argument that it is "on the relative quantity of labour which is necessary for its production" that the value of a commodity depends, "*and not* on the greater or less compensation which is paid for that labour".‡ He then takes up Smith's well-known example of the beaver and the deer ("if it usually cost twice the labour to kill a beaver which it does to kill a deer, one beaver should naturally exchange for, or be worth two deer") and declares that the principle which it is used to illustrate, that labour "is really the foundation of the exchangeable value of all things, excepting those which cannot be increased by human industry, is a doctrine of the utmost importance in political economy". He then criticises Smith for

---

* *Works and Correspondence of Ricardo*, ed. Sraffa, Vol. I, p. 105.
† Cited in Sraffa's Introduction to Vol. I of *Works and Correspondence*, p. xxxiv; *cf.* Vol. VI, p. 348 (Letter of 30 Dec. 1815).
‡ This was the wording of the heading of Section I of this Chapter in Edition 2 (in the first edition the Chapter is undivided into Sections).

proceeding to speak of a thing as being more or less valuable according to "not the quantity of labour bestowed on the production of any object, but the quantity which it can command in the market".

Extending the beaver–deer example to cover the case where capital, in the shape of some weapon, "would be necessary to enable [the hunter] to kill his game", he showed that its use does not necessarily impugn his principle (as Adam Smith had implied): the comparative prices of beaver and deer "would be in proportion to the actual labour bestowed, both on the formation of the capital, and on the destruction of the animals"; this being unaffected by the fact that "the implements necessary to kill the beaver and deer might belong to one class of men, and the labour employed in their destruction might be furnished by another class", or by whether those furnishing the capital "might have a half, a fourth or an eighth of the produce obtained", since "whether the profits of the capitalist were greater or less . . . or whether the wages of labour were high or low, they would operate equally on both employments".*

It is to be noted that he was implicitly assuming here that the proportions in which capital was used (or what Marx was to call 'the organic composition of capital') were equal in the various lines of production considered, whether in hunting beaver and deer or in catching fish or in shooting game, or in manufacturing stockings. What he was concerned to show was that "the accumulation of stock . . . in the hands of particular persons" and "the appropriation of land" did not (as Smith had claimed)† per se invalidate the principle of exchange in proportion to labour employed in production. It is also to be noted that the importance attached to what we have seen that he called "the sheet anchor" of his position explains his concern, in a later section added to his third edition,‡ with "an invariable measure" of value and the conditions necessary to render such a standard invariable: a matter to which we shall,

---

* Ibid., Vol. I, pp. 23–4; and cf. his own emphatic explanation of the point in a letter to Mill, cit. ibid., pp. xxxvi–xxxvii.

† See Chapter 2, p. 45.

‡ Added to the 3rd edition where it was to become Section VI of this chapter.

again, return. At the conclusion of the argument about value that we have just summarised, he writes: "If we had an invariable standard, by which we could measure the variation in other commodities, we should find that the utmost limit to which they could permanently rise was proportioned to the additional quantity of labour required for their production, and that unless more labour were required for their production, they could not rise in any degree whatever."*

Contrary to Adam Smith's contention, a rise in wages would *not* result in a general rise in prices: instead it would result in a reduction of profits, and this to a balancing extent. De Quincey was to sum up the Ricardian view of the relation of wages to profit in the following way. "It might be said of profits – that they are *the leavings of wages*: so much will the profit be upon any act of production . . . as the wages upon that act permit to be left behind . . . But do not wages and profits as a whole, themselves, on the contrary, predetermine the price? No, that is the old superannuated doctrine. But the new economy has shown that all price is governed by proportional quantity of producing labour, and by that only . . . Any change that can disturb the existing relations between wages and profits, must originate in wages: whatever change may silently take place in profits, always we must view as recording and measuring a previous change in wages."†

Many, if not most, readers of this Chapter On Value are puzzled to find themselves confronted immediately after this with what appears to them as a contrary argument, to be summarised in the heading to Section IV in the third edition as: "The principle that the quantity of labour bestowed on the production of commodities regulates their relative value, considerably modified by the employment of machinery and other fixed and durable capital."‡ Here he proceeds to take account of the fact that "the tools, implements, buildings, and machinery

---

* *Ibid.*, p. 29.
† Thomas de Quincey, *The Logic of Political Economy* (Edinburgh and London, 1844) pp. 204–5. In his Preface he had spoken of "the revolution affected in that science by Ricardo".
‡ *Works and Correspondence of Ricardo*, ed. Sraffa, Vol. I, p. 30.

employed in different trades may be of various degrees of durability, and may require different portions of labour to produce them ... the proportions, too, in which the capital that is invested in tools, machinery and buildings, may be variously combined". Thereby is introduced "another cause, besides the greater or less quantity or labour necessary to produce commodities, for the variations in their relative value" – adding (perplexingly at first sight) "this cause is the rise or fall in the value of labour".* For many this reference to a second 'cause' of value, especially as it is presented sharply in the third edition, appears as evidence of a contradiction and of a shift away from a 'primitive' theory with which he started at the time of the *Essay* towards something like a Cost of Production Theory such as it was to become later in the century,† not in essentials different from Adam Smith's theory of the 'component parts of price'.

Since the publication of Mr Sraffa's famous Introduction we should by now have become familiar with the view that there is little or no ground for this interpretation, and that the situation is really otherwise. It was after the appearance of the *Essay on Profit* and in the course of writing the *Principles* that Ricardo made the "discovery" of "the curious effect", as he called it, of a rise of wages on the products of industry in which a relatively large amount of fixed capital was used: namely, it caused their prices actually to *fall* (because of the consequential fall of profits). This it was that formed the basis of the reference

---

* This is the wording of the relevant paragraph in the third edition (*ibid.*, p. 30). In the earlier editions the wording was different, *e.g.* "Besides the alteration in the relative value of commodities, occasioned by more or less labour being required to produce them, they are also subject to fluctuations from a rise of wages, and consequent fall of profits, if the fixed capitals employed be either of unequal value, or of unequal duration" (*ibid.*, p. 53).

† As an example of this interpretation *cf.* Erich Roll, *A History of Economic Thought*, 1st ed. (London, 1938) p. 185: "We see once again that the difference between price and value caused by the existence of different capital structures was leading Ricardo, not to the distinction between value and prices of production which Marx worked out, but to a cost-of-production theory of value"; and the reference on p. 181 to "modifications in the law of value, which he appears to have regarded with increasing concern and to which he gave more and more space in successive editions". A similar interpretation was offered by both Cannan and Hollander, and hinted at by Marshall.

we have quoted to a 'second cause' (what in the first edition appears as a reference to the relative value of commodities being "also subject to fluctuations from a rise of wages, and consequent fall of profits, if the fixed capitals employed be either of unequal value, or of unequal duration").* But on the contrary to regarding this as a concession, he regarded it as a discovery of his own that represented a *reinforcement* of his argument against Adam Smith; and as such he triumphantly announced it in his *Principles* of 1817. Not only did a rise of wages *fail* to raise the prices of commodities, but it actually caused the prices of some commodities to *fall*.† Thus the secondary effect of unequal proportions of capital, far from qualifying and weakening the anti-Smith corollary of his primary value principle, served to reinforce it with something of the effect of paradox. It was hardly surprising in the circumstances that he should have treated his primary cause (quantity of labour) as being "never superseded" by the 'second cause' (variation in capital proportions and durability) "but only modified by it".‡

Actually the element of paradox in this 'curious effect' – the conclusion that no prices rose and things made with fixed capital *fell* (as it appears in the first edition of 1817) depended upon an assumption that his invariable standard, or money, in terms of which commodity-prices were measured, was produced by "unassisted labour". Four years later in the third edition he shifted the definition of his standard to one "produced with such proportions of the two kinds of capital as approach nearest to the average quantity employed in the production of most commodities"; and in terms of this, when

* *Cf. Works and Correspondence of Ricardo*, ed. Sraffa, Vol. I, p. 53.

† "It appears, then, that in proportion to the quantity and the durability of fixed capital employed in any kind of production, the relative prices of those commodities on which such capital is employed, will vary inversely as wages; they will fall as wages rise. It appears too that no commodities whatever are raised in absolute price, merely because wages rise; that they never rise unless additional labour be bestowed on them; but that all commodities in the production of which fixed capital enters, not only do not rise with a rise of wages, but absolutely fall" (*Principles of Political Economy and Taxation* (London, 1817) pp. 41–2; *Works and Correspondence*, ed. Sraffa, Vol. I, pp. 62–3).

‡ *Ibid.*, Vol. I, p. xxxvii, and Vol. VII, p. 377 (Letter to Mill, 28 Dec. 1818).

wages rose, some things would rise in price (those "which had less fixed capital employed upon them than the medium in which price was estimated" and/or with a more rapid turnover of fixed and circulating capital), while other things (those with more fixed capital) would fall; the price-level on the average remaining unchanged as his anti-Smith corollary (as we have called it) required.* He thereby came nearer, it may be noticed, to the standpoint that Marx adopted in his theory of Prices of Production in Volume 3 of *Capital*.

The place occupied in this argument by the notion of 'an invariable standard' explains his concern with finding the proper way of defining an invariable measure of value as well as the close connection in his mind between the two problems of the measure and the cause or principle of value. The connection between them, as he envisaged it, is clearly expressed in the opening sentence of the section 'On an invariable measure of value' (Section VI in the third edition): "When commodities varied in relative value, it would be desirable to have the means of ascertaining which of them fell and which rose in real value, and this could be effected only by comparing them one after another with some invariable standard measure of value, which should itself be subject to none of the fluctuations to which other commodities are exposed."† He forthwith goes on to say that "of such a measure it is impossible to be possessed, because there is no commodity which is not itself exposed to the same variations as the things, the value of which is to be ascertained". But, while there was no shift in his standpoint on "the real foundation of exchangeable value", hesitation and doubt become increasingly evident in his search for a precise definition of the conditions necessary to make such a standard invariable. In his third edition he seems to have accepted the view that invariability in a standard was not only impossible to find in practice but was impossible in principle. The reason he gives

---

* *Ibid.*, Vol. I, pp. xxxix, xlii–xliv, pp. 43, 63. In edition 2 he had added in deference to Torrens "the unequal times that the circulating capital may circulate" to the other two sorts of variation in capital, which he had called "differences in the durability of fixed capital" and "variety in the proportions in which the two sorts of capital may be combined".   † *Ibid.*, p. 43.

is that even supposing "the same quantity of labour to be always required to obtain the same quantity of gold, still gold would not be a perfect measure of value, by which we could accurately ascertain the variations in all other things, because it would not be produced with precisely the same combinations of fixed and circulating capital as all other things; nor with fixed capital of the same durability; nor would it require precisely the same length of time, before it could be brought to market". Thus it could only "be a perfect measure of value for all things produced under the same circumstances precisely as itself, but for no others". Thus in seeking a measure one seemed to be faced with a dualism of two incommensurable entities, labour and time (*i.e.*, the length of time over which labour was 'advanced', or alternatively stored-up): it was in this context that he made the percipient remark that all differences in capital can be reduced to differences of time.* One had to content oneself, therefore, with "as near an approximation to a standard measure of value as can be theoretically conceived": namely, "gold considered as a commodity produced with such proportions of the two kinds of capital as approach nearest to the average quantity employed in the production of most commodities".† Yet so important did he hold this search for an absolute value to be as to cause him to spend the last summer of his life in an intensive correspondence with Malthus on the subject of the measure of value (following publication of the latter's pamphlet of that name), and in the closing weeks of his life to compose several incomplete drafts of a paper on 'Absolute Value and Exchangeable Value?'‡ According to his own confession in a last letter to Mill, he had "been thinking a good deal on the subject lately, but without much improvement".§

* "All the exceptions to the general rule come under this one of time" (*ibid.*, Vol. VIII, p. 193. Letter to McCulloch, 13 June 1820). *Cf.* also: "In this then consists the difficulty of the subject that the circumstances of time for which advances are made are so various that it is impossible to find any one commodity which will be an unexceptionable measure" (*ibid.*, Vol. IV, p. 370).

† *Ibid.*, Vol. I, p. 45.

‡ Published for the first time (after discovery along with a series of letters to Mill among some Cairnes family papers in Ireland) *ibid.*, Vol. IV, pp. 361-412.

§ *Ibid.*, p. 359, and Vol. IX, p. 387.

To a modern ear this search for a notional measure or invariable standard is apt to appear curious, even meaningless: so much so that it is sometimes dismissed as a phantom problem, or else as being just the familiar 'index-number problem' in an old-fashioned guise. Possibly the position occupied in economic controversy of recent years by questions of measurement of capital and the influence of distribution upon prices will serve to win for Ricardo's preoccupation a more understanding attention. We are indebted, again, to Mr Sraffa for revealing the true nature of Ricardo's problem. He has shown that what troubled Ricardo was that the size of the national product appears to change when the division of it between classes changes. "Even though nothing has occurred to change the magnitude of the aggregate, there may be *apparent* changes due solely to a change in measurement, owing to the fact that measurement is in terms of value and relative values have been altered as a result of a change in the division between wages and profits." Had Ricardo been interested primarily in the question of "why two commodities produced by the same quantities of labour are not of the same exchangeable value", this need not have worried him. But since his primary concern was with the effect of a rise or fall of wages – with 'change' rather than with 'difference' – it was crucial for his analysis to "find a measure of value which would be invariant to changes in the division of the product; for if a rise or fall of wages by itself brought about a change in the magnitude of the social product, it would be hard to determine accurately the effect on profits".*

III

Ricardo's primary interest in Distribution as "the principal problem in Political Economy" is probably too familiar to need repeating, as may be also the main dynamic corollary derived from his Theory of Distribution in the shape of a conditional forecast of the future. Yet this has been sufficiently misinterpreted for an emphasis on certain aspects of it not to

* Editor's Introduction to *Works and Correspondence of Ricardo*, Vol. 1, pp. xlviii–xlix. For Mr Sraffa's own proffered solution see Chapter 9.

be entirely otiose. An initial object of misunderstanding has
been his use of proportions in connection with changing income-
shares, and hence the proper interpretation of certain of his
statements. Needless to say, the income-categories that he took
as the subject of his enquiry were not adopted arbitrarily as
abstract categories of instrumental productive factors, but were
chosen as corresponding to the three main classes of the community as he (and other economists of the time) saw them. In
this he followed in the footsteps of Adam Smith; and here at
the ground-floor of his structure an important sociological
datum was introduced. (In those much-thumbed opening words
of his Preface: "The produce of the earth – all that is derived
from its surface by the united application of labour, machinery
and capital, is divided among three classes of the community;
namely, the proprietor of the land, the owner of the stock or
capital necessary for its cultivation, and the labourers by whose
industry it is cultivated.") When he spoke of these shares rising
or falling (and the direction of their relative movement was his
principal concern) he generally meant rising or falling in what
he called "real value" in terms of an invariable money: in
other words in terms of the amount of labour required to produce the share in question. Here his statements stood firmly
within the category of (absolute) value, as measured by quantity of labour. With a given scale of production measured in
terms of employment of labour, this was accordingly the same
thing as saying that the proportion of the total value produced
going to the share in question had risen or fallen; and it is in
this sense that his references to a rise of wages causing a fall in
profits must be understood. Thus the phrase 'real value of
wages' that comes strangely to a modern ear is defined by
Ricardo as "the quantity of labour, and capital employed in
producing them": wages are to be estimated by this "and not
by their nominal value either in coats, hats, money or corn".*

* *Ibid.*, Vol. I, p. 50. In his *Notes on Malthus* he says: "I should think it a great
error to say that wages had fallen, when it was agreed that the labourer 'had an
increased proportion of the value of the whole produce obtained by a given
quantity of capital'. Value is I think measured by proportions" (*ibid.*, Vol. II,
p. 138). This in particular was the language sharply criticised by Bailey (among

In this connection there was some ambiguity over the share of rent as to whether this would tend to rise as a proportion with progress in capital accumulation and increasing population; and in view of this Ricardo has sometimes been interpreted as claiming that rent would rise, not merely absolutely, but relatively to profit and wages, or as a proportion of total product.* To begin with, it is true, he came very close to saying that rents would rise, not merely as a share of total surplus, and hence at the expense of profit, but as a proportion of the whole. In the *Essay* of 1815 he certainly speaks of rent "in a progressive country" as "not only absolutely increasing", but also "increasing in its ratio to the capital employed on the land" and says that "the landlord not only obtains a greater produce, but a larger share". In the first edition of the *Principles* this 'double benefit' to the landlord is repeated and reference is made to "the proportion of raw produce paid to the landlord for rent" as rising.† In face of criticism from Malthus (in his own *Principles*) for having handled rent in terms of proportions, Ricardo, in his *Notes on Malthus*, admitted that his "language about proportions may not have been so clear as it ought to have been" and that if he had fallen into the error of stating‡ that "the proportion of the whole produce which falls to the landlord's share" increases, he wished to "correct the passage" by substituting the word 'portion' for proportion, "or if the word proportion be retained, it must be the proportion of the produce obtained on the more fertile lands".§ In accordance with this, among his revisions in the third edition of *Principles*

others) as "strange language" and a "singular perversion of terms" (*A Critical Dissertation on the Nature, Measure and Causes of Value* (London, 1825) p. 50); and referred to by Malthus as "this unusual application of common terms which has rendered Mr Ricardo's work so difficult to be understood by many people" (*Principles of Political Economy, considered with a view to their practical application* (London, 1820) p. 214). Malthus followed Smith in using 'real wages' and 'real rent' to refer to "power of commanding labour, and the necessaries and conveniences of life".

* Professor M. Blaug, for example, apparently interprets him in this sense (*Economic Theory in Retrospect* (London, 1964 and 1968) p. 111).

† Ed. 1 of *Principles* (London, 1817) p. 76; *Works and Correspondence of Ricardo*, ed. Sraffa, Vol. I, p. 83.

‡ This is prefaced by the statement: "I do not know where I have said this."

§ *Ibid.*, Vol. II, p. 197; *cf.* Editor's Introduction to Vol. I, p. lvi.

Ricardo included a change in the Chapter On Rent from the words "proportion of the whole produce" to "proportion of the produce obtained with a given capital on any given farm".* It seems clear, therefore, that Ricardo had in mind the produce of *previously cultivated land*, when speaking of the share of rent as increasing when the margin of cultivation was extended. A glance at any simple textbook rent-diagram will show that in this he was right, but that it is quite possible at the same time for rent as a proportion of *all* produce, from previously cultivated *and* from newly cultivated land, to fall as the margin of cultivation is extended.† Clearly nothing in his general argument about rent and profits is affected by whether rent as a relative share rises or falls, as some seem to have supposed it to be.

Into his long-term forecast (resting as we have seen on the assumption of negligible, or at least restricted, imports of corn) enters the notion of the stationary state, which in slightly different guises and with varying degrees of emphasis occupied a place in much of the writing of the classical period. Were one painting the scene in dramatic colours, one might be tempted to speak of this as a nightmarish phantom lurking just over the horizon; its possible emergence being a constant preoccupation whenever the long-term effects of policy-measures were considered. The progress of capital accumulation was the constant goal of endeavour and the guarantee of material prosperity for the community at large and for all classes. Adam Smith had

* *Ibid.*, Vol. i, p. 83.

† The rise or fall depending on the shape of the cost-curve. Obviously cost swallows proportionately more (and rent equivalently less) under higher-cost production near the margin than it does on more fertile land; while the degree to which rents on the latter rise depends on how rapidly cost (and hence price) rises as the margin is extended. Thus in the attached diagram, using a straight-line curve of costs, the rent-triangle remains a constant proportion of the whole; while rent as a share of the produce on *old* land, OA, rises proportionately when cultivation expands to OB and price equivalently rises from OP_1 to OP_2; *cf.* Blaug, *Ricardian Economics*, p. 110, where *per contra* average and marginal productivity curves are used in illustration.

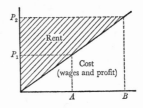

his "progressive state . . . in reality the cheerful and hearty state to all the different orders of society" (by contrast with which "the stationary is dull, the declining melancholy"). This progressive state, "while the society is advancing to the further acquisition, rather than when it has acquired its full complement of riches" is when "the conditions of the labouring poor, of the great body of the people, seems to be the happiest and the most comfortable".* Ricardo, inclined to pessimism of dynamic vision, at any rate in the absence of free trade, held out the possibility, "notwithstanding the tendency of wages to conform to their natural rate", of the market price of labour "in an improving society, for an indefinite period be[ing] constantly above it; for no sooner may the impulse, which an increased capital gives to a new demand for labour be obeyed, than another increase of capital may produce the same effect". This possibility will be reinforced if circumstances permit "an addition to the food and clothing of a country . . . [to] be made by the aid of machinery, without any increase, and even with an absolute diminution in the proportional quantity of labour required to produce them". Then indeed "the condition of the labourer will be very greatly improved"; and if there should happen to be "an abundance of fertile land: at such periods accumulation is often so rapid, that labourers cannot be sup- plied with the same rapidity as capital". There is also a hint of a further favourable influence of which John Stuart Mill was later to make much more: that the 'natural price of labour', depending as this does "on the habits and customs of the people", should itself be raised by upward changes in the latter. Of this he wrote (in his second edition): "The friends of humanity cannot but wish that in all countries the labouring classes should have a taste for comforts and enjoyments, and that they should be stimulated by all legal means in their exertions to procure them. There cannot be a better security against a superabundant population."†

Despite this, however, the more general or likely picture as

---

* *Wealth of Nations*, p. 83.

† *Works and Correspondence of Ricardo*, ed. Sraffa, Vol. i, pp. 94–5, 98, 100.

he probably saw it in circumstances such as those prevailing in England, was that population would tend to outdistance capital accumulation, and "as population increases, these necessaries will be constantly rising in price, because more labour will be necessary to produce them". If money-wages in these circumstances should rise in whole or partial compensation to the labourer, this "would necessarily diminish the profits of the manufacturer", with a tendency to discourage accumulation further. While the stationary state ("from which I trust we are yet far distant") is mentioned explicitly only in the context of the Poor Laws and their effect on population, it seems fairly clear that it was in his mind's eye as the ultimate destination of that "natural tendency of profits to fall" which was constantly threatening to undermine the "progressive state", especially in face of hindrances to importation. Although "checked at repeated intervals" by improvements in agricultural machinery and discoveries in the science of agriculture, this tendency, long before its limit is reached, "will have arrested all accumulation, and almost the whole produce of the country, after paying the labourers, will be the property of the owners of land and the receivers of tithes and taxes".*

It has become not uncommon for these Ricardian dynamic tendencies to be dismissed by setting them in contrast with actual events in the second half of the nineteenth century. Such pessimism – not only in his case but surrounding all talk of a 'stationary state' – has been dismissed as a curiosity in the history of thought or even as a salutary example of the result of following out "long trains of deductive reasoning" such as Marshall† counselled economists to eschew. Such criticism, however, in Ricardo's case seems to be less than fair: indeed, confrontation of his 'forecast' with actual events in a century that was to witness English free trade and a revolution in both sea and land transport is scarcely appropriate in view of his explicit mention of "hindrance to free importation" in the

---

* *Ibid.*, pp. 101–2, 109, 120–1.
† *Principles of Economics*, 7th ed. (London, 1916) p. 781.

context of the tendencies described. It can be said that in the *Principles* these hindrances to importantion are too little emphasised as a condition; and that since they are not firmly placed in the centre of the picture, the impression is conveyed that they are a reinforcing influence only, affecting merely the time-scale of the depicted "natural tendency" which would operate in any case, if more slowly in their absence. In his own mind, however, it seems clear that the Corn Laws were prominent, if not central, in the context of his dynamic forecast. In the argument of the *Essay* they evidently were; and their prominence was the occasion of Edwin Cannan's statement that we quoted in Chapter 1, that as "basis for an argument against the Corn Laws it would have been difficult to find anything more effective than the Ricardian theory of distribution".* Free imports, in Ricardo's view, were the essential offset to diminishing returns – essential to keep at bay the bogey of relapse into a stationary state. Writing in 1819, and referring to "the scarcity, and consequent high value of food and other raw produce" as "the only obstacle" to increasing wealth and population "for an indefinite time", he says this: "Let these [*i.e.* food and raw products] be supplied from abroad in exchange for manufactured goods, and it is difficult to say where the limit is at which you would cease to accumulate wealth and to derive profit from its employment." To this he adds: "This is a question of the utmost importance to political economy."† A year later, in writing to Trower, he says: "I contend for free trade in corn on the ground that while trade is free, and corn cheap, profits will not fall however great the accumulation of capital. If you confine yourself to the resources of your own soil, I say, rent will in time absorb the greatest part of that produce which remains after paying wages, and con-

---

* E. Cannan, *op. cit.* p. 391.

† Contribution to *Encyclopaedia Britannica, Works and Correspondence of Ricardo*, ed. Sraffa, Vol. IV, p. 179. *Cf.* Prof. M. Blaug: "The alleged 'pessimism' of Ricardo was entirely contingent upon the maintenance of the tariff on raw produce ... the notion of an impending stationary state was at most a useful device for frightening the friends of protection ... [it was] a methodological fiction" (*Ricardian Economics*, pp. 31–2).

sequently profits will be low."* This interpretation of his own intentions in the *Principles* (he was referring to "misrepresentation" of it in Malthus's book) would seem to be decisive.

We have so far said nothing directly about the place occupied by the Malthusian theory of population in Ricardo's system, although this must have been implied in what has already been said. Suffice to say that Ricardo fully accepted this theory, and felt indebted to his friend and epistolary sparring-partner for it. What it served to do was to provide Ricardo with a supply-theory of wages. It provided a mechanism of supply-adjustment whereby wages, or the current 'market price', became adjusted to the 'natural price of labour'; this latter being defined as "that price which is necessary to enable the labourers to subsist and perpetuate their race, without either increase or diminution".† In other words, the price of labour was governed by its own cost of production, in the sense of a level of wages that sufficed to maintain a given labouring population (or alternatively a population increasing about as fast as capital accumulates – which of the possible alternatives never being made quite clear). We have seen that this notion of a given, or independently determined, level of corn-wages was the basis of this theory of profits as initially formulated. But we have also seen that he did not give it a crudely physical-subsistence interpretation as some have imagined and as such have lightly dismissed it. 'Habits and customs' entered into what was conventionally 'necessary' at any period or place. Thus in his Chapter On Wages there is the much-quoted passage: "It is not to be understood that the natural price of labour, estimated even in food and necessaries, is absolutely fixed and constant. It varies at different times in the same country, and very materially differs in different countries. It essentially depends on the habits and customs of the people. An English labourer would consider his wages under their natural rate, and too scanty to support a family, if they enabled him to purchase no

* *Works and Correspondence of Ricardo*, ed. Sraffa, Vol. VIII, p. 208 (Letter to Trower, 21 July 1820). *Cf.* also in Notes on Malthus, *ibid.*, Vol. II, p. 222: "but I have added this will not be the case if you can and will get cheap food from abroad".
† *Ibid.*, Vol. I, p. 93.

other food than potatoes, and to live in no better habitation than a mud cabin; yet those moderate demands of nature are often deemed sufficient in countries where 'man's life is cheap' and his wants easily satisfied."* It was the enhanced importance of this social or conventional element at times when the market price of labour rose above the natural price on which "the permanence" of this rise "will depend" and on which "the friends of humanity" could place their hopes as "security against a superabundant population".

An account of Ricardo's theory can scarcely be closed without some reference to his discussion with Malthus on the cause of 'gluts' and the possibility of general overproduction. Here it is that Ricardo relied on what has come to be called Say's Law, while Malthus has been hailed as precursor of twentieth-century doctrine which, in denial of Say's Law, lays emphasis upon the level of effective demand. Together with Sismondi, Malthus was here fathering what was to be regarded for a century or more as the heresy of underconsumption. A substantial part of Ricardo's 'Notes on Malthus' is occupied with this theme.

Malthus starts with the case where there is a 'parsimony' by capitalists that is utilised to employ additional workers (in common with Ricardo he has in mind the case where capital consists exclusively of circulating capital and all new capital accordingly goes to provide wages and raw materials with which new workers are set to work). "It is undoubtedly possible by parsimony", he says, "to devote at once a much larger share than usual of the produce of any country to the maintenance of productive labour; and it is quite true that the labourers so employed are consumers." "But ... the consumption and demand occasioned by the persons employed in productive labour can never alone furnish a motive to the accumulation and employment of capital; and with regard to the capitalists themselves, together with the landlords and other rich persons, they have, by the supposition, agreed to be parsimonious, and by depriving themselves of their usual conveniences and

---

* *Ibid.*, Vol. I, pp. 96–7. To this in the 2nd edition he added a footnote to acknowledge his indebtedness to Torrens.

luxuries to save from their revenue and add to their capital. Under these circumstances, I would ask, how it is possible to suppose that the increased quantity of commodities, obtained by the increased number of productive labourers, should find purchasers, without such a fall of price as would probably sink their value below the costs of production."* This could almost be a passage from J. A. Hobson or any other under-consumption (or over-saving) theorist; but yet it does not strike one as specifically Keynesian (on first glance at any rate), since the additional parsimony is matched forthwith by additional investment. Concern would seem to be directed towards the productive effect of additional investment, and to this being un-matched by any expansion of demand (thus giving it something of a Kaleckian savour).

Referring to Say and his 'Law of Markets', Malthus goes on to say that, although "it has been thought by some very able writers" that there cannot be a general overproduction or glut of *all* things because "commodities being always exchanged for commodities, one half will furnish a market for the other half", yet in his opinion "it is by no means true . . . that commodities are always exchanged for commodities. The great mass of commodities is exchanged directly for labour." Hence "it is quite obvious that this mass of commodities, compared with the labour with which it is to be exchanged, may fall in value from a glut just as any one commodity falls in value from an excess of supply".† Here, it would seem, his concern is with a rise in real-wages in consequence of an increase in the rate of accumu-lation, with a resulting squeeze on profits. This might seem to come oddly from the pen of the author of the *Essay on Population* (as, indeed, J.-B. Say remarked).‡

* Rev. T. R. Malthus, *Principles of Political Economy* (London, 1820) pp. 352–3. A few paragraphs later he puts it even more sharply, thus: "a great increase of produce . . . with wants diminished by parsimony, must necessarily occasion a great fall of value estimated in *labour*, so that the same product, though it might have *cost* the same quantity of labour as before, would no longer *command* the same quantity; and both the power of accumulation and the motive to accumu-late would be strongly checked" (*ibid.*, p. 355).   † *Ibid.*, pp. 353–4.
‡ *Letters to Mr Malthus on several subjects of Political Economy and on the Cause of Stagnation of Commerce*, by J.-B. Say (trans. John Richter, London, 1821) p. 30.

His emphasis, however, later shifts back to the deficiency of demand for commodities. "No productive labour can ever be in demand with a view to profit unless the produce when obtained is of greater value than the labour which obtained it. No fresh hands can be employed in any sort of industry merely in consequence of the demand for its produce occasioned by the persons employed."* Since a too rapid rate of accumulation was quite possible, it followed that there was an advantage in having a class of 'unproductive consumers', such as he evidently regarded the landed gentry as being. Their self-indulgent demand would serve to offset the excessive parsimony of capitalists, and an economic as well as social balance would then be struck. He concludes that "no nation can *possibly* grow rich by an accumulation of capital, arising from a permanent diminution of consumption; because, such accumulation being greatly beyond what is wanted, in order to supply the effective demand for produce, a part of it would very soon lose both its use and its value, and cease to possess the character of wealth".†

Ricardo, not surprisingly, answered with Malthus's own view of population. In the first place, he denied that parsimony, if matched by investment in additional circulating capital, could result in any deficiency of demand (unless the investment were misdirected): the "wants of consumers" would simply be "transferred with the power to consume to another set of consumers"; "the power to consume . . . is not annihilated but is transferred to the labourer".‡ Secondly, if wages should be raised, this could be no more than a temporary state of affairs unless the cost in labour of subsistence had risen. In the circumstances supposed "the specific want would be for population". While admitting that "on the supposition that population does not increase with the same rapidity as the funds which are to employ it", there would be a check to accumulation, this would be no more than a temporary check until population had caught up again. In the meantime "the condition of the

* T. R. Malthus, *Principles of Political Economy* (London, 1820) pp. 348–9.
† *Ibid.*, p. 370.
‡ 'Notes on Malthus', *Works and Correspondence of Ricardo*, ed. Sraffa, Vol. II, pp. 309, 311.

labourer would then be most happy", the power of labourers to consume having been increased. True, "profits would be low because wages would be high", but "would only continue so till population increased and labour again fell".*

Malthus's views on effective demand and upon the beneficial rôle of a class of 'unproductive consumers' had been anticipated at the beginning of the century by the Earl of Lauderdale by whom he was very probably influenced (as he undoubtedly was in his views on the Corn Laws), even while stating that "Lord Lauderdale appears to have gone as much too far in deprecating accumulation, as some other writers in recommending it".† Although the latter's views about the evils of parsimony, as we shall see, were expressed more strongly than by Malthus, any analysis connected with the statement of them was much weaker. In addition to being an "instigator and champion of the Corn Law", so beneficial to the landowning interest, he was to become "a leading champion ... of extreme Tory policies" in the House of Lords.‡ Malthus, although more cautious as a reasoner and more moderate in his statement of any argument, clearly sympathised with Lauderdale's views in essentials and leaned fairly consistently to the conservative side. This would seem a more revealing clue to the disagreement between him and Ricardo than whether he chanced to be biassed towards attending to "immediate and temporary effects", and Ricardo towards the long-run and more permanent results of economic change (as Ricardo himself expressed it).§

---

* *Ibid.*, pp. 303, 318.
† Malthus, *Principles of Political Economy*, p. 352n.
‡ Morton Paglin, *Malthus and Lauderdale: the Anti-Ricardian Tradition* (New York, 1961) p. 90. In earlier years he had been a Whig follower of Charles James Fox.
§ In a letter to Malthus of 24 Jan. 1817, *Works and Correspondence of Ricardo*, ed. Sraffa, Vol. VII, p. 120.

4

THE REACTION AGAINST RICARDO

I

In the years following Ricardo's death a considerable volume of criticism of his doctrine accumulated, and such was its impact, already before the end of the decade, as to make one wonder whether respect for his doctrine would have continued to be anything like so great as it was in the middle of the nineteenth century without the loyal championship (as well as popularisation) of his main doctrines by John Stuart Mill. By 1831, indeed, the Political Economy Club was holding a discussion on the question (tabled by Torrens) "whether any of the principles first advanced" in Mr Ricardo's work are "now acknowledged to be correct"; Torrens affirming in the discussion that "all the great principles of Ricardo's work have been successively abandoned, and that his theories of Value, Rent and Profits were now generally acknowledged to have been erroneous".*

Already in Ricardo's lifetime, of course, there had been rival poles of doctrine. Most definite and outspoken in its conservatism we have seen was the Earl of Lauderdale, no negligible economic thinker and one who swam boldly against the incoming tide of *Smithianismus*. Not only was he in policy protectionist, at least so far as the Corn Laws were concerned, but a leading pre-

* *Political Economy Club: Centenary Volume*, Vol. VI (London, 1921) pp. 35, 36, 223. Torrens's question was discussed on 13 Jan. and then again on 14 April. According to Mallet, in the second discussion, however, "it was generally admitted that . . . his [Ricardo's] principles are in the main right. Neither his Theories of Value nor his Theories of Rent and profits are correct, according to the very terms of his propositions; but they are right in principle" (*ibid.*, p. 225). *Cf.* also Blaug, *Ricardian Economics*, pp. 62–3; Meek, *Economics and Ideology and Other Essays* (London, 1967) pp. 67–8; and for a contrary view *cf.* the remarks of Lionel Robbins, *The Evolution of Modern Economic Theory* (London, 1970) p. 59. Professor Meek observes that "Marx saw the year 1830 as marking the end of 'Ricardian' economics – and, indeed, not only of 'Ricardian' but also of 'Classical' and even of 'scientific' economics. From then on, the scientists were obliged to give way to the hired prize-fighters" (*ibid.*, p. 52). It was with special reference to these post-1830 trends that Marx's term *vulgarökonomie* was coined.

occupation with him was to denounce the "baneful passion for accumulation that has been falsely denominated virtue" and to demonstrate "the full extent of the evil that must arise from indulging" it. The evil consisted in the "diminution of value" that "must be produced . . . in the articles for which parsimony occasions an abstraction of demand" and hence "a similar diminution of the productions of the country".* It followed that "accumulation of capital must at all times have its bounds".† Another butt for his criticism was the Smithian view of profit as a deduction; of the ideological implications of which he was perspicaciously aware. As against it he saw the origin of profit in capital's capacity for "supplanting a portion of labour, which would otherwise be performed by the hand of man; or – from its performing a portion of labour, which is beyond the reach of personal exertion of man to accomplish‡. Although Malthus we have seen was undoubtedly influenced by him, the former by contrast chose the rôle of a supporter of Smithian tradition on points where Ricardo had been critical of the *Wealth of Nations* and had given its essential doctrines a more radical twist. This is apparent not only in Malthus's tenacious defence of Adam Smith's 'labour commanded' measure of value, but also in his habit of visualising questions of exchange-value within a general supply–demand framework (as Smith had done in his 'Adding-up-components Theory'). It was nowhere more evident than in his treatment of the theory of profits.§ Yet by the time that the reaction against Ricardo was

* Earl of Lauderdale, *An Inquiry into the Nature and Origin of Public Wealth* (Edinburgh, 1804) pp. 218, 220, 248. As such he might seem to have been voicing no more than a crude under-consumption view. He does add that the formation of an accumulating fund would have caused "real wealth to be extinguished" (due to the fall in demand) "before this accumulating fund . . . could have in all probability converted . . . revenue into capital" (*ibid.*, p. 249), which some might regard as anticipating Keynesian reasoning about saving and investment and the immediate effect of a change in the propensity to consume.

† *Ibid.*, p. 265.

‡ *Ibid.*, pp. 161 *seq*. He goes on to speak of "five modes . . . by which capital becomes entitled to a profit".

§ *E.g.* Malthus's statement in summary towards the end of his Chapter 'Of the Profits of Capital': "We only take a view of half the question if we advert exclusively to a rise in wages of labour without referring to a fall in the prices of commodities. Their effects on profits may be precisely the same; but the latter

in full tide, these differences apparently came to be regarded as secondary and Malthus himself, to a larger view, as leaning towards the Ricardian side.*

The gathering criticism of Ricardo in the years following his death was mainly directed against his theories of value and of profit; secondarily against his theory of rent, so far at any rate as this was presented in such a way as to represent the interests of the landowner as being opposed to the social interest. Professor R. L. Meek has explained the vehemence and quick success of this criticism by the fact "that the majority of economists were very much aware of the dangerous use to which a number of radical writers were putting Ricardian concepts"†; these writers including Thomas Hodgskin in particular, and later other so-called 'Ricardian Socialists'. Although McCulloch in the middle 1820s had undertaken a series of annual lectures in honour of Ricardo (and was later to edit a collection of Ricardo's works), he was by training and

case, where there is no question respecting the state of the land, shews at once how much profits depend upon the prices of commodities, and upon the cause which determines these prices, namely the supply compared with the demand" (*Principles of Political Economy* (London, 1820) p. 334).

* This may have been because Bailey joined criticism of Malthus with his attack on Ricardo, and Malthus retorted, as we shall see, with contemptuous dismissal of Bailey's pamphlet. Dr Robert M. Rauner in his essay on Bailey speaks of "the fact that both Ricardo and Malthus became increasingly attached to a value which was not relative" and of Malthus "being one with Ricardo in believing that 'value' would remain the same if cost remained constant" (*Samuel Bailey and the Classical Theory of Value* (Harvard, 1961) p. 66 and *cf.* p. 119).

† Meek, *Economics and Ideology*, p. 70. Hodgskin's *Labour Defended against the Claims of Capital* was published in 1825 and his *Popular Political Economy* in 1827, by which date he was a considerable influence in Mechanics Institute circles. James Mill's view of Hodgskin's ideas as given in a letter to Brougham was that "if they were to spread they would be subversive of civilised society" (*cit.* Robbins, *The Theory of Economic Policy in English Classical Political Economy* (London, 1952) p. 135). Of the whole group of economists of this period from Bailey to Longfield Professor M. Blaug has said: "It is significant that the writers who attacked the views of the 'labour theorists' – Scrope, Read and Longfield – were also among the first to advance the abstinence theory of profit. In this sense, the theoretical innovations of the 'neglected British economists' were not unrelated to the nature of the class struggle after 1830 . . . And if we choose to regard the labour cost theory of value as the kernel of Ricardian economics we are driven to assert that the vital influence of Ricardo came to an end in the 1830s" (*Ricardian Economics*, pp. 224–5).

inclination less than equal to the task of answering this criticism effectively; being a fluent (and intelligent) journalist and populariser rather than a subtle or original thinker. Moreover, he was himself in the course of time to move progressively further away from Ricardo's position.

The first and perhaps most influential of the attacks on Ricardo was the work of Samuel Bailey in 1825, a Sheffield merchant of some consequence in that city, who was later to engage, *inter alia*, in some quite acute philosophical criticism which included a critique of Bishop Berkeley's theory of vision. His polemic against Ricardo took the form of a 200-page essay entitled *A Critical Dissertation of the Nature, Measure and Causes of Value: chiefly in reference to the writings of Mr. Ricardo and his followers*, which was at first published anonymously, and has been hailed by some twentieth-century economists as a remarkable anticipation of modern notions. Although Torrens was quick to endorse it (in the 1831 discussion at the Political Economy Club), Seligman has classed Bailey among "Neglected British Economists".*

The main butt of his criticism was Ricardo's notion of absolute value, and with it the notion of an invariable standard. Bailey was a thorough-going relativist, and he started by defining value as solely consisting in what Ricardo had termed 'relative value' or 'exchangeable value'. "Value", he said, "denotes ... nothing positive or intrinsic, but merely the relation in which two objects stand to each other as exchangeable commodities ... it denotes a relation between two objects", thus "bear[ing] a resemblance to distance".† It followed that "the very term absolute value implies the same sort of absurdity as absolute distance", and that Ricardo's search for a commodity of unvarying value as a standard was pointless, since there was no way of defining 'unvarying value'. "My proposition is that, if the causes affecting any one commodity continued unaltered, this commodity would not be invariable in value, unless the causes affecting all commodities compared with it continued

* *Economic Journal*, Vol. XIII, 1903, pp. 352–5.
† *A Critical Dissertation*, pp. 4–5.

unaltered."* In presenting this purely relative notion of value (and denying any other) he spoke incidentally of "value, in its ultimate sense" as meaning "the esteem in which any object is held. It denotes strictly speaking an effect produced on the mind."† (This remark, needless to say, has caused him to be hailed as a progenitor of the Jevonian Revolution.)‡ De Quincey comes in for special attack as exponent of Ricardo, and even Malthus for sponsoring the notion of "invariable, absolute, natural" value (in his *Measure of Value*) by contrast with "nominal or relative value".

Regarding the theory of profits he has little to contribute beyond the statement that profits denote "only a share or proportion of commodities" and a rise in them can only mean that "the gain of the capitalist bears a higher ratio to the capital employed"; from which the conclusion is drawn that when profits are defined in this way, "the proposition that when labour rises profits must fall is true only when its rise is not owing to an increase in its productive power" (he is, of course, here talking of wages as 'real wages' in the Smith-cum-Malthus sense and *not* of wages as a proportion, or 'the real value of wages' in Ricardo's sense). Reverting to the question of value, he asserts that the cost of production governing value under competition "may be ... either a quantity of labour or a quantity of capital", and concludes, in agreement with Torrens, that as a proximate cause operating on the minds of capitalists "the amount of capital expended is the cause which determines the value of the commodity produced".§

A minor curiosity in his treatment of value is a reference to monopoly. This he distinguishes as being of two main types, one "in which there is only one interest", the other "in which there are separate interests". In the former it may be in the interest of the monopolist to withhold part of the supply. But in the latter case this will not be the case: even if "he is fenced in by an exclusive privilege [*e.g.* a gild or an industry with high

---

* *Ibid.*, p. 20.   † *Ibid.*, p. 180.
‡ *Cf.* Rauner, *Samuel Bailey*, pp. 5–7.
§ Bailey, *A Critical Dissertation* ..., p. 201.

costs of entry] or possession from the competition of the public ",
"he is obliged . . . to produce the greatest supply in his power,
so long as the average price pays him a higher profit than the
ordinary employment of capital ".* He goes on to include in
this latter category most short-period situations (as they would
be called to-day) and most temporary deviations of market
price from cost of production. "All commodities which require
any considerable length of time for their production are liable
to be occasionally forced into the class of articles owing their
value to this second kind of monopoly by a sudden alteration in
the relative state of the demand and supply. Hence arises what
is called by economists market value." Should demand increase,
"the possessors of the commodities would enjoy a temporary
monopoly", whereas should demand decrease they would
suffer the disadvantage that "the competition among them
would force the whole of their supply into the market".† He
ends by introducing what is virtually a third type of monopoly:
"the case where competition cannot increase except at greater
cost". Rent is thus treated as an example of "monopoly-value"
due to limitation of lands of superior fertility, and "proceed[ing]
from the extraordinary profit which is obtained by the possession
of an instrument of production protected up to a point from
competition".‡

Bailey's *Dissertation* was quoted approvingly, and as being
decisive in its criticism of Ricardo On Value, by Torrens in his
aforementioned discussion at the Political Economy Club;§ and
in the same year Cotterill, who was also much influenced by
Bailey, referred laconically to "some Ricardians still remaining".‖ *The Dissertation* received rough treatment, however,
from a reviewer in the *Westminster Review* of January 1826 (who
seems likely to have been James Mill,¶ although the attribution
has varied between father and son). Malthus answered back
with some asperity in his *Definitions in Political Economy* of 1827,
where he speaks of Bailey as applying his own exclusive defini-

* *Ibid.*, p. 187.   † *Ibid.*, pp. 188–9.   ‡ *Ibid.*, pp. 185, 195–6.
§ Mallet's diary *cit.* in *Political Economy Club: Centenary Volume*, Vol. VI, p. 223.
‖ *Cf.* Cotterill, *An Examination of the Doctrines of Value* (London, 1831) p. 8.
¶ *Cf.* Rauner, *Samuel Bailey*, pp. 149–57.

tion of value "to try the truth of a number of propositions advanced by different writers, who, according to his own showing, have used the term in a very different sense". The work is curtly dismissed as "peculiarly calculated to retard the progress of that science which it must have been intended to promote".*
Malthus proceeds to defend the use of a distinction between relative and absolute-value by saying that "to compare a commodity either with the mass of other commodities or with the elementary cost of production, is most essentially distinct from comparing it with some particular commodity named . . . it is essential to the language of political economy that they should be distinguished by different terms". To this he adds that "nothing is more common than the use of the terms real, positive and absolute, in contradistinction to relative, when the former terms have relation to some more general object, particularly to anything which is considered as a standard".†
Marx, not surprisingly, spoke of it "as a work not having positive value"; whereas in recent times Schumpeter *per contra* has hailed it as "a masterpiece of criticism".‡

Evidently as a dismissal of Ricardo On Value it can be seen to have much less cogency than its contemporary and modern admirers have attributed to it, and little of the finality. To *define* value as *relative*-value, or exchange-value, is not *per se* a refutation of those who, concerned with finding a basis or 'cause' of this exchange-value, seek this in cost of production (or, indeed, in anything else), and define the latter by means of a distinctive term, whether 'natural', 'real' or 'absolute' value. Here Malthus's retort was, surely, entirely just. What needs to be shown is that no such concept can consistently be maintained. Although this is implied in Bailey's *Dissertation*, it certainly cannot be said to be demonstrated. So far as realism is concerned, it by no means suffices to render a notion 'metaphysical' that it should be held (like Smithian 'natural value') to exist only under certain hypothetical conditions – unless

---

* T. R. Malthus, *Definitions in Political Economy* (London, 1827) pp. 145, 201–2.
† *Ibid.*, pp. 148–9, 151.
‡ Marx, *Theorien über den Mehrwert*, ed. Karl Kautsky (Berlin, 1923) Vol. III, p. 146; Schumpeter, *History*, p. 486.

everything arrived at by deductive reasoning is to be dismissed in this way.

II

The retreat from a Ricardian theory of profit into something resembling modern theories is associated mainly with the names of Mountifort Longfield and Nassau Senior in works that appeared within two years of one another, in 1834 and 1836. Both consisted, wholly or partly, of lectures, delivered respectively in Dublin and Oxford. The former, in his *Lectures on Political Economy*, expounded something akin to a marginal productivity theory of profits (profits were due to the additional productivity given to labour when capital was invested in machines); the latter, in his *Outline of Political Economy*, propounding his well-known theory of profit as a reward for abstinence; thereby implying a dualistic interpretation of 'real cost', in its rôle of determinant of value, as consisting in labour *plus* abstinence. Schumpeter says of Longfield that he "produced a system that would have stood up well in 1890" and "anticipated the essentials of Böhm-Bawerk's theory".*

Senior probably deserves initial mention since he really had priority in the field; his lectures having been delivered before 1830. Appointed to the newly-founded Drummond Professorship of Political Economy at Oxford in 1825 for a five-year term, he was later to occupy the Chair again for a second term from 1847 to 1852. It was the lectures delivered during his first tenure of the Drummond Chair in Oxford that formed the basis of his *Outline of Political Economy*, to be published in the same year as the posthumous second edition of Malthus's *Principles*. From 1830 as a member of the Whig Party he was its adviser on economic matters, and he was a member of the notorious Poor Law Commission of 1832–4. His well-known "violent opposition to trade unionism", as it has been called,† shows that he was by no means unaware of, or unmoved by, the social implications of what he was saying.‡

* Schumpeter, *History*, p. 465.
† By Sir Erich Roll, *A History of Economic Thought* (London, 1938) p. 351.
‡ For Senior's later reaction to 1848 in France and the importance he attached in that event to socialist ideas germinated among the working class, cf. Robbins, *The Theory of Economic Policy in English Classical Political Economy* (London, 1952) p. 136.

About Abstinence he does not say a great deal beyond postulating it as the cause and explanation of Profit: "Profit is the remuneration of abstinence, and abstinence is the deferring of enjoyment", while capital owes its "existence and preservation" to this. Elsewhere he says that Labour and Nature are the only primary productive powers, but "they require the concurrence of a third Productive Principle to give them complete efficiency. To the Third Principle ... we shall give the name of Abstinence", which "stands in the same relation to Profit as Labour does to Wages".* This he proceeds to qualify, however, by stating that Capital continually tends to approximate to Land (and hence Profit to Rent) by losing its mobility once it is invested in durable goods. Again (introducing a different consideration) "for all useful purposes, the distinction of profit from rent ceases as soon as the capital from which a given revenue arises has become, whether by gift or by inheritance, the property of a person to whose abstinence and exertions it did not owe its creation. The revenue arising from a dock or a wharf or a canal, is profit in the hands of the *original constructor*. It is the reward of *his* abstinence in having employed capital for the purposes of production instead of for those of enjoyment. But in the hands of his heir it has all the attributes of rent. It is to him the gift of fortune, not the result of a sacrifice."† It is, perhaps, not surprising that this qualification should have received so little emphasis from those who, in the wake of Senior, have 'justified' profit and interest in terms of abstinence (or 'waiting' which is a less colourful word for the same thing) and have sought to assimilate profit and wages as payments for 'real costs'; for the qualification leaves precious little of the justification (or explanation – call it what one will) behind it.‡ Edwin Cannan's comment here is appro-

---

* *An Outline of the Science of Political Economy* (London, 1836) pp. 58–9.
† *Ibid.*, p. 129. He goes on to say that if such a revenue or inherited property were to be regarded as "the reward for the owner's abstinence in not selling the dock or the canal and spending its price in enjoyment", then "the same remark applies to every species of transferable property" and most rent would have to be called profit.
‡ Schumpeter suggests (*History*, p. 926) that the theory of abstinence and of what he calls 'limitation' (that the supply of capital is limited rather than indefinitely

priate: "In modern civilised and wealthy communities inherited property is far greater than the property which has been acquired by the saving of living persons."*

In discussing wages Senior departs from a Subsistence Theory to the extent of saying that wages depend "on the Extent of the Fund for the maintenance of Labourers, compared with the number of Labourers to be maintained".† Thus far he could be classified as a sponsor of a simple-minded Wages Fund Doctrine. But this general statement he proceeds to qualify or extend in several respects. (Simultaneously, indeed, he is careful to posit as inconsistent with his own theory the view "that the Rate of Wages depends solely on the proportion which the number of Labourers bears to the amount of Capital in the country".)‡ As regards the size of the Fund, this depends, first "on the productiveness of labour in the direct or indirect production of the commodities used by the labourer", secondly "on the number of persons directly or indirectly employed in the production of things for the use of labourers, compared with the whole number

expansible) are really identical. But this is really not the case, or at least not necessarily so. To say that the capital stock is of limited size at any one date because of this or that limit on the rate of investment is one thing: this would be consistent with treating profit as analogous to rent. On the other hand, to 'explain' profit in terms of 'real cost' only makes sense if there is some reasonably close and direct connection between the incurring of this 'real cost' and the accrual of profit as income (an explanation that is particularly unconvincing when all but marginal amounts of any existing capital stock was the result of saving and investment decisions in *the past*). To overlook such a consideration is, surely, a sign of exclusive preoccupation with the formal technique of economic analysis.

Böhm-Bawerk conceded that "Lassalle is for the most part right as against Senior – that the existence and the height of interest by no means inevitably correspond with the existence and the height of a 'sacrifice of abstinence'"; and attributed the popularity of Senior's theory "not so much to its superiority as a theory, as that it came in the nick of time to support interest against the severe attacks that had been made on it" (*Capital and Interest*, trans. W. Smart (London, 1890) pp. 277, 286).

* *History of Theories of Production and Distribution*, 2nd ed. (London, 1903) p. 198. He has earlier said that Senior had simply taken for granted that profit was the reward for a sacrifice "and makes no attempt to prove it" (p. 197), and again says later that his theory "does not really take us beyond the proposition that capital is the result of saving" (p. 214).

† Senior, *Outline of Political Economy*, p. 154.

‡ *Ibid.*, p. 154. *Cf.* on this Marian Bowley, *Nassau Senior and Classical Economics* (London, 1937) pp. 197–200.

of labouring families".* So far he might seem to remain fairly close to Ricardo who, we have seen, treated profits as being determined by the productivity of labour in producing wage-goods in relation to the level of real-wages, or alternatively by the proportion of the labour force needed to produce wage-goods. It is significant, however, that Senior should see such a ratio as determining, not profits in relation to wages, but on the contrary the *demand for labour* expressed in real terms. Moreover, in further stating how his second ratio is determined, he expressed this in the reverse order of determination from Ricardo: it is determined by "Causes which Divert Labour from the Production of Commodities for the use of Labouring Families": namely "I Rent. II Taxation. III Profit". In other words, instead of Profits being determined "as the leavings of wages", as de Quincey put it† (taking productivity of labour into account as affecting the size of these 'leavings'), Profit is treated (along with Rent) as being prior-determined, and Wages, apparently, as the residual after these prior deductions have been made.‡ This is in the tradition of Adam Smith, in one sense; with the not-unimportant difference that Profit is explained (if not at all clearly) by Abstinence. In answering the question as to what determines the *rate* of profit, he introduces the notion of the 'average period of advance of capital' – the time for which wages have to be advanced; and in explanation of international wage-differences, he offers the interesting suggestion (in *Three Lectures on the Cost of Obtaining Money*, 1830) that these are due to differences in value, in terms of precious metals, of exportable commodities producible by an average worker in a given period, after allowance for deduction of profit, according to the rate of profit and the 'period of advance'.

Regarding Value, Senior seems in large degree to have followed J.-B. Say and Lauderdale in treating it as depending on Utility, conditioned by limitation of supply and transferability; adding that of these limitation was "by far the most

* Senior, *Outline of Political Economy*, p. 174.
† *Cit.* above, pages 70, 79.
‡ Professor M. Bowley says of Senior's attempt to determine wages residually that he does so "unsuccessfully" (*Nassau Senior*, p. 185).

important". "Utility", he writes, "denotes no intrinsic quality
in the things which we call useful, it merely expresses their
relations to the pains and pleasures of mankind." Some have
hailed him as anticipating the Law of Diminishing Utility in
his statement that "not only are there limits to the pleasure
which commodities of any class can afford, but the pleasure
diminishes in a rapidly increasing ratio long before those
limits; . . . two articles of the same kind will seldom afford
twice the pleasure of one".* Some again may detect a modern
ring in his statement that, while "our desires do not aim so much
at quantity as at diversity", the desire for diversity is "weak
compared with the desire for distinction".†

Mountifort Longfield was an Irish Judge who was appointed
in 1832 to the Chair of Political Economy founded at Trinity
College, Dublin, by Archbishop Whately. The lectures in
question were delivered in 1833 and published in the following
year. In his Preface (p. vii) he expresses his concern to prove
"how impossible it is to *regulate wages generally*, either by combinations of workmen, or by legislative enactment"; so that his
concern, if not preoccupation, with the emerging 'Labour
question' is clear. So is his rejection of Ricardo, at least so far as
the theory of profits is concerned. He starts his discussion of
Profits by attacking Ricardo's proposition that the rate of
profits can only fall under the operation of diminishing returns
on land, which by raising the cost of subsistence raises Wages.
He first considers capital invested as fixed capital in improved
machinery or tools as aids to labour. The profit on capital first
invested in this way will tend to be governed by the "sum which
can be paid for the use of any machine" and this "by its
efficiency in assisting the operations of the labourer". This will
set what he terms the "maximum limit" of profit. But "its
lesser limit is determined by the efficiency of that capital which
without imprudence is employed in the least efficient manner",
to which level competition will tend to reduce *all* profit on
fixed capital.‡ From this he concludes that increase of capital

* Senior, *Outline of Political Economy*, p. 11.   † *Ibid.*, pp. 11–12.
‡ M. Longfield, *Lectures on Political Economy* (Dublin, 1834), p. 188.

per se "has a tendency to diminish the rate of profits" even "without an increase of population" and rise in corn-prices. Profits on circulating capital "must be regulated by the profits of fixed capital".* His 'marginal efficiency' notion of profit (as it substantially is) is summed-up in the following sentence. "In every case the profits of capital will be regulated by that portion of it which is obliged to be employed with the least efficiency in assisting labour."† It is evident that we have here quite a number of preliminary sketches for economic theory at the end of the century.

As for "the wages of the labourer", these "depend upon the value of his labour and not upon his wants". Like Senior he maintains that real wages "depend entirely on the rate of profits and on the efficiency of labour in producing those articles on which the wages of labour are usually expended".‡ The grand corollary that he derives is the comforting one that "the amount of profits and wages is confined within limits which it is beyond the power of the legislature, by any direct exertion of their authority, to extend. Here legislation and combination may do mischief, but cannot do good".§ And in his eleventh and final lecture he epitomises the result of his enquiries (which "will not, I trust, be unpleasing to the benevolent mind") with the statement about economic laws that we quoted in Chapter 1.|| To this is appended the remark: "We shall find that all the causes which diminish any source of wealth originate in vice or folly."¶ The laws of production and distribution, apparently, are not merely made of iron but are of divine origin.

As regards Value, Longfield also paid more attention to utility than had been customary, at any rate in England "The value of every article depends upon the demand and the supply and . . . indirectly the cost of production of any commodity, as well as its utility, has an effect upon its price."**He speaks of varying "intensities of demand", and concludes that "the

---

* *Ibid.*, p. 198.   † *Ibid.*, p. 193.   ‡ *Ibid.*, pp. 206, 212.
§ *Ibid.*, p. 159. || Above, page 23n.   ¶ *Ibid.*, pp. 222–3.
** *Ibid.*, p. 110.

market price is measured by that demand, which being of the least intensity yet leads to actual purchases. If the existing supply is more than sufficient to satisfy all the demand equal or superior to a certain degree of intensity, prices will fall, to accommodate themselves to a less intense demand."* This is certainly a foretaste of a Jevonian Law of Diminishing Utility.

The successor to Senior's first tenure of the Drummond Chair at Oxford was Richard Whately, who was in turn succeeded in 1831 by W. F. Lloyd. Both Whately and Lloyd published their lectures (to do so, indeed, being one of the conditions of occupying the Chair); the former in 1831 under the title of *Introductory Lectures on Political Economy*, the latter in 1834 as *A Lecture on the Notion of Value*. The views of both of them were similar to Senior's and to those of their Dublin colleague; and both are generally classified among the group of economists of the anti-Ricardian reaction who anticipated some of the main ideas of the 'Jevonian Revolution' of forty years later.

Whately, whose general approach may well have influenced Senior†, suggested 'Catallactics' as a more appropriate name for Political Economy to emphasise the fact that it was primarily concerned with the mechanism of *Exchange* (Marx's 'sphere of circulation', which the latter treated as belonging to 'phenomena' rather than 'essence'). W. F. Lloyd was no doubt the more important of the two as a discoverer of the marginal utility principle (the rôle in which many have viewed him): he spoke of value as "undoubtedly signif[ying] a feeling of the mind, which shows itself always at the margin of separation between satisfied and unsatisfied wants", and explained that "an increase of quantity will at length exhaust, or satisfy to the utmost, the demand for any specific object of desire".‡

Other writers belonging to this period if not to this group shew even more clearly (as Professor Meek has pointed out) preoccupation with the social implications of Ricardian doctrine which they were opposing.§ Samuel Read spoke strongly

* *Ibid.*, p. 113.　　† *Cf.* Schumpeter, *Economic Analysis*, p. 484.
‡ *A Lecture on the Notion of Value* (London, 1834) pp. 9, 16.
§ *Cf.* R. L. Meek, *Studies in the Labour Theory of Value* (London, 1956) pp. 124–5:
"Some of Ricardo's opponents (Scrope, Read and Longfield, for example) seem

of what he held to be implied by Ricardo's theory (that "labour is the only source of wealth") as a "mischievous and fundamental error" at the heart of his system.* Poulett Scrope, author of *Principles of Political Economy* of 1833, said of the works of the Ricardian School (in which he included both Malthus and Whately) that he "could not discover in them any answer likely to satisfy the mind of a half-educated man of plain commonsense and honesty who should seek there some justification for the immense disparity of fortunes and circumstances that strike the eye on every side. On the contrary, these works appeared to me to contain many obvious inconsistencies and errors, to inculcate many false and pernicious principles."† Elsewhere in the same work (*Political Economy for Plain People*) he refers to "mistaken hostility to Capital" and the "Right to Profit on Capital", mentioning Hodgskin and his "robbery of labourers".‡ In his *Principles* he makes specific mention of those who "declaim against capital as the poison of society, and the taking of interest on capital by its owners as an abuse, an injustice, a robbery of the class of labourers"; and he condemns the labour theory for not recognising profit as compensation for "the time during which the owner of capital has allowed it to be employed".§ It is hardly surprising that he should have advanced the notion of abstinence (independently of Senior, it would seem) as an explanation of profit.‖ Was Marx's "bad conscience and evil intent of apologetic" too strong a characterisation of such as these?

to have been fairly well aware of what they were doing: it was the *dangerous* character of Ricardo's doctrines, rather than what they believed to be their falsity, with which they were primarily concerned." Also *cf.*: "Their fundamental approach . . . was determined by a belief that what was socially dangerous could not possibly be true" (Meek, *Economics and Ideology and Other Essays*, p. 71).

* Samuel Read, *An Inquiry into the Natural Grounds of Right to Vendible Property or Wealth* (Edinburgh, 1829) p. xxix.

† Preface to *Political Economy for Plain People*, cit. Meek, *Economics and Ideology*, p. 71.

‡ *Political Economy for Plain People* (London, 1833); (2nd edn, 1873) pp. 103, 105.

§ *Principles of Political Economy* (London, 1833) p. 150.

‖ Schumpeter even speaks of the "Scrope–Senior Abstinence Theory of Interest" (*History of Economic Analysis*, p. 659).

III

Sometimes the group of economists of whom we have been speaking has been represented, not as unseating Ricardianism as a system (or seeking so to do), but as playing on the whole a reconciling and 'improving' rôle – improving the defects and one-sidedness of Ricardian doctrine, much in the way that later, and more painstakingly, Marshall claimed to be doing. Thus Senior, it has been said, "endeavoured to reconcile Say and Ricardo".* Speaking of Longfield, Schumpeter more cautiously says that he "did not fail to keep contact with Ricardian teaching" and was careful to supplement the latter with "a more perfect analysis gently and without any violent break".† It is, of course, true that new ideas when first introduced often (perhaps more often than not) appear in the guise of mere extensions of an existing conceptual structure, or even appear as attempts to reconcile this structure with what had previously been treated as inconsistent notions or observations (as with epicycles and the Ptolemaic system). Subsequently only will the new ideas or observations find more convincing expression as crucial elements or relations of a quite new conceptual structure that challenges the old one in its entirety. So it was with the new theoretical system of the post-1870 period, associated in this country with the name of Jevons. Yet in retrospect to interpret early ideas of a Bailey, Senior or Longfield about utility or marginal productivity, still crude and lacking more general formulation, as merely attempts to improve or extend Ricardianism, reconciling this with its critics, is to do much less than justice to their novelty and to their critical and eventually disruptive rôle. There can be small doubt from the evidence available that the group associated with Senior (and this included Longfield) were quite consciously in retreat from the most characteristic doctrines of Ricardo, and especially from those (such as his theory of profit and its stress on the antagonistic relationship between wages and profit and between

* Erich Roll, *History of Economic Thought*, p. 341.
† Schumpeter, *History of Economic Analysis*, p. 464.

profit and rent) which they regarded as socially dangerous and hence untenable.

Even if we confine our attention, with Schumpeter, to the analytical pattern of doctrines, it is clear that there were, broadly speaking, two quite distinct and rival traditions in nineteenth-century economic thought as to the order and mode of determination of phenomena of exchange and income-distribution. One of these deriving from Adam Smith treated the value of any commodity as being determined as the sum of the various expenses or costs involved in its production; these expenses depending upon the necessary payments for land, capital and labour and upon the various amounts of these needed to produce the commodity in question. Determination of these necessary payments was viewed in a general supply-and-demand framework, and in Adam Smith was treated as the problem of the general *rate* of profits and rate of wages and rent of land, which together constituted the 'component parts of price'. Various writers treated one or other of these components as 'residual' in the global picture, in the sense that it received what was left over of the total product after certain pre-determined shares had been met. We have seen that in Adam Smith's treatment property-income (*i.e.* both profit and rent) appeared as a prior deduction, in a context mildly suggestive of an exploitation theory (many have thought so, at least, including Bortkievicz). This seemed to leave wages as a residual; although a residual subject to a minimum ("there is a certain rate below which it seems impossible to reduce, for any considerable time, the ordinary wages even of the lowest species of labour"); the possibility of a rise above this minimum being (rather inconsistently perhaps) conditioned upon an "increase of the funds which are destined to the payment of wages"; this latter occasioning "a competition among masters, who bid against one another, in order to get workmen, and thus voluntarily break through the natural combination of masters not to raise wages".*

It was this type of conception, etched in lightly and suggest-

* Adam Smith, *Wealth of Nations*, pp. 70, 71.

ively rather than rigorously by Smith, that the economists of
the Senior–Longfield group in the 1820s and 1830s sought to
develop into what was to become known as the Cost of Production Theory of Value. As such it descended through John
Stuart Mill (though incongruously sailing under the flag of
Ricardo) to Alfred Marshall; and as such it was now equipped
with a theory of real cost subjectively conceived (echoing Adam
Smith's 'toil and trouble') and accordingly capable of being
used as the basis of a theory of profit, in addition to a theory of
wages. (Quite early Cotterill had said quite plainly: "there are
two ingredients in cost of production, wages of labour . . . and
profits of stock".)* Rent of land still remained, in this view, a
residual surplus, since there was no real cost, however subjectively conceived, corresponding to the use of gifts of nature
(other than the foregoing of alternative possibilities of use). The
sting had thus been drawn from the suggestion of profit being
a 'prior deduction' from the product of labour, since capital
and labour were placed on a level as factors of production having
joint, if not coequal, responsibility for the product. Moreover,
the whole notion of treating some forms of revenue as 'prior
deductions' and others (or another) as 'residual' became pointless, indeed meaningless, in view of the subsequent introduction
of the notion of 'simultaneous determination'; the latter being
applied *both* to the pricing of different productive factors or
agents *and* to the respective rôles of supply-conditions and
of demand-conditions (Marshall making differences in the
latter turn on the question of time by his well-known
distinction between the assumption of a short-period or
of a long-period in which adaptive supply-changes could
occur).

It was only with the later and more sophisticated versions of
the supply-demand-cum-component-parts-of-price line of tradition, especially with versions stressing primarily demand-
influences, that we meet a rather essential consideration on
which we have previously touched and to which we shall later
return. This is that the theoretical framework of determination

* Cotterill, *Doctrines of Value*, p. 22.

lay entirely within the exchange process (or what is commonly called to-day the pricing process); product-prices and income-distribution being assimilated and integrated within one system of mutual or simultaneous determination of product-prices and factor-prices in interaction. This was specially true, as we shall see, of the Austrian School, for whom the notion of 'real cost' is replaced by an assumption of *given* supplies of various factors, with consequential demand-determination of all prices (and, incidentally, the notion of surplus, applied to rent as much as to profit, losing all meaning in this context). This was not just a peculiarity of the Austrian treatment: it is true of the Walrasian system and of its derivatives as well. Even if (as with Marshall) subjective real cost is retained as a determinant, at the margin, of the supplies of capital and labour, increasing emphasis is inevitably thrown upon conditions of demand (and its subjective determinants) compared with which the Cost of Production Theory inevitably fades into the background. The sole way in which conditions of production obtrude into this essentially exchange-process or market process is in the form of 'technical coefficients' defining the possibilities of factor-combination, and what is commonly called to-day a 'production-function' setting the range of alternative technical coefficients. Social conditions and relations, or institutions such as the pattern of ownership, do not appear at all;* being treated, indeed, as having no determining rôle and as irrelevant to the result. It follows, as one could expect, that a concept like 'exploitation' or a surplus-value (or even something milder, implying a Ricardian long-run income-antagonism) can have neither place nor meaning, since the validity of such a concept rests on something about price-relations hingeing on some characteristic of the institutional structure (and if *nothing* about normal price-relations is dependent upon the social or institutional background, these price-relations can *only* reflect the requirements of the economic problem *per se, e.g.* the pattern

* These may possibly be admitted as influencing *personal* income-distribution, by contrast with distribution between *factors*; but if so at the risk (as we shall see below) of introducing a damaging circularity into the system of demand-governed distribution.

of Walrasian *raretés*, which would remain the same whatever the institutional system happened to be, given only the existence of free exchange). The intrusion of monopoly is, of course, another matter (this is a feature of the market-situation); and it is characteristic of the 'modern' approach that the term 'exploitation', if it is used at all, is employed in a quite different sense to signify some *departure* from 'normal' price-relations, due to the presence of some monopolistic element or market 'imperfection'.*

The second main line of tradition also derived from Smith, even if in a quasi-Hegelian manner from certain doctrines or propositions of Smith inverted (and hence transmuted) by Ricardo. First, Smith's peculiar theory of value (with its polarised distinction between "the early and rude state" and developed capitalist society) was refashioned by Ricardo so as to make conditions of production, and in particular quantities of labour expended in production, the basic determinant alike in capitalist and in pre-capitalist society. In doing so he rejected the Adding-up-components Theory, and by implication rejected the possibility of treating the sphere of exchange-relations as an 'isolated system', and anchored the explanation of these exchange-relations firmly in conditions and circumstances of production. Secondly, whatever his reason may have been for regarding distribution as the central problem, his instinct in doing so was undoubtedly right, and his mode of treating distribution was crucial. He saw that this had to be explained in terms peculiar to itself and not as an outcome of general supply–demand exchange-relations, as Smith had treated it. The latter at any rate was incapable of yielding precise results in the rather loose manner in which Smith and Malthus alike formulated it. Moreover, for Ricardo an answer to the question about distribution was a necessary and prior condition for calculating the effect of a change in wages on prices (both general and individual prices): in other words for calculating

---

* *Cf.* Pigou's use of the term to refer to payment of workers at *less* than the equivalent of their marginal net product (A. C. Pigou, *The Economics of Welfare* (London, 1920) pp. 511 *et seq.*).

the 'modifications' of relative prices introduced by differences in technical conditions of production, affecting particularly the use of fixed capital. (As we noted above, the 'curious effect' of a rise of wages on the prices of things produced with a disproportionate amount of fixed capital was his own innovation and treated by him as a reinforcement of his own position and *not* as a concession to that of Adam Smith.)

So far as distribution is concerned Ricardo could be regarded as extending and developing the brief section on the subject in the *Wealth of Nations*. But the extension contained a crucial additional element. This was the introduction, implicitly if not explicitly, of a social or institutional datum in the shape of the socio-economic conditions defining the level of real-wages. In Ricardo this was not very carefully or fully defined: it seemed to rest on a Malthusian view of population-increase, although we have remarked that he was careful to include the element of 'habit and customs' in his notion of subsistence-requirements at any given date or in any country. But it was this way of presenting distribution and its determinants that opened the door through which Marx introduced into economic theory those crucial 'social relations of production', and in particular the historically-conditioned emergence of a proletariat, as the pivot of his theory of surplus-value. A main consequence of this was (more explicitly, perhaps, in Ricardo than in Marx) that once the level of real-wages was taken as given in this way, the conditions of production in the industry or industries producing necessities for wage-earners played a key rôle in determining the ratio of profits or surplus to wages, and hence (given necessary labour-expenditures in various lines of production) relative exchange-values. The crucial ratio here was that of the produce of a day's labour to the wages of a day's labour, or alternatively on a global scale the proportion of the total labour-force needed to produce subsistence, or necessary wage-goods, for that labour-force. It was the little-known Russian economist, W. K. Dmitriev, at the turn of the century, who seems to have been the first both to appreciate and to formulate concisely the distinctive novelty of Ricardo's analytical structure and approach – something which had become submerged and forgotten amid the revisions and reinterpretations that he had suffered in the interval. In answering a criticism of which we shall speak below* Dmitriev showed that the essence of Ricardo's theory could be represented in the following equation applying to a simplified two-product case, where one of the two products, A, is input in the production both of itself and of B. He writes the equation:

$$\Upsilon_{AB} = \frac{N_A a x_a (1 + r)^t_A}{N_B a x_a (1 + r)^t_B},$$

where Υ is the price-ratio of A to B; the real-wage per unit of labour-time is a units of wage-good A; price per unit of A is x_a; N_A and N_B are the number of units of labour required to produce respectively a unit of A and B; r is the rate of profit and t is the time over which labour is advanced (or the production-period). This, of course, bears close analogy with Ricardo's case of agriculture, producing corn as the wage-good, and manufactures. Dmitriev then shows that r can be directly derived from N and t in the wage-good industry once a (the real wage) is known. N, t and a are part of the data in the aforementioned equation; N and t depending on the technical conditions of production in A; and it is *not* necessary for the *price* of A *first* to be determined before r can be derived. Accordingly this single equation suffices in the two-product case to determine the price-ratio of A to B, given the N's and the t's and a.†

---

* See Chapter 7, pp. 177–8.
† *Essais Économiques*, V. K. Dmitriev (trans. Bernard Joly, Paris, 1968) p. 47 and *cf.* pp. 38, 45. Also *cf.* on both Dmitriev and the Ricardian theory of profit P. Garegnani, *Il Capitale nelle teorie della Distribuzione* (Milano, 1960) pp. 3–34, 54–9. Dmitriev himself remarks that "exaggerated importance" has often been ascribed to Ricardo's proposition about the inverse relationship between profit and wages, whereas "the principal merit of Ricardo's theory of profit lay not in this but in establishing the laws determining the absolute level of profit" (*op. cit.*, p. 45n). It was, however, the former proposition that the anti-Ricardians found socially disturbing.

It may be noticed incidentally that in the above equation the inclusion of x_a is, strictly speaking, unnecessary in the two-product case, since the quantities concerned can be expressed in physical units of the wage-good A.

It was against this whole mode of approach to a theory of profit that the Senior–Longfield school reacted so strongly – not merely against it as an inapposite analytical tool (which in common with most critics of Ricardo then and since it seems probable that they imperfectly grasped), but against its wider implications and corollaries. In reacting in this way, it was almost inevitable that they should be carried in the wake of (and eventually join) the other and rival tradition deriving from Smith, reinforcing it by so doing. If they are properly described at all as 'improvers' or 'conciliators', such a term should really be applied to their rôle in developing *this* Smithian tradition and *not* the Ricardian branch. This was to be the case, as we shall see, with J. S. Mill, despite the inhibitions imposed by filial piety; so that his eventual influence was to define and develop, not the Ricardian tradition, but its rival and eventual supplanter; this fact being obscured at the time (and since) by his insistence that he was preserving and improving Ricardo's doctrine. The latter was to reappear, towards the end of the reign of Mill, in Marx who adapted and extended it in his own dialectical manner. Scarcely surprising that it should thereafter have lived on in what Keynes called "the underworld of heretics" and kept at arm's length by the academic *élite* as the unfortunate begetter of Marx – only to re-emerge in the 1960s in what has been christened 'neo-Ricardianism', a minority movement associated with critique of orthodox doctrine.

A concluding remark, almost in parenthesis, is possibly in place here, alluding to another matter that has often obscured the true nature of Ricardian doctrine. It should be fairly clear from what has been said that a system which determines distribution in terms of exchange and its emergent prices must, in one way or another, with possibility of varying emphasis, be cast in terms of supply and demand;* but *au contraire* the Ricardian system, which explains exchange in terms of distribution, and distribution itself in terms of productivity and conditions of production in one industry or sector of industry (given the real-wage), has no place for the relations of supply

* Needless to say, 'scarcity' is essentially a supply–demand notion.

and demand – at least, until it comes to *movements* in relative prices, and in particular of Smithian market prices. On a number of occasions Ricardo, in controversy with the position of Smith and of Malthus, criticised and dismissed explanations in terms of 'supply and demand'; and for doing so Ricardo has in turn been criticised for primitive incomprehension of the fact that both blades of the Marshallian 'scissors' are needed to do the cutting. Schumpeter, for instance, has written as follows: "Thus, for Ricardo, the main point at issue was from the first labour quantity *versus* supply and demand . . . The true enemy was the supply-and-demand theory, which 'has become almost an axiom in political economy, and has been the source of much error' (Ch. 30, third paragraph). . . It implies, of course, that Ricardo was completely blind to the nature, and the logical place in economic theory, of the supply-and-demand apparatus and that he took it to represent a theory of value distinct from and opposed to his own. This reflects little credit on him as a theorist. For it should be clear that his own theorem on equilibrium values is only tenable, so far as it is tenable at all, by virtue of the interplay of supply and demand."*

This is a strange charge, and one only explicable by basic (and by no means uncommon) misunderstanding. Of course, Ricardo would not have denied (no more than would Marx† whom Schumpeter also includes in this criticism) that in the context of market-price, their variations and adjustments, shifts in supply–demand relations act as proximate causes of price-movements. What Ricardo had in mind was the use of the notion of supply–demand relations by Smith in his system as a whole – as the vehicle and framework of determination. Ricardo was using it, in other words, as a label for the rival theory of value and distribution that he was combating. Significantly enough, Malthus in turn used it as a generic

---

* Schumpeter, *Economic Analysis*, pp. 600–1.
† There is a good deal about supply and demand in the chapter on 'Market Prices and Market Values' in Vol. III of *Capital*, and more in Chapter 3 of *Wage-Labour and Capital*, which refers to 'competition among buyers' and 'competition among sellers' and the effect of these severally on price.

phrase in opposition to Ricardo's system. He wrote in his *Principles* of "the two systems, one of which accounts for the prices of the great mass of commodities by the cost of their production, and the other accounts for the prices of all commodities, under all circumstances, permanent as well as temporary, by the relation of the demand to the supply, though they touch each other necessarily at a great number of points, have an essentially different origin, and require, therefore, to be very carefully distinguished". He concluded by asserting his belief "that the great principle of demand and supply is called into action to determine what Adam Smith calls natural prices as well as market prices".* On this Ricardo's comment was: "The author forgets Adam Smith's definition of natural price, or he would not say that demand and supply could determine natural price. Natural price is only another name for cost of production. When any commodity sells for that price which will repay the wages for labour expended on it, will also afford rent, and profit at their then current rate, Adam Smith would say that commodity was at its natural price. Now these charges would remain the same, whether commodities were much or little demanded, whether they sold at a high or low market price."† Does not this comment of Ricardo place it beyond doubt that he was thinking of both wages and profit as being determined *independently* of and prior to market-price or even of natural value?

---

* Malthus, *Principles of Political Economy* (London, 1820) pp. 73, 75.
† 'Notes on Malthus', *Works and Correspondence of Ricardo*, ed. Sraffa, Vol. II, p. 46. To this he adds that "market price will depend on supply and demand" and "the supply will be finally determined by ... the cost of production" (*ibid.*, p. 47). *Cf.* also Chapter xxx of his *Principles* (*ibid.*, Vol. I, p. 382) which is entitled 'On the Influence of Demand and Supply on Prices.'

JOHN STUART MILL

I

At first sight it is very difficult to place J. S. Mill (1806–73) in the hierarchy of descent, especially in relation to the two branches, or lines of tradition, of which we spoke in the last chapter. From one aspect he was a direct lineal descendant of Ricardo, and according to his own statements and belief he was at the same time the defender of Ricardian doctrine against its critics and its elaborator. Certainly at the time he was regarded as the embodiment of Ricardian orthodoxy; and from 1848 until Marshall his *Principles of Political Economy with some of their applications to social philosophy* held a unique place as the accepted textbook on the subject. Bagehot spoke of his "monarchical influence" over his contemporaries, and said that from then on all students "see the whole subject with Mill's eyes"; adding that "they see in Ricardo and Adam Smith what he told them to see".* As son of James Mill, Ricardo's close friend at whose instigation the latter had written his *Principles* of 1817 and had entered Parliament, John Stuart as a youth had known Ricardo personally, had visited Gatcomb Park and been taken on walks by him; moreover he was trained in Political Economy by his father (at the age of 13) on Ricardo's *Principles*. At the same time he was by nature a systematiser and synthesiser (some would say eclectic); and in the Preface to his own book of 1848 he states it as his aim to write a treatise containing "the latest improvements which have been made in the theory". "Many new ideas, and new applications of ideas", he wrote, "have been elicited by the discussions of the last few years . . . and there seems reason that the field of Political Economy should be re-surveyed in its whole extent, if only for the purpose of incorporating the results of these speculations, and bringing

* In an obituary article in *The Economist*, 17 May 1873 (No. 1551) pp. 588–9.

DTV

them into harmony with the principles previously laid down by the best thinkers on the subject."

He took *The Wealth of Nations* advisedly as his model, rather than Ricardo, since "the most characteristic quality" of that work of Adam Smith had been that it "invariably associates the principles with their application", and this "implies a much wider range of ideas and topics, than are included in political economy considered as a branch of abstract speculation". "For practical purposes", Mill added, "political economy is inseparably intertwined with many other branches of social philosophy" – a truth of which "Adam Smith never loses sight".* These sentiments could well imply that in his heart his devotion was to the Smithian approach and tradition in either of its interpretations and that his defence of Ricardo's doctrine against its critics was no more than an act of piety.

In any case, when looking back on him from a distance one can see quite clearly that in major respects his own work was much nearer to Marshall than it was to Ricardo; and that so far as his theory of value was concerned, on the contrary to continuing and improving on Ricardo, in essentials he took his stand on the position of Smith where Ricardo had been opposing him. We shall see that he ended-up, at any rate, with a Cost of Production Theory which was essentially the Adding-up-of-Components Theory of Smith, borrowing something from Senior and even Say, on the one hand, and trying to reconcile the result with some Ricardian propositions, on the other. Schumpeter speaks of the "Smith–Mill–Marshall line", and refuses to include J. S. Mill in Ricardo's school on the ground that "the economics of the *Principles* [of 1848] is no longer Ricardian". This forthright opinion he supports and expands as follows: "This is obscured by filial respect and also, independently of this, by J. S. Mill's own belief that he was only qualifying Ricardian doctrine. But this belief was erroneous. His qualifications affect essentials of theory and, still more, of course, of social outlook. Ricardianism meant no doubt more

---

* J. S. Mill, *Principles of Political Economy, with some of their applications to social philosophy* (London, 1848) Vol. I, pp. iii, iv.

to him that it did to Marshall ... From Marshall's *Principles*
Ricardianism can be removed without being missed at all.
From Mill's *Principles* it could be dropped without being missed
very greatly."*

Since John Stuart (who was born in Pentonville, London, on
20 May 1806 as the eldest son of James Mill) wrote in later life
an autobiography, there is no need to recount any of the strange
details of his upbringing or of the influences upon him even
where these are important to an understanding of his ideas.
Apart from the influence of his father's intensive education, one
could say, perhaps, that most worthy of being singled out as
post-adolescent influences upon his socio-philosophic attitude
and standpoint were the Utilitarian Society and the foundation
of the *Westminster Review*. The former was a small gathering (of
never more than ten) "composed of young men agreeing in
fundamental principles" which started meeting at Bentham's
house in the winter of 1822–3, and continued to do so for rather
more than three years. It was "the first time anyone had taken
the title of Utilitarian". About the same time (in 1823)
Bentham founded the *Westminster Review* as a Radical organ "to
make head against the Edinburgh and the Quarterly"; and in
this new review John Stuart participated as a frequent contri-
butor of articles and reviews. (His father had contributed to the
first number an article criticising the Whig Party and the
Edinburgh Review as its chief literary organ.) Of the 'Philosophic
Radicalism' (as it came to be called) of the group of young men
round the *Westminster*, John Stuart (as one of them) writes as
follows: "Their mode of thinking was not characterised by
Benthamism in any sense which has relation to Bentham as a
chief and guide, but rather by a combination of Bentham's
point of view with that of the modern political economy and
with the Hartleian metaphysics."† They championed Malthusian restriction of births among the labouring population
as "the sole means of realising improvement in their economic
conditions"; and in politics they advocated representative

---

* *History of Economic Analysis*, pp. 529, 530.
† *Autobiography* (London, 1873) p. 105.

government and freedom of discussion. Mill refers to their "unbounded confidence" in representative government and in freedom of discussion in politics as weapons against minority class-rule: "when the legislature no longer represented a class interest it would aim at the general interest". He also speaks of himself and his friends, in connexion with the conduct of the *Westminster Review*, as having, as one of two principal aims, the freeing of "philosophic radicalism from the reproach of sectarian Benthamism . . . to give a wider basis and a more free and genial character to Radical speculations; to show that there was a Radical philosophy, better and more complete than Bentham's, while recognising and incorporating all of Bentham's which is permanently valuable". An example of what to-day would be called the 'committed' standpoint of these young Radicals of whom Mill was one is his description that we cited in Chapter 1 of his *System of Logic* (even) of 1843 as "a textbook . . . which derives all knowledge from experience", as opposed to "the German or *a priori* view of knowledge and of the knowing faculties" which served as "the great intellectual support of false doctrines and bad institutions".*

After 1828 Mill gave up journalistic activities and went in for more serious study and writing; which included, in 1830–1, the five essays (published later, in 1844) entitled *Essays on Some Unsettled Questions of Political Economy* of which we shall presently speak. From this time also dated the signal influence upon his life that was eventually to render him a self-styled 'socialist': namely his meeting (in 1830) with Mrs Harriet Taylor, who twenty-one years later was to become his wife, three years after the appearance of his *Principles of Political Economy*.

This influence of his wife-to-be upon this work (which, as Leslie Stephen remarks, "became popular in a sense in which no work upon the same topic had been popular since the *Wealth of Nations*")† was sufficiently great for a few words

---

* *Autobiography*, p. 225.

† Leslie Stephen, *The English Utilitarians* (London, 1900) Vol. III, p. 53. He goes on to say that in the 1850s and 1860s "a large school looked up to Mill as an almost infallible oracle".

to be said of it here, if only by way of parenthesis. In Mill's own words, it gave to the book its "general tone by which it is distinguished from all previous expositions of Political Economy"; this consisting "chiefly in making the proper distinction between the laws of the production of wealth, which are real laws of nature, dependent on the properties of objects, and the modes of its Distribution, which, subject to certain conditions, depend on human will". Other economists, in his opinion, confused the two "under the designation of economic laws . . . incapable of being defeated or modified by human effort".* In other words, he regarded Distribution of Income as being the product of alterable social institutions – as being 'institutional' and historical-relative, not 'natural' or universal. This explicit avowal was certainly an advance, both on what had been implied by his predecessors and on what was to come later with theories of 'imputation' of which we shall presently speak. It was to be underlined by Marx as a reason why "it would be very wrong to class [those like J. S. Mill] with the herd of vulgar economic apologists",† even though for Marx, of course, such a statement as the one quoted was an inadequate indication of the connection between Distribution and the social relations of production.

More specifically Mill speaks of the change in his social philosophy under her influence in this way. "I was [formerly] a democrat, but not the least a Socialist." Then, speaking of himself and his wife: "Our ideal of ultimate improvement went far beyond Democracy and would class us decidedly under the general designation of Socialists . . . We looked forward to a time when society will no longer be divided into the idle and the industrious."‡ In the *Principles* these new opinions "were promulgated less clearly and fully in the first edition, rather more so in the second, and quite unequivocally in the third". The chapter that he attributed entirely to her, and one which he held to have had "a greater influence on opinion than all

---

* *Principles of Political Economy*, p. 246.
† *Capital*, Vol. 1 (Aveling and Moore edn) p. 623n.
‡ *Autobiography*, p. 231.

the rest", was one entitled 'The Probable Futurity of the Labouring Classes'. This did not exist at all "in the first draft of the book".* It ends, rather tamely to modern eyes if radical-sounding in its day,† with advocacy of some kind of profit-sharing and copartnership. It may be added that when in 1865 he stood as a Parliamentary candidate for Westminster, it was as a Liberal – but then so did the trade unionists of the time who ran for Parliament. After losing his seat in 1868, he did not himself stand again but lent support and money to George Odger and other trade unionists standing for Parliament.

II

Of the doctrines that were characteristic of Mill, it may be convenient to deal first with his theory of profit, before mentioning his treatment of value, about which there is very little of interest to say. Indeed his treatment of the former is in many ways a key to the latter (as it had also been with Ricardo). Profit was the subject of the fourth and most significant essay of his early work, *Essays on Some Unsettled Questions*; where he puts forward what he claimed to be a restatement of Ricardo's theory, and one that appears to be wholly Ricardian in *form*.

Ricardo's theory, as we have seen, was that Profits depend exclusively on Wages in the sense of being the difference between the *value* of wages paid to labour and the value of labour's product; or in other words on real wages as a proportion of the value produced when both are expressed in terms of the labour required to produce them. This according to Mill was "the most perfect form in which the law of profits seems to have been yet exhibited" and to be "the basis of the true theory of profits".‡

---

* *Ibid.*, p. 245.

† This chapter contains *inter alia* such forthright and radical statements as: "I cannot think it probable that they [the working classes] will be permanently contented with the condition of labouring for wages as their ultimate state. To work at the bidding and for the profit of another, without any interest in the work – the price of their labour adjusted by hostile competition . . . is not, even when wages are high, a satisfactory state to human beings of educated intelligence, who have ceased to think themselves naturally inferior to those whom they serve" (*Principles*, Vol. II (2nd ed., 1849) p. 324).

‡ *Essays on Some Unsettled Questions* (London, 1844) pp. 94–5, 98. Marx, perhaps rather unfairly, criticises Mill here for failing to see that, while this is true of the rate of surplus value, it is not necessarily true of profit and the rate of profit

He translates this into his own terminology by making this equivalent to the statement that profits depend upon "the cost of production of wages"; but then goes on to point out that part of the requisites of production (*e.g.* "tools, materials and buildings") consists of products of labour expended *in the past*. Hence "the *whole* of their value is not resolvable into the wages of the labourers by whom they were produced", but in part consists of profit to the capitalists who have advanced these wages of the labour expended in the past.* This is illustrated with an example that has puzzled some and been called curious. Actually it is a remarkably simple way of making the point in question. It consists of a comparison of two cases in both of which 100 men, working for a year and each receiving a quarter of corn as wages, produce 180 quarters as final product. In the first example part of the labour, that of 40 men, is expended in the *previous* year to produce seed corn and tools "amounting to the value of 60 quarters"; and in the second year, with the aid of this "fixed capital and seed", 60 men work to produce the final product of 180 quarters. In the second example all the labour, namely that of 100 men, is expended in the *current* year, and since it is working without the aid of fixed capital its productivity is lower, and this labour of 100 men (instead of 60) yields the same final product of 180 quarters. Yet, although the total expenditure of labour in the two cases is the same, and also the cost in wages, the rate of profits in one case is 50 per cent

$$\left(= \frac{180 - (60 \text{ seed corn and tools}\dagger + 60 \text{ wages})}{120} \right),$$ and in the other

case 80 per cent $\left(= \frac{180-100}{100} \right)$; the difference being due to that

part of the capital (20 quarters) that in the former case repre-

(*Theorien über den Mehrwert*, ed. Karl Kautsky (Berlin, 1923) Vol. II, pp. 230 *seq.*). But if it is true of profit or surplus-value as a ratio to wages, then it is presumably true also, *ceteris paribus*, of its derivative, ratio of profit to total capital. True, if the latter changes, the *rate* of profit, *ceteris paribus*, will be affected; but this indeed is just the point of Mill's example.

* Mill, *Essays on Some Unsettled Questions*, p. 98.

† The value of the seed corn and tools produced in the previous year is made up of 40 quarters as wages of 40 men employed in that year and (at the prevailing rate of profit) 20 quarters as profit on the capital advanced in that year as wages.

sented profit upon the wages advanced in the previous year. Hence "Ricardo's theory is defective" in that "the rate of profit does *not* exclusively depend upon the value of wages in his sense, namely the quantity of labour"; accordingly the "cost of production of wages", upon which profits depend, must be so interpreted as to include in "cost of production" the profits advanced as well as the wages advanced. He concludes: "Mr. Ricardo's principle that profits cannot rise unless wages fall, is strictly true, if by low wages he meant not merely wages which are the produce of a smaller quantity of labour, but wages which are produced at less cost, reckoning labour and previous profits together."*

How is one to take this emendation? How large a departure from the Ricardian theory did it represent? Throughout this essay, it may be noted, Mill was concerned with the *rate* of profit, and the focus seems to have been shifted from the determination of total profit, or profit as a proportion of any given value produced (and hence as a ratio to wages),† which was Ricardo's main concern, to the ratio of this profit to the capital advanced. Mill's emendation amounts to pointing out, quite correctly, that with fixed capital in the picture this latter ratio will be smaller, *ceteris paribus*, the larger the proportion of fixed to circulating capital, or the longer the time over which the expenses of production, or the labour, have to be advanced: a point which Ricardo never seems to have made explicitly, and even to have ignored, presumably because he was not very much concerned with profit as a ratio to total capital. Formally this emendation can be treated as analogous to Marx's criticism that Ricardo ignored so-called 'constant capital' as a factor in the determination of the profit-rate, or alternatively treated profit and surplus-value as identical. Mill *could* have said that Ricardo's principle that profits depended on the value of wages

* *Ibid.*, p. 104.
† It is to be noted that with Ricardo's implicit assumption of an annual harvest cycle and of capital consisting of wage-advances the rate of profit was the same as the ratio of profit to wages and no problem of a difference between the two arose. (Seed-corn would be a qualification of this, of course, if it were treated as as an advance of capital and not merely as a deduction from the gross product at the *end* of each year.)

was quite true of *total profits*, or of the amount of profit yielded by any given value total produced; but that when expressed as a ratio to capital it depended, naturally, on the size of the total capital and this in turn on how much fixed capital was used in production (compared to current expenditure on wages). But he did not in fact say this; he preferred to say that Ricardo's "cost of production of wages" must be interpreted to consist of "two parts", wages and "the profits of those who, in any antecedent stage of the production, have advanced any portion of those wages"; and the handling of his example might be taken to imply that the time over which labour is advanced influences not merely the *rate* of profit (by influencing the size of the capital to be advanced) but also the size of the total profit available.

Later, in his *Principles*, he introduces the notion of a *minimum* profit if capitalists are to continue to accumulate capital and to invest it in industry, and he has by this time adopted Senior's notion of interest as a reward for abstinence and the notion of profit as being (or including) the 'wages of superintendence'.* Although he tries to marry these ideas with his own rather cloudily amended version of Ricardo's principle that profits depend upon the 'cost of production of wages',† he ends up with a theory that is much closer to Marshall's theory of 'normal profit' than it is to anything specifically Ricardian.

Mill's treatment of the theory of value‡ is prefaced by the confident statement: "Happily there is nothing in the laws of Value which remains for the present or any future writer to clear up; the theory of the subject is complete."§ Here again he starts by claiming that he is doing no more than tidy up, expand a little and restate Ricardo. What in fact he does is to return to the 'adding-up-the-components-of-price' theory of Adam Smith, and in his restatement of this to bring it very close

* *Principles*, Vol. i (London, 1848) Ch. xv, pp. 477–9.
† Mill here interprets this as "the labourers' proportional share" and renders "profits depend on wages" as profits "depend on the *cost of labour*" (*ibid.*, pp. 492–3).
‡ In his chapter 'On Value' in Book iii, Ch. i, *ibid.*, pp. 513 *seq.*
§ *Ibid.*, p. 515.

to Marshall's theory of long-period 'normal value'. Ricardo's
theory of profits is translated into the proposition that profits
depend on the 'cost of production of wages' so as to include
profits on the time for which the wages have been advanced in
cost of production. Mill then goes on to say that "things on the
average exchange for one another in the ratio of their cost of
production", and to define cost of production explicitly to
mean wages *plus* profit on the amount of capital employed together with the labour at a rate the expectation of which is
necessary to persuade capitalists to continue producing.

"If we consider as the producer the capitalist who makes the
advances, the word Labour [in Ricardo's theory] may be
replaced by the word Wages: what the produce costs to him is
the wages which he has had to pay." But since capital is "the
result of abstinence", it follows that "the produce, or its value,
must be sufficient to remunerate, not only all the labour required, but the abstinence of all the persons by whom a
remuneration of the different classes of labour was advanced.
The return for abstinence is Profit".* "As a general rule, things
tend to exchange for one another at such values as will enable
each producer to be repaid the cost of production with the
ordinary profit . . . The latent influence by which the values of
things are made to conform in the long run to the cost of production, is the variation that would otherwise take place in the
supply of the commodity." The chapter 'Of Cost of Production'
(Chapter III of Book III) concludes in the "strain of metaphor":
"demand and supply always rush to an equilibrium, but the
condition of *stable* equilibrium is when things exchange for each
other according to their cost of production, or, in the expression
we have used, when things are at their Natural Value".†

Thus in a formal sense he still retains a Ricardian base to his
renovated Smithian structure by admitting that profits depend,
inter alia, upon wages, in his amended and qualified interpretation of this proposition. But since he regards profit as tending
always to the minimum level at which they just remunerate
'abstinence' and 'labour of superintendence' and no more

---

* *Ibid.*, pp. 540, 546.   † *Ibid.*, pp. 534–5, 539.

(apart from risk-bearing), and cannot fall below this without adversely affecting the supply, the Ricardian proposition would seem to be left without a place.

Schumpeter has pointed out that his conception of value is entirely in line with Bailey's criticism of Ricardo and leaves no room for anything in the nature of 'absolute value'. "The energy with which he insisted on the relative character of [Value] completely annihilated Ricardo's Real Value and reduced other Ricardianisms to insipid innocuousness."* Looking at the result from a different angle, it was Cairnes who made the comment that Mill had shifted the perspective "to the partial and limited stand-point of the capitalist employer" by framing his theory in terms of *expenses* of production, rather than of any form of real cost, whether objectively or subjectively conceived.† To a certain extent this comment is, no doubt, appropriate, and certainly indicates the affinity of Mill's treatment with Smith's. But as a critique it is, surely, secondary to the fact that in Mill's theory Ricardian determination of the profit–wage ratio is replaced by the notion of a 'minimum level' of profit, which, if it is to be more than an empty box, must rest, presumably, on rather misty and contingent entrepreneurial 'propensities-to-accumulate'.

III

Thirdly and lastly, the doctrine that is best known among those characteristic of Mill is probably the Wages Fund: no doubt by reason of his dramatic recantation of it in face of the criticism of W. T. Thornton in his book *On Labour* (which may well have convinced him of the reactionary uses to which the doctrine was being put).‡ This, briefly, was the view that total wages

* Schumpeter, *History of Economic Analysis*, p. 603. This is evidently a reference to Mill's forthright statement (*Principles*, Vol. 1, p. 543) that "the value of a commodity is not a name for an inherent and substantive quality of a thing itself, but means the quantity of other things which can be obtained in exchange for it. The value of one thing must always be understood relatively to some other thing or to things in general."

† J. E. Cairnes, *Leading Principles of Political Economy Newly Expounded* (London, 1874) p. 53.

‡ Three years previously, indeed, in a letter to Henry Fawcett (of 1 Jan. 1866) he had dissented from Fawcett's chapter on wages and said: "I think I could show

were limited by the existing fund of capital, moreover by that part of capital that was earmarked (in some fashion unexplained) for paying wages. Given this total, wages per head were arrived at by a simple process of dividing the total by the labouring population that competed for employment. This view that wages are "paid out of capital" regarded as advances of wages, and hence "limited by capital", is what Marshall called the "vulgar form of the Wage-Fund theory": a form in which it "cannot be defended".* As such it was first cousin, on the one hand, to the doctrine which many have seen as implicit in classical political economy that industry (and hence in the long run population) is limited by capital, and on the other hand to another contentious proposition of Mill to the effect that "demand for commodities is not demand for labour" (*i.e.* that it is not income *spent* on consumption that creates employment, but income invested as wage-advances to labour).

The most succinct expression of his doctrine in Mill's *Principles* is as follows. "Wages, then, depend upon the demand and supply of labour; or, as it is often expressed, on the proportion between population and capital. By population is here meant the number only of the labouring class, or rather of those who work for hire; and by capital, only circulating capital, and not even the whole of that, but the part which is expended in the direct purchase of labour . . . Wages (meaning, of course, the general rate) cannot rise, but by an increase of the aggregate funds employed in hiring labourers, or a diminution of the number of the competitors for hire."† And again: "Since therefore the rate of wages which results from competition distributes the whole wages-fund among the whole labouring population; if law or opinion succeeds in fixing wages above this rate, some labourers are kept out of employment."‡

that an increase of wages at the expense of profits would not be an impracticability on the true principles of political economy" (*The Letters of J. S. Mill,* ed. H. S. R. Elliot (London, 1910) Vol. ii, p. 52).

* A. Marshall, *Principles of Economics* (London, 1916) p. 823.

† Mill, *Principles,* Vol. i, Book ii, Ch. xi, 'Of Wages', pp. 401, 402.

‡ *Ibid.,* p. 426. This is prefaced by the statement: "It is a mistake to suppose that competition merely keeps down wages. It is equally the means by which they are kept up . . . Wages can only be lowered by competition until room is made

This doctrine, appearing as it did with the simplicity and force of an arithmetical truism, manifestly served as a persuasive answer to the claims of trade unionism to be capable of affecting the general level of wages. Leslie Stephen was to dismiss it as "an identical proposition: the wage-fund means simply the wages, and the rate of wages is given by the total paid divided by the number of receivers".* Such a dismissal, while being fair comment on some of the cruder versions of the doctrine,† seems to be too sweeping a dismissal, since Mill and his disciples clearly did not intend to *define* the fund as total wages, but were maintaining, rather, that total wages, and hence the average wage-level, were determined by some independently determined entity called the Wages-Fund. Refutation required one to show that no such independent and pre-determining entity existed; which is what Thornton in fact did when he posed the question: "Is there really any such fund? Is there any specific portion of any single individual's capital which the owner must necessarily expend upon labour?"‡

Mill's recantation (in which according to Marshall "he

to admit all the labourers to a share in the distribution of the wages-fund. If they fall below this point, a portion of capital would remain unemployed for want of labourers; a counter-competition would commence on the side of the capitalists, and wages would rise" (*ibid.*, pp. 425–6).

* *The English Utilitarians* (London, 1900) Vol. III, p. 216.

† It might well be a valid comment, *e.g.*, on Mrs M. G. Fawcett's statement that "wages depend on the proportion between the wages-fund and the number of the labouring population. If this proportion remains unchanged, the average rate of wages cannot be raised" (*Political Economy for Beginners* (5th ed., London, 1880) p. 102); perhaps also Prof. Henry Fawcett's statement: "The circulating capital of a country is its wage fund. Hence, if we desire to calculate the average money wages received by each labourer, we have simply to divide the amount of this capital by the number of the labouring population. It is therefore evident that the average money-wages cannot be increased unless either the circulating capital is augmented or the number of the labouring population is diminished" (*Economic Position of the British Labourer* (Cambridge and London, 1865) p. 120). Sidgwick declared that in the form in which it was stated by Mill "it would be merely saying that a quotient can only be made larger by increasing the dividend or diminishing the divisor", but that "what Mill really meant was that . . . the amount of wealth devoted to the payment of wages is mainly determined . . . by saving" (*The Principles of Political Economy*, 2nd edition (London, 1887) p. 299). To this he later adds the remark that "the commodities consumed by hired labourers is not divided by a sharp line from those consumed by other classes" (*ibid.*, p. 305).

‡ W. T. Thornton, *On Labour* (London, 1869) p. 84.

yielded too much, and overstated the extent of his own past error")* came in the course of reviewing Thornton's book in the *Fortnightly Review* of May 1869. These were his words: "There is no law of nature making it inherently impossible for wages to rise to the point of absorbing not only the funds which he [the employer] had intended to devote to carrying on his business, but the whole of what he allows for his private expenses beyond the necessaries of life. The real limit to the rise is the practical consideration how much would ruin him, or drive him to abandon the business, not the inexorable limits of the Wages-fund." But although disowned by one of its main exponents,† the doctrine, with its implications, was destined to live on in other guises, either that of a Böhm–Bawerkian 'subsistence fund', or in some version of marginal productivity doctrine. We have already noted Marshall's opinion that there was a sense in which it could be held to be true. Wicksell was to point out that the Austrian theory of capital in effect substituted for the simple relation $W = C/L$ of wage-fund theory that of

$$C = \frac{Lwt}{2},$$

where C is a fund of subsistence goods for workers, w is the wage and t is the length of the period of production; together with the further relation $p = w + t(\mathrm{d}p/\mathrm{d}t)$ to determine t (p being annual production per worker), or else, to determine t, the condition that

$$(p - w) : \frac{wt}{2}$$

is a maximum.‡

---

* Marshall, *Principles*, p. 825.
† His disciple, J. E. Cairnes, does not seem to have abandoned the doctrine, although in a letter to Mill he apparently expressed agreement with the *Fortnightly Review* article (*The Letters of J. S. Mill*, ed. Hugh S. R. Elliot, Vol. II, p. 207).
‡ K. Wicksell, *Value, Capital and Rent* (London, 1954) pp. 145–6. "The great importance" of Böhm-Bawerk's theory "consists partly in the fact that in this theory for the first time a real substitute is provided for the obsolete wage fund theory which several writers have tried to overthrow by cheap criticism without being able to replace it by a better" (p. 145).

Needless to say, one respect in which Mill was entirely traditional and made no change in accepted doctrine was in his belief in 'Say's Law'. Here he spoke forthrightly and without making any concession: "A general over-supply, or excess of all commodities above the demand, so far as demand consists in means of payment, is thus shown to be an impossibility . . . It is evident enough, that produce makes a market for produce."*

One cannot close a review of Mill's economic views without a brief reference to the distinctive view he took on the question of the 'stationary state'. The notion of such a state in which capital accumulation would be halted we have seen appeared in the work both of Smith and Ricardo, but had been treated by them as lying some way in the future, and according to Ricardo would continue to lie in the future so long as free trade in corn and agricultural improvements enabled the tendency to diminishing returns to be held at bay and the rate of profit maintained. Mill's attitude towards it was marked by two special peculiarities. First, he regarded the 'stationary state' as only just round the corner – at most a few years ahead and no more; its arrival only being postponed by such things as government borrowing, export of capital and wastage of capital by misdirection. Secondly, he regarded its arrival with much less gloom than had his forbears because he hoped that it would provide the occasion for improving the distribution of income. "I cannot regard the stationary state of capital and wealth with the unaffected aversion so generally manifested towards it by political economists of the old school."† He held that, were it not for export of capital and wastage of it and government loans for unproductive expenditure, none of which he supposed could be relied upon to continue indefinitely, only a few years more of capital accumulation at its existing rate (if "annually invested in really productive employment within the country") would suffice to reduce profits to their minimum level at which inducement to further investment would cease. Profits,

* *Principles of Political Economy*, Vol. II (2nd ed., 1849) p. 94.
† *Ibid.*, p. 310.

he thought, were "within a hand's breadth of the minimum", and the country therefore "on the very verge of the stationary state".* This he was able to regard with equanimity since he held that one should "fix attention upon improved distribution, and a large remuneration of labour, as the true desiderata", rather than on "mere increase of production" to which "inordinate importance" was usually "attached".† Luke-warm as such an aspiration may appear to modern eyes, in days when a prevalent view was that to let the poor die off from starvation was the only effective cure for poverty ("the rich man in his castle, the poor man at his gate") this was, indeed, a quite daringly radical doctrine.

This improvement in income-distribution, however, could not occur if population continued to increase at a Malthusian rate: it was conditional upon the growth of "provident habits of conduct" among the working classes, which he hoped for and anticipated with their growing independence and educa-tion. Given the spread of these "provident habits", the result should be that "population will bear a gradually diminishing ratio to capital and employment".‡

Were one listing in full the achievements of Mill's analysis, it would be an omission to fail to enlarge on his contribution to the theory of international trade, where he was the first to combine a theory of reciprocal demand with Ricardian com-parative costs, in order to show how the gains of trade were shared between the countries concerned (the latter alone being capable of defining the limits, only, within which the terms of trade could lie). Moreover, in the course of doing so he intro-duced the *notion* of elasticity of demand, although without the name or precise definition. In the case of the present work, whose theme is centred on theories of value and distribution, and in the main on relations internal to a closed economic system, failure to enlarge on such questions may perhaps be excused.

* *Ibid.*, pp. 289, 290.   † *Ibid.*, p. 315.   ‡ *Ibid.*, p. 322.

6

KARL MARX

I

We have seen that there were critics of post-Ricardian trends, particularly as regards the theory of profits, who tried to carry Ricardian theory further and to turn it into a critique of Capital itself. These were writers and pamphleteers like Thomas Hodgskin and William Thompson and J. F. Bray and John Gray, to whom the name of 'Ricardian Socialists' has been given; and although they inhabited what Keynes, a century later, was to call the "underworld of heretics", their significance did not go unnoticed by economists of gentry-breed in Dublin or Oxford. Although their audience was to be found in Mechanics Institutes and among incipient trade unions and radical fraternities, rather than in the cloisters of ancient universities, their actual or potential influence was evidently feared by writers such as Scrope and Read.*

Hodgskin presented his rather undeveloped concept of exploitation from the standpoint of a believer in a Smithian 'natural harmony' of natural laws†; and from this standpoint he was a critic of Ricardo, especially the latter's theory of wages and theory of rent. His claim that labour had a right to the whole produce, and that profit and rent were alike filched from labour, was essentially a natural right doctrine, such as Marx's surplus-value is commonly, but erroneously, interpreted as being.‡ Natural right to property in the fruit of one's own

---

* *Cf.* G. Poulett Scrope's reference (cited above, p. 110) to persons who "declaim against capital as the poison of society, and . . . robbery of the class of labourers", with a footnote reference to Hodgskin (*Principles of Political Economy* (London, 1833) p. 150), and again to Hodgskin's talk of "robbery of labourers" and "mistaken hostility to Capital" (in *Political Economy for Plain People* (London, 1833; 2nd ed. 1873) pp. 103, 105); Samuel Read, *An Inquiry into the Grounds of Right to Vendible Property* (Edinburgh, 1829) esp. pp. xxx–xxxi. More generally *cf.* Blaug, *Ricardian Economics*, pp. 140–50.

† *Cf.* E. Halévy, *Thomas Hodgskin* (London, 1956) pp. 58–9, 64–6, 80.

‡ Halévy, speaking of "the true psychological origin of the labour theory of value", says that "Hodgskin, a philosopher at the same time as he is an economist, finds the true source of the labour theory of value in Locke" (*ibid.*, p. 181).

labour was sharply contrasted with 'the legal or artificial' right of property to appropriate the product of the labour of others. He speaks of Capital as "engross[ing] the whole produce of a country, except the bare subsistence of the labourer, and surplus produce of fertile land", of "the all-engrossing nature of compound interest", and in a well-known passage throws down the challenge: "I am certain . . . that till the triumph of labour be complete; till productive industry alone be opulent, and till idleness alone be poor, till the admirable maxim that 'he who sows shall reap' be solidly established; till the right of property shall be founded on principles of justice, and not on those of slavery . . . there cannot and there ought not to be either peace on earth or goodwill amongst men."* Two years after the publication of *Labour Defended* came the publication of his lectures at the London Mechanics Institution (of which he had been a co-founder) under the title of *Popular Political Economy*.

Already in the year following Ricardo's death William Thompson, in *An Inquiry into the Principles of the Distribution of Wealth*, had deduced the right of labour to the whole produce from the postulate that labour is the sole (active) creator of wealth. In existing society this right was obstructed by a system of 'unequal exchanges' which resulted in part of labour's product being appropriated by the possessors of economic power and advantage. Apart from its injustice and its offence against the Benthamite maxim of 'greatest happiness', such a system deprived labour of much of its incentive (and in place of this made want the spur to labour): for which reason it was inimical to the production of wealth.

G. D. H. Cole, in his Introduction to the 1922 reprint of Hodgskin's *Labour Defended*, had this to say of Hodgskin and Thompson: "Hodgskin, in *Labour Defended*, and William Thompson in his *Inquiry into the Principles of the Distribution of Wealth* (1824) and *Labour Rewarded* (1827), were the first to formulate clearly the working-class criticism and inversion of the Ricardian economic system. In their constructive work the

---

* *Labour Defended against the Claims of Capital, or the Unproductiveness of Capital Proved*, by a Labourer (London, 1825), pp. 7, 23, 32.

two men differed widely. Thompson was, on the whole, a Cooperative Socialist of the school of Robert Owen; Hodgskin a philosophic anarchist following the tradition of William Godwin. But, in essence, their deductions from Ricardian assumptions are the same."*

Even before this, in 1821 Piercy Ravenstone (who might be called a conservative traditionalist rather than a Ricardian Socialist among the ranks of whom he is sometimes classed†) had propounded a 'deduction' or 'appropriation' theory of property-income bearing close analogy at several points with the ideas of Thompson and Hodgskin. He had spoken of the "pretension of the landowner" as being "the basis of the property of every description, which is seen to multiply so rapidly with the growth of civilisation"; on it "are built the pretensions of the master-manufacturer, of the tradesman, of the capitalist". "From this moment labour ceases to be free. A man cannot exercise his faculties without paying for the permission so to do. He cannot make use of his limbs without sharing the produce of his labour with those who contribute nothing to the success of his exertions. The exercise of industry is as effectively barred in manufactures as on land; everywhere the toll must be paid before industry is allowed to go to work . . . Everywhere the labourer must purchase the permission to be useful."‡ A not dissimilar emphasis, anticipating Marx's, is to be found also in Richard Jones, who in speaking of rent declared that "in the actual progress of human society, rent has usually originated in the appropriation of the soil, at a time when the bulk of the people must cultivate it on such terms as they can, or starve; and . . . are chained . . . to the land by an overpowering necessity; the necessity then which compels them to pay a rent . . . is wholly

* Introduction to Thomas Hodgskin in *Labour Defended against the Claims of Capital* (London, 1922) p. 12.
† Professor M. Blaug speaks of him as "the first of the so-called Ricardian social-ists" (*Ricardian Economics*, p. 141).
‡ P. Ravenstone, *A Few Doubts as to the Correctness of some opinions generally entertained on the subjects of Population and Political Economy* (London, 1821) pp. 199–200. Speaking historically, he says also that "rent and slavery cannot exist together, they are different modes of obtaining the same end . . . Slavery is the natural consequence of property in a thinly-peopled country, as rent is where population

independent of any difference in the quality of the ground they occupy, and would not be removed were the soil all equalised."*

Although they can scarcely be said to have constituted a school of economic theory, one should not omit to mention that on the continent, in addition to the utopian socialism of Saint-Simon and Fourier, who preached equality and the natural harmony of men cooperating as producers, there were in France Proudhon and his followers, author of *Qu'est-ce que la Propriété* and coiner of the adage "Property is Theft". This latter was Proudhon's answer to the Lockean right to property by labour, and an assertion of the two aspects of property-right on which both Ravenstone and Hodgskin had insisted. Yet Proudhon could be called a 'distributivist' as much as (probably more than) a socialist: one commentator has said of him that "he was always at heart a peasant".† His influence has been in the direction of anarchism rather than of socialism, with equality and individual freedom as two of his central ideas; while he preached against communism and the authoritarian State and sought an answer to the evil of interest on capital in a system of universal, interest-free credit organised through a Mutual Credit Bank.‡ In Germany there was the more considerable economic writer Rodbertus with his theory of surplus-value and rent (to whom Marx was to devote a longish critical chapter in his *Theorien über den Mehrwert*), not to mention the later Eugen Dühring,§ with his 'force theory', who was to raise the ire of Friedrich Engels.

Such were the forerunners of Marx's *Das Kapital*, or those

---

is more abundant" (p. 211). Again he says that "the fund for the maintenance of the idle is the surplus produce of the labour of the industrious" (p. 233).

* Rev. Richard Jones, *An Essay on the Distribution of Wealth* (London, 1831) p. 11. Marx attributed to Jones the distinction of having "a sense of historical distinction between modes of production" which has escaped "all English economists since James Steuart" (*Theorien über den Mehrwert*, Vol. III, ed. Kautsky (Berlin, 1923) p. 450).

† Alexander Gray, *The Socialist Tradition* (London, 1946) p. 256.

‡ Schumpeter classes him as an anarchist and speaks of "Marx's scathing criticism (*Misère de la philosophie*, 1847)" as being "fully deserved, though not well aimed in every respect" (*History of Economic Analysis*, pp. 457–8).

§ He was, of course, a contemporary of Marx, and not a forerunner: born in 1833 he actually lived until 1921, and Engels's polemic was not until the late 1870s.

who have sometimes been called 'anticipators'* of this theory of surplus-value. Apart from Rodbertus and Proudhon, Marx was to single out Ravenstone and Hodgskin (also as we have seen Richard Jones) for fairly extensive comment in *Theorien über den Mehrwert*; particularly Hodgskin whose two booklets are referred to as "among the most significant products of English political economy".† Stronger in intuition and sense than they were in rigorous analysis, they were writers who shared the discovery of an important clue, to which the orthodox were blind, even while they failed to approach a complete solution. One thing in particular that they failed to do was to show how 'unequal exchanges' or 'surplus-value' could be reconciled with the existence of 'perfect competition'.

II

Marx himself has been more variously estimated, as well as more misinterpreted, than almost any other economist of note. This is hardly surprising in view of the acute ideological issues involved in both the positive and the polemical sides of his doctrines. He also enjoys the distinction of being more frequently explained away or refuted. Böhn-Bawerk, who at least took him seriously (deeming him to have "the same mixture of positive and negative merits as his prototype Hegel", both "philosophical geniuses"), heralded what he called the "downfall of Marx's system" (in his polemical work of 1896 entitled *Zum Abschluss des Marxschen Systems*), with the dubiously prophetic declaration that "the Marxian system has no abiding future".‡ Marshall dismissed him as a tendentious thinker who had mischievously misunderstood Ricardo.§ Edgeworth estimated "the importance of Marx's theories" as being "wholly emotional".‖ Keynes, in so far as he noticed him at all, treated

---

* *E.g.* Alexander Gray, *Socialist Tradition*, pp. 257, 262.
† *Theorien*, ed. Karl Kautsky (Berlin, 1923) Vol. III, p. 313 (treatment of this group of writers as a whole occupies pp. 281–381).
‡ See page 158.
§ *Principles*, 7th ed. (London, 1916) p. 503.
‖ F. Y. Edgeworth, *Papers relating to Political Economy* (London, 1925) Vol. III, p. 275 (the occasion was a review of Achille Loria's *Karl Marx* and J. S. Nicholson's *Revival of Marxism*).

him as a luminary of the dim underworld of heretics, with less
to teach than the relatively obscure monetary reformer Silvio
Gesell;* and Samuelson has loftily dubbed him "a minor
Post-Ricardian" – and withal "an autodidact".† More cate-
gorical than any is Ludwig von Mises with his "Marxism is
against logic, against Science, and against the activity of
thought itself";‡ while in our own country an historian of
economic thought has spoken contemptuously of a "pedantic
parade of learning", "dexterous skating on thin ice, the
subtlety approaching at times perilously near to sophistry",
"nowhere in print such a miracle of confusion, such a supreme
example of how not to reason".§ Distinctly more respectful
than most as well as more percipient, Joseph Schumpeter speaks
of "the totality of his vision", which "asserts its right in every
detail and is precisely the source of the intellectual fascination
experienced by friend as well as foe who makes a study of him";
and he ranks Marx as being "Ricardo's only great follower".‖

Ricardo's follower in an important sense he was; for which
reason he has sometimes been called, if in a special, almost
Hegelian, sense of *aufhebung*, 'the last of the classical economists'.¶ What can certainly be said is that he was in a direct
line of descent from Ricardo, and that his understanding and
interpretation of Ricardian doctrine has been substantially

---

* J. M. Keynes, *General Theory of Employment, Interest and Money* (London, 1936)
p. 355.

† 'Wages and Interest: Marxian Economic Models', *American Economic Review*,
Vol. XLVII, No. 6, Dec. 1957, p. 911.

‡ *Socialism*, trans. J. Kahane (London, 1936) p. 17.

§ Sir Alexander Gray, *The Development of Economic Doctrine* (London, 1931)
pp. 300–2.

‖ Schumpeter, *History of Economic Analysis*, pp. 384, 596. *Cf.* also J. Schumpeter,
Economic Doctrine and Method (London, 1954) p. 72: "he considered himself as
one who continued Ricardo"; also pp. 119–22: "At the time when his [Marx's]
first volume appeared there was nobody in Germany who could have measured
himself against him either in vigour of thought or in theoretical knowledge."

¶ The school of Classical Political Economy was a term coined by Marx himself
to describe the theoretical system constructed by Adam Smith and Ricardo and
their immediate contemporaries – the period "notable in England for scientific
activity in the domain of Political Economy" when "splendid tournaments
were held", and when "the class struggle is latent" still, or else "manifests itself
only in isolated and sporadic phenomena" (Author's Preface to Second Edition
of *Das Kapital*, Vol. I, 1872: in Eng. ed. (trans. Moore and Aveling) p. xxii).

borne out, and certainly not weakened, by the new material embodied in Piero Sraffa's edition of Ricardo's *Works and Correspondence*, so copiously cited in Chapter 3. Schumpeter explains the reference to "Ricardo's follower" in this way: "Ricardo is the only economist whom Marx treated as a master ... Marx used the Ricardian apparatus: he adopted Ricardo's conceptual lay-out and his problems presented themselves to him in the forms that Ricardo had given to them. No doubt, he transformed these forms and he arrived in the end at widely different conclusions. But he always did so by starting from, and criticising, Ricardo. Criticism of Ricardo was his method in his purely theoretical work."*

To obtain a correct perspective, however, upon his economic theory, especially upon its original elements, this needs to be seen within the setting of his general concept of historical development, of which *Das Kapital* was designed as a special application. It is even desirable to appreciate the specifically Hegelian roots of this conception, in order at any rate to catch the finer shades of meaning. As is sufficiently familiar, the dialectic as a structural pattern of development started with Hegel from abstract Being as Mind or 'Spirit'. For Marx, *per contra*, the dialectic of development started from Nature and from Man as initially an integral part of Nature. But although part of Nature and subject to the determinism of natural laws, Man as a conscious being had the distinctive capability of struggling with and against Nature – of subordinating and ultimately transforming it for his own purposes. This was the

* Schumpeter, *History of Economic Analysis*, p. 390. It is quite evident that, while criticising his limitations and going beyond him, Marx held Ricardo in high esteem: *vide* his reference to Smith, in contrast to Ricardo, being prevented "from reaching a uniform and comprehensive theoretical view of the abstract, general foundations of the capitalist system"; and again to "the great historical significance of Ricardo for the science ... With this service to economic science is closely linked the fact that Ricardo discovers and proclaims the economic contradiction between the classes – as shown by the intrinsic relations – and hence the historical struggle and process of development is grasped at its roots and disclosed in economic science" (K. Marx, *Theories of Surplus Value: a selection*, trans. G. A. Bonner and Emile Burns (London, 1951) pp. 129, 203–4; Karl Marx, *Theories of Surplus Value*, Part I (Moscow, n.d.) p. 86; Part II (Moscow, 1968) p. 166).

unique rôle of human productive activity, or human labour, which differentiated man from all (or nearly all) other animate creatures; and for this reason the various and successive forms of productive activity, and especially the relations between human beings in society in the course of this activity, formed the ground-plan of human history.

A leading feature of this dialectic of Man *versus* Nature, a *sine qua non*, indeed, of its progressive issue, was the invention and use of productive instruments that were simultaneously durable embodiments of labour and productive aids to labour – instruments "which the labourer interposes between himself and the subject of his labour, and which serve as the conductor of his activity"*; and it is these which make of productive labour a collective or social process, and are the principal clue to the division of labour. "In production men not only act on nature but also on one another. They produce only by co-operating in a certain way and mutually exchanging their activities." And again: "By thus acting on the external world and changing it, he at the same time changes his own nature."† Hence the importance of the productive forces to an understanding of human history, although only in closest conjunction with the social relations between men in the course of production associated with these productive forces (a purely technological interpretation which some have seen in it is an impoverishment and distortion of the concept). Thus the clue to the periodisation as well as the movement of human history lay in the successive modes of production, severally characterised, not only by technical forms, division of labour and exchange, but also by different forms of 'social relations of production' between human beings and classes.

It was natural that an historical conception of this kind, when applied to a particular economic system, should approach the matter from the angle of conditions of production, including such *socio*-economic factors as ownership or non-ownership of means of production and the respective effects of these upon the

---

* *Capital*, Vol. i (trans. Moore and Aveling) p. 158.
† *Ibid.*, p. 157.

situation and behaviour of social groups or classes. Not only is the main order of determination – conditions and relations of production to relations of exchange – immediately indicated, but the boundaries of the subject (as we have previously said) are drawn differently and more widely than has become customary with an economic theory conceived as the 'laws of the market' (or *a fortiori* conceived as a formal study of "the adaptation of scarce means to given ends" in Lord Robbins's much-quoted phrase of forty years ago). Such an approach serves also to explain the place assigned to Labour as human productive activity: why it was natural for Marx to place it in the very centre of the stage. Implied in this, indeed, is a virtual definition of productive *activity*,* and correlatively of appropriation or exploitation, in the sense of the annexation or receipt of part of the fruits of production by those who have contributed no productive activity and lack any personal participation in the process of production *per se*. As such 'exploitation' is neither something 'metaphysical' nor simply an ethical judgement (still less "just a noise") as has sometimes been depicted† : it is a factual description of a socio-economic relationship, as much as is Marc Bloch's apt characterisation of Feudalism as a system where feudal lords "lived on the labour of other men". If history is viewed as a succession of modes of production, characterised in historical times to-date by such appropriation, it is natural that enquiry should start by asking what were the means and instruments, political, military, legal, economic, by virtue of which such appropriation occurred. It was accordingly

* Not indeed of 'productive' which in various contexts can be applied to anything the presence or absence of which makes a difference to the amount produced: *vide* Marx's statement that "it would be wrong to say that labour which produces use-values is the *only* source of the wealth produced by it, that is of material wealth" (*Critique of Political Economy*, trans. S. W. Ryazanskaia (London, 1971) p. 36). Even L. Rogin (*The Meaning and Validity of Economic Theory* (New York, 1956) p. 338) attributes to Marx's theory the premise that "living labour is the sole source of output, of value added". For Marx's use of the term 'productive labour' see above, Chapter 2, page 60n, 61n.

† *E.g.* Prof. M. Blaug: "Marx is caught up in the purely metaphysical problem of whether capital is barren or productive, whether interest or profit are a payment for services rendered or merely income stolen from workers"; and Marx's "emotive arguments about the nature of surplus value" (*Economic Theory in Retrospect* (New York, 1962; London, 1964) pp. 243, 247).

quite natural for Marx, sensing an analogy in nineteenth-century conditions with previous forms of class society, to start by enquiring wherein such appropriation consisted under capitalism, and how it was possible at all in a society in which free contractual relations ruled all things and market competition, according to the economists, ensured that exchange was always of equivalents for equivalents, at their Smithian 'natural values'. And if exchange was always, or predominantly, one of equivalents, whence could a surplus arise?

Some have supposed that the notion of exploitation, and hence of surplus-value, was in some way derived from the proposition that things exchange according to the amounts of labour embodied in them, presumably with the aid of some Lockean 'natural right' doctrine to the effect that labour gives right of ownership over its own product. To this view the law of value is premiss and surplus-value consequent. Of the Ricardian Socialists this, or something like it, is true. They started from the position, either that labour gives a right to the whole product, or that labour alone creates 'value' (whether in the sense of use-value or of exchange-value not always being made clear). But this was precisely why Marx regarded their theories, though suggestive, as inadequate; and as applied to Marx himself it is a definite misconception. The analogy between capitalism and earlier forms of society, as regards appropriation of a surplus by those contributing no productive activity, was for him an historical datum: an observation from social experience. It was this analogy with cases where appropriation of surplus-labour or surplus-product was plainly written in political terms or by virtue of legal enactment or military force, and was recognised as such, that he sought to emphasise by talking of a specifically capitalist form of exploitation. The specifically *economic* problem consisted, not in proving this, but in *reconciling* it with the law of value: in explaining how this could happen in the economists' realm of competition and 'unseen hand' where everything exchanged at its 'natural value'. In a popular vein in his *Value, Price and Profit*, he says: "To explain the *general nature* of profits, you must start from the theorem that, on an average, commodities are *sold at their real values*, and *that profits are derived from selling them at their values* . . . If you cannot explain profit upon this supposition, you cannot explain it at all."*

For such a purpose the theory of value as he found it in Ricardo was evidently highly congenial. This placed Labour as human productive activity in the forefront and made it the basis of explanation of exchange-value. It was quite natural that he should start expounding his theory of surplus-value in Volume I on the assumption that things exchange at their *values* (*i.e.* proportionately to labour): this was not only, for the purpose, a simple way of doing so, it was also a way of demonstrating the origin and persistence of surplus-value in the *strong* case. Moreover, it enabled the emergence of surplus-value, as well as the measure of it, to be firmly located in facts and relations of production (by contrast, for example, with William Thompson's 'unequal exchanges'). That he was well aware of what he was doing, and of the limitations of this case as a 'first approximation', is shown by his statement in Volume I: "If prices actually diverge from values, we must first of all reduce the former to the latter, in other words treat the difference as accidental in order that the phenomena may be observed in their purity, and our observations not interfered with by disturbing circumstances that have nothing to do with the process in question."†

But in addition to its simplicity and appropriateness for his purpose, there was a formal reason why he should have concentrated upon Values in terms of Labour, and hence trodden

---

* *Value, Price and Profit*, by Karl Marx, ed. Eleanor Aveling (London, 1899) pp. 53–4. Italics in the original.

† *Capital*, Vol. I, trans. Moore and Aveling (London, 1886) p. 144. An alternative way perhaps of explaining the approach would be to say with Oskar Lange (in an early article) that "Marx developed his theory of value first for an *einfache Warenprodukt*" [simple commodity production], later introducing the "slight modification . . . unessential from his point of view" ('Marxian Economics and Modern Economics', *Review of Economic Studies*, Vol. II, 1934–5, p. 198). It is to be noted that 'simple commodity production' implies producers owning their own means of production, so that while there will be mobility of labour together with its means of production between different industries, there will be no separate 'mobility of capital' in the modern sense.

closely in Ricardo's footsteps. This is something that nearly all commentators on Marx seem to have missed, at any rate until quite recently. It will be clear from what has been said that the nature of his approach required him to start from the postulation of a certain rate of exploitation or of surplus-value (or profit–wage ratio in Ricardo's terms); since this was *prior* to the formation of exchange-values or prices and was not derived from them. In other words, this needed to be expressed in terms of production, *before* bringing in circulation or exchange.

How then to express the rate of surplus-value as initial *datum*? It would not have been satisfactory to express it in terms that were themselves relative to changes in the ratio itself. It could have been expressed, as we have seen that Ricardo initially did, in terms of a single commodity such as Corn, thus rendering it a *product*-ratio, unaffected by changes in exchange-value or prices. Alternatively, if the notion had been invented by then, it could have been in something like Sraffa's standard composite commodity of which we shall presently speak. But much better for his immediate purpose than a single commodity (because more generalised) was its expression in terms of Labour; as indeed Ricardo had done with his profit – wage ratio as determined at the margin of the wage–goods industry. The rate of exploitation could then be unambiguously expressed as a ratio between two quantities of (average) labour, as well as the source of surplus-value being simultaneously revealed. If things were exchanged in proportion to labour expended, changes in this rate could not *per se* affect relative exchange-values, nor could changes in the latter react upon the exploitation-ratio when represented in this way. The (Labour) Value category, or the 'approximation' of Volume I, thus embodied something essential that would otherwise have been lacking.*

* To the view that the Law of Value was a 'first approximation' based on simplified assumptions Professor Samuelson has retorted that "modern science and economics abound with simplifying first approximations, but one readily admits their inferiority to second approximations, and drops them when challenged" (*The Collected Economic Papers of Paul A. Samuelson*, Vol. I (Cambridge Mass., 1966) ed. J. E. Stiglitz, p. 348). This light-hearted retort might have some point where the 'first approximation' contains nothing essential that cannot be ex-

In writing to-day, when economic analysis has become so exclusively quantitative in character, one should perhaps add this further comment – if it does not lay superfluous emphasis on what has already been implied. While he was concerned no less than was Ricardo to exhibit the quantitative relationship between conditions of production and actual exchange-values or prices (if only because otherwise a link would have been lacking between the analysis in value-terms in Vol. I and actual market phenomena), he was concerned at least as much to demonstrate the qualitative, or relational, aspect of things, especially as regards income-distribution. He deemed this as crucial to understanding the specific character and functioning of the capitalist type of class society. He called it revealing the 'hidden essence' and 'inner form' lying beneath the superficial 'outward disguises' or 'market appearance' of things. This is what some have meant by saying that his theory has to be viewed as 'economic sociology' and not only as economic analysis in the narrower and more modern sense of the term. Oskar Lange expressed something of the kind by saying that "the superiority of Marxian economics" lies in its "exact specification of the institutional datum distinguishing Capitalism from the concept of an exchange economy in general", thus permitting "the establishment of a theory of economic evolution" which ordinary economic theory ignores.* This was certainly the main emphasis – and the signal contribution – of his analysis at the Value-level of Volume I.

To conduct analysis within the category of Value involved certain implicit assumptions of the same kind as Ricardo made at the beginning of his chapter on Value, but by him more quickly abandoned. These consisted in a uniformity in specific respects in the conditions of production of constituent industries

pressed equally well and easily in other terms. But it ceases to do so when there is something in the first approximation which is lacking in later approximations, or cannot be expressed so easily in their terms (*e.g.* the first approximation may be a device for emphasising and throwing into relief something of greater generality and less particularity).

* *Political Economy*, pp. 196, 201. The words "exchange economy in general" is a rendering of *einfache Warenprodukt* referred to in an earlier footnote (page 147) and more usually rendered as "simple commodity production".

or lines of production (alternatively one could speak of ignoring for the time-being the effects of lack of uniformity and focusing attention upon the global configuration – or yet again, referring to a situation where there was mobility of labour between industries but as yet no separate mobility of capital in the modern sense). This uniformity can be expressed in terms of the capital-to-labour ratios,* or what Marx was to call 'the organic composition of capital', or alternatively (and differently) by saying that all capital is assumed to consist of wage-advances to labourers, advanced in all lines of production for similar periods of time.† In modern terminology one could say that, since he was at this stage interested in the *macroscopic* picture, the general and overall pattern] of distribution and exchange, he considered this degree of abstraction as both legitimate and appropriate. The *minutiae* of *microscopic* relations, with their additional complications, including divergence of individual prices from values (which then, at the microscopic level, admittedly became important) were for him of secondary interest‡ and to be handled later. These he was content to treat, like Ricardo, as secondary modifications of the main principle.

Marx's answer to the question about reconciling surplus-value with the prevalence of the 'law of value' was fairly simple, once the problem had been posed, and the answer is to-day fairly familiar. It turned on a distinction to which he attached crucial importance, between labour and labour-power. The latter he defined in *Capital* as "energy transferred to a human organism by means of nourishing matter" and as "the aggregate of those mental and physical capabilities existing in a human being which he exercises whenever he produces a use-value of any description".§ The "nourishing matter"

---

* This includes the circulation-periods of circulating capital and the durability of fixed capital.

† In terms of Dmitriev's equation cited above, page 117, this amounts to uniformity of the t's.

‡ Provided, of course, that they were of a kind and magnitude not to impugn the generalisations reached at the macroscopic level.

§ *Capital*, Vol. 1 (ed. Moore and Aveling) pp. 145, 198. He also spoke of "creation of value [as] transformation of labour-power into labour" (*ibid.*, p. 198).

needed to replace the energy used-up in work was the material
input into human labour; and the possibility and dimensions
of surplus-value depended upon the value of the former being
less than the value 'created' as output by the labour it sustained.
The difference between the two he spoke of as the difference
between 'necessary labour-time' (the input) and the total
labour-time actually expended in production.* It was completely analogous to Ricardo's difference between "production
and the consumption necessary for that production". What
established, and maintained, the difference – and it was here
that the crucial historical or institutional *datum* came in – was
the existence of a proletariat, dispossessed of land or other forms
of property and hence completely dependent for a livelihood
upon the sale of labour-power for a wage. (Perhaps one should
add to this as a condition of existence, not merely a sufficiency,
but an actual surplus of labour-power beyond the amount
purchased and employed.) "The historical conditions of its
[Capital's] existence", Marx writes, "are by no means given
with the mere circulation of money and commodities. It can
spring into life only when the owner of the means of production
and subsistence meets in the market with the free labourer
selling his labour-power."† Labour-power, in other words, had
itself to become a marketed commodity, and consistently with
the competitive 'rules of the game' to sell at its value.‡ What
Marx called the 'rate of surplus-value' (the ratio of the surplus-

* The question could here be asked: if one is speaking of inputs creating more of
themselves as output than is needed for their own replacement, and treating this
as *fons et origo* of surplus product, why should this not be the case also with *other*
inputs than labour: in which case why should special significance be attached
to a difference of this kind in connection with labour? The answer (as reflection
will show) is that when one is speaking of a surplus-*value* as a category of income-
distribution, a difference attaching to labour as an input is a necessary condition
for such a result. Professor M. Morishima (*Marx's Economics: A Dual Theory of
Value and Growth* (Cambridge, 1973)) has put the matter thus: "exploitation of
labourers by capitalists is a necessary and sufficient condition for the existence
of a set of non-negative prices and the wage rate yielding positive profits in every
industry", and calls this "the Fundamental Marxian Theorem".
† *Ibid.*, p. 148.
‡ In the popular lecture reprinted as *Wage-Labour and Capital* (London, 1933,
pp. 26–7) he spoke of the "cost of production of labour-power" and of "the cost
of the existence and propagation of the worker" as "setting the minimum of
wages".

value to the wage-advance, or to the purchase-price of labour-power) depended, when viewed on a global scale, upon the reciprocal of the proportion of the total labour-force required to produce subsistence for that labour-force. This was the crucial exploitation-ratio which lay at the base both of the structure of income-distribution (and especially distribution between propertied and propertyless) and of the structure of relative prices. The result, we repeat, was to make income-distribution an historically-relative product of a given set of historical or institutional conditions.

Not uncommonly this has been dismissed, in company with Ricardo's theory, as depending upon a subsistence theory of wages, and hence on something which can no longer be entertained.* Two things can be said about this. First, just as Ricardo had done, Marx made it plain that he did not intend the 'value of labour-power' in the sense of purely physical subsistence: into the practical definition of what was deemed 'necessary' at any time and place there entered an "historical and moral element".† In the same way, for trained or skilled labour – "labour-power of a special kind . . . a special education or training is requisite, and this, on its part, costs an equivalent in commodities of greater or less amount. The amount varies according to the more or less complicated character of the labour-power. The expenses of this education . . . enter *pro tanto* into the total value spent in its production."‡ It is clear, therefore, that Marshall's "conventionally necessary"§ ele-

---

* Prof. N. Kaldor, for example, in his Pekin lecture of 1956, held that "the Marxian scheme operates . . . in the early stages of capitalist development" only ('Capitalist Evolution and Keynesian Economics', *Essays on Economic Stability and Growth* (London, 1960) pp. 243–58).

† *Capital*, Vol. 1 (trans. Moore and Aveling) p. 150. To this he adds the words: "in contradistinction to the case of other commodities". "The number and extent of his so-called necessary wants, as also the modes of satisfying them, are themselves the product of historical development, and depend therefore to a great extent on the degree of civilisation of a country, more particularly on the conditions under which, and consequently on the habits and degree of comfort in which, the class of free labourers has been formed" (citing Torrens and Thornton). The same point is emphasised in his popular lecture, *Value, Price and Profit*, ed. Eleanor Aveling (London, 1899) pp. 85–8).

‡ *Capital*, Vol. 1, pp. 150–1.

§ A. Marshall, *Principles of Economics*, 7th ed. (London, 1916) p. 70: things such that "in order to obtain them the average man and woman will sacrifice some things which are necessary for efficiency".

ments are included here; and one could as well use his term a 'supply-price' theory of wages as being implied in some form, rather than a strictly subsistence theory. Secondly, Marx clearly had in mind initially a 'pure' labour market, characterised by perfect competition and individual bargaining. He fully admitted, however, that the price of labour-power could rise above (or alternatively in special circumstances be depressed below) its value, not only temporarily but also permanently to the extent that conditions of a 'pure' market for labour-power were modified or disturbed. In this connection he treated collective bargaining by trade unions as a potentially important modifying influence, and spoke of "every combination of employed and unemployed" in trade unions as "disturb[ing] the 'harmonious action'" of the law of supply and demand.*
In a situation of general collective bargaining, to become characteristic of advanced industrial countries in the ensuing century, a new institutional element admittedly entered in; the influence of which would need to be included in order to postulate the rate of surplus-value.†

To this it should be added that a key rôle was occupied in all his thinking about surplus-value by the so-called 'industrial reserve army'. Whereas Ricardo's theory of wages depended upon Malthus's law of population – upon the assumption of a highly elastic labour-supply for Malthusian reasons – Marx strongly repudiated this, and relied instead on the chronic existence, and periodic re-creation (by labour-saving technical innovation prompted by any tendency for rising wages to encroach on surplus-value), of an unemployed reserve of surplus labour. This was "a law of population peculiar to the

---

* *Capital*, Vol. I (trans. Moore and Aveling) p. 655. This qualification, which comes at the end of the section where 'absolute impoverishment' is elaborated, seems to have been overlooked by most commentators. In his argument against 'Citizen Weston' from which we have already quoted he maintains that workers "ought to combine and struggle for a rise of wages" and within certain limits can be successful (*Value, Price and Profit*, p. 12).
† For formal purposes one might then have to stipulate a certain real-wage level (or a certain share of surplus-value accruing to the wage additional to the 'value of labour-power'). *Cf.* remarks below, page 262 on a device adopted by Sraffa.

capitalist mode of production".* This it was that performed the crucial function for the system of restraining the tendency of wages to rise in face of advancing capital accumulation,† and provided the answer to the question: if there is a difference between the value of labour-power and of its product, why does this not disappear in the long-term with the progress and expansion of the system itself? A situation in which surplus labour disappeared, and full employment prevailed, would be one of extraordinary instability for the capitalist mode of production and one that it might well be unable to survive.‡

Having enunciated his theory of surplus-value as arising from the difference between the value of labour-power itself when sold as a commodity and the value of its poduct, Marx proceeded to classify ways of increasing the rate of surplus-value into two broad types. The one, which retained some potential importance, at least, in the mid-nineteenth century and which he termed increase of Absolute Surplus-Value, consisted of a lengthening of the working day (or week), whereby 'surplus labour-time' of the existing labour force was enhanced both absolutely and relatively to 'necessary labour-time' (spent in replacement of the value of labour-power, or the wages-bill). The other he called increase of Relative Surplus-Value, and consisted in reduction of 'necessary labour-time' as a proportion of total working-time, mainly as a consequence of raised labour-productivity in the wage-good sector of production. It is to be noted that only improvements in productivity in the wage-goods sector will have this effect; improvements in productivity elsewhere merely reducing equivalently the value of their product and leaving the value of labour-power itself unchanged.§ Although, unlike Ricardo, he was not a believer in

* *Capital*, Vol. I, p. 645. He adds: "In fact every special historic mode of production has its own special laws of population, historically valid within its limits alone. An abstract law of population exists for plants and animals only, and only in so far as man has not interfered with them."

† By means of it "the rise of wages is confined within limits that . . . leave intact the foundations of the capitalist system" (*ibid.*, p. 634).

‡ Unless by introducing some form of servile 'Corporate State', or at the least legal wage-control.

§ *Cf.*: "The general rate of surplus-value is, therefore, ultimately affected by the whole process, only when the increase in the productiveness of labour has seized

diminishing returns as a long-run tendency (in the historical sense), it may have been the fact that agriculture bulked so large in the wage-goods sector, and in his day was subject relatively little to the march of modern industrial methods, that caused him to give relatively little weight to this tendency in certain contexts (*e.g.* falling profit-rate) where one might have expected him to give more.

III

It is not until his third volume that Marx comes to the qualifications introduced by varying 'compositions of capital' as between industries (also of what he terms the 'turnover-period of variable capital').* This he deals with by introducing the category of 'Prices of Production', which diverge from the 'Values' of the Volume I analysis because of the need for an equal profit-rate on capital – which he dubbed facetiously "unconscious capitalist communism", and without which capital would tend to migrate from industries of low profit-rate to industries of high profit-rate, until, by virtue of the competition thereby engendered the requisite equality was achieved. It follows that the rate of surplus-value (or ratio of surplus-value to the wage-bill) is no longer uniform between industries. He has earlier introduced his own distinction between Constant Capital and Variable Capital as overriding the traditional distinction between Fixed and Circulating; the Variable being the capital advanced as wages in the direct purchase of labour-power, the Constant being what is invested in commodity-inputs, whether serving as once-for-all inputs like raw materials, fuel and components, or as durable instruments and structures

upon those branches of production that are connected with, and has cheapened those commodities that form part of, the necessary means of subsistence, and are therefore elements of the value of labour-power" (*ibid.*, p. 308).

* Marx had previously (Vol. II, trans. E. Untermann, Kerr ed. (Chicago, 1925) pp. 336 *seq.*) made a distinction between the 'simple rate of surplus-value' (rate of surplus to wages expended during a single cycle of production) and the 'annual rate', which was equal to the former multiplied by the number of times that variable capital expended as wages turned over in the course of the year. It was, of course, the latter that was relevant to the formation of the annual rate of profit (*cf.* also Vol. III, trans. Untermann, Kerr ed. (1909) pp. 87–91).

usually classed as fixed capital. (The actual dividing line between the two types of capital will manifestly depend on the degree of vertical integration in industry.) Whereas the rate of surplus-value was denoted by s/v, the rate of profit was $s/(v+c)$; writing v and c for variable and constant capital respectively.* The ratio c/v was called the organic composition. Prices of Production were defined by Marx as the Cost-Price (equal to the wage cost *plus* the elements of constant capital entering into output)† *plus* the average or normal rate of profit on the capital employed.‡

It can be seen to follow that, given the simple rate of surplus-value or the exploitation-ratio of which we have spoken, the rate of profit will be higher the *shorter* the period of turnover of the variable capital, and will be lower the higher is the ratio of the constant to the variable capital, or the 'composition of capital'. The former is evidently equivalent to Ricardo's 'durability of circulating capital' and the latter to his 'proportions of capital' and 'durability of fixed capital'.§ The result was that where the composition of capital was above the general average (and/or the turnover of variable capital below it) competition in the form of 'migration' of capital would cause prices of production to be in excess of values, and conversely in the opposite case. Whereas Ricardo had expressed the effect of different proportions and durabilities of capital in terms of the differential effect on prices of a rise of wages, Marx

* *Cf.* "the surplus-value measured by the variable capital is called the rate of surplus-value. The surplus-value measured by the total capital is called the rate of profit . . . The rate of profit may remain unchanged and yet express different rates of surplus-value" (*Capital*, Vol. III, trans. Untermann, Kerr ed. (Chicago, 1909) p. 55).

† In the case of durable elements it was, of course, the 'used-up', or depreciated, part only of this stock that entered into Cost-Price.

‡ *Ibid.*, p. 186.

§ As a matter of fact, for most of his exposition of Prices of Production Marx ignored the effect of the latter by using a 'working capital model' and adopting the simplifying assumption that the constant capital turned over once in each year (a common classical assumption, as Sraffa has pointed out). *Cf. ibid.*, p. 183: "we assume for the sake of simplicity that the constant capital is transferred everywhere uniformly and entirely to the annual products of the capitals named". Three pages below (p. 186) he emphasises that in calculating prices of production the rate of profit must be calculated "on the total capital invested (not merely consumed)".

expressed it in terms of divergence of prices of production in individual cases from values.*

It is in the same context, and immediately following (in Part III of Volume III) that Marx gives his own answer to the classical problem of the so-called tendency of the rate of profit to fall. Around this answer much discussion has gathered, as well as variety of interpretation, both as regards the long-term dynamic movement of the system and the interpretation of periodical economic crises. If differences in the organic composition of capital between industries were responsible for 'redistributing' surplus-value between industries in proportion to capital, it seemed reasonable to suppose that changes in this composition over time could account for long-run changes in the rate of profit. In place of Ricardo's resort to diminishing returns, Marx substituted the effect of technical change in raising the ratio of constant to variable capital, in particular of fixed capital to wage-labour, thereby lowering the rate of profit that a given rate of surplus-value could yield. Having said this, he proceeded to list a number of 'counteracting causes', including an increase in 'relative surplus-value' (consequent on improved productivity in wage-goods industries) and 'cheapening of the elements of constant capital' itself. Apart from the latter, there is no hint that the progress of technique could result in what to-day are called 'capital-saving' inventions as well as 'labour-saving' (in the nineteenth century it would seem that the bias of technical advance was towards the latter); nor is there any statement about the anticipated relative strength of 'tendency' and 'counter-tendencies'.† It seems probable that Marx, in common with other economists of the early and mid-nineteenth century,

---

* Price of production "is, as a matter of fact, the same thing which Adam Smith calls *natural price*, Ricardo *price of production* or *cost of production*, and the physiocrats *prix necessaire*, because it is in the long run a prerequisite of supply" (*ibid.*, p. 233; italics in original).

† Merely the rather vague statement that "the rise in the rate of surplus-value . . . does not suspend the general law. But it causes this law to become more of a tendency, that is, a law whose absolute enforcement is checked, retarded, weakened by counteracting influences" (*Capital*, Vol. III, trans. Untermann, Kerr ed. (1909) p. 275).

assumed that this was an actual trend for which an explanation was called for; and treated it as such rather than as a dogmatic forecast for the future. Whether or not he assigned to it in his mind a significant place as a contributory factor in the causation of periodic crises seems to be an open question. He had already said that at times when capital accumulation outruns the supply of labour-power, reducing the industrial reserve army to a low level (as tends to happen in a boom), investment tends to be arrested until the upward pressure of wages upon profits is relieved; which suggests that he might well have considered this to be a sufficient, as well as more plausible, reason for the halting of a boom.

It was Marx's 'admission' (as critics called it) in Volume III that exchange under capitalism normally took place at Prices of Production that was seized upon by Böhm-Bawerk and hailed as the 'Great Contradiction' on which the Marxian system foundered.* Referring to Volume III, he declared: "I see here no explanation and reconciliation of a contradiction, but the bare contradiction itself. Marx's third volume contradicts the first. The theory of the average rate of profit and of the prices of production cannot be reconciled with the theory of value. This is the impression which must, I believe, be received by every logical thinker." He concludes: "I have no manner of doubt. The Marxian system has a past and a present, but no abiding future."† It is quite true that Marx never satisfactorily demonstrated how these Prices of Production were related to or 'derived' from Values; and without such a demonstration there was no logical ground for declaring that the former were determined by the conditions of production and the social relations of production that he had dealt with in Volume I. Indeed, the arithmetical examples that he uses to show the connection are unsatisfactory, since the transformation into Prices of Production is only applied to outputs, and not to inputs (whence it follows that he uses the same rate of profit as in the value situation). Although Marx shows awareness of the

---

* *Zum Abschluss des Marxschen System*, 1896; Eng. trans. by Alice M. Macdonald, *Karl Marx and the Close of his System* (London, 1896).
† *Ibid.*, pp. 64, 218.

incompleteness of his own solution and hints at the real nature of the problem, he nowhere improves on these examples* – possibly because of the incompleteness of the manuscript of Volume III, which he never succeeded in finishing, let alone rewriting. Moreover, he seems to maintain *both* that total prices will equal total values *and* that total profit will equal total surplus-value: two conditions that are incompatible save in exceptional circumstances.†

Subsequent discussion of the 'Transformation Problem' (as it has come to be called) has shown, however, that Böhm-Bawerk's lucid polemic was too superficial to grasp the essence of the problem (which he seems to have imperfectly understood), and that Values and Prices of Production do not necessarily stand in contradiction even if they are contrasted. The latter, in other words, are derivable from the former (or from the conditions of production, including the labour-expenditures of which Values are the expression, *plus* the crucial exploitation-ratio). But since both inputs, including labour-power, and outputs have to be transformed into price-terms, and hence in all probability the rate of profits will be affected,‡ these have all to be determined simultaneously and

* *Cf.* Marx, *Capital*, Vol. III, p. 194: "Now, the price of production of a certain commodity is its cost-price for the buyer, and this price may pass into other commodities and become an element of their prices . . . There is always a possibility of error, if we assume that the cost-price of the commodities of any particular sphere is equal to the value of the means of production consumed by it." *Cf.* also *Theorien über den Mehrwert*, Vol. III, ed. Kautsky (Berlin, 1923) pp. 200–1, 212.

† *Capital*, Vol. III, pp. 185 *seq*. Different authorities have stressed equality of different relationships between the value-situation and the price-situation as being more essential to Marx's purpose. Professor Meek, for example, suggests that what Marx wished to emphasise was that "after the transformation of values into prices the fundamental ratio upon which profit depended could still be said to be determined in accordance with the Volume I analysis" – namely the ratio between total output and total wages: an equality which is fulfilled when "the organic composition of capital in the wage-goods industries is equal to the social average" (Meek, *Economics and Ideology and Other Essays*, p. 154). *Cf.* also A. Emmanuel, *Unequal Exchange*, trans. Brian Pearce, London, 1972, pp. 390 *seq*. It would seem, however, that the possibility of fulfilling any such particular condition is of secondary importance to that of deriving price-relations *in general* from value relations, or the value-situation. Given the latter, does the former essentially matter?

‡ The exceptions to this are when there is no constant capital in the wage-goods industry, only variable (*i.e.* the simple Ricardian case), and the rate of profit in the price situation is equal to the rate of surplus-value, and also the case referred to by Professor Meek in the previous footnote.

interdependently, *i.e.* by solving a set of simultaneous equations. The first to demonstrate the possibility of this, adapting equations of Dmitriev (to whom we referred above), was Bortkievicz. Bortkievicz used a three-sector model; one sector producing wage-goods, another elements of constant capital and the third luxury goods consumed out of surplus-value. On the assumption of static conditions with zero net investment (Marx's 'simple reproduction'), it followed that the supply of output from each sector or department of industry must equal the demand for it arising from the sum of the relevant incomes generated in the three departments (in his tables the sum of the columns must equal the sum of the relevant rows; *e.g.* total price of wage-goods equal to the sum of the wages paid in all three sectors). A curiosity of his solution which has occasioned some discussion is that it exhibits the rate of profit as depending exclusively on the production-conditions (in particular the composition of capital, given the rate of surplus-value) in the sectors producing respectively capital-goods and wage-goods. The circumstances of the third sector producing luxuries for capitalist consumption are irrelevant ("The rate of profit, given a certain rate of surplus-value, depends exclusively on the organic composition of the capital in Departments I and II"). Bortkievicz proceeds to claim that "this result is hardly surprising from the point of view of the theory of profit which sees the origin of profit in 'surplus-labour'",* and that it lends support to what, following Adam Smith, he calls a "deduction theory" of profit. "If it is indeed true that the level of the rate of profit in no way depends on the conditions of production of those goods which do not enter into real wages, then the origin of profit must clearly be sought in the wage-relationship and not in the ability of capital to increase production. For if this ability were relevant here, then it would be inexplicable why certain spheres of production should become irrelevant for the question of the level of profit."†

---

* Appendix to *Karl Marx and the Close of his System by E. von Böhm-Bawerk and Böhm-Bawerk's Criticism of Marx by Rudolf Hilferding*, ed. Paul M. Sweezy (New York, 1949) p. 209.

† L. von Bortkievicz, 'Value and Price in the Marxian System', *International Economic Papers*, No. 2, p. 33. In this case luxury goods are what Mr Sraffa (as we shall see below) calls "non-basics".

Actually there is here a close parallel with Ricardo, who, as we have seen, treated Profit as determined exclusively by conditions in the wage-goods industry (agriculture). Since Ricardo neglected fixed capital so far as production of wage-goods was concerned, and treated capital as consisting exclusively of 'wage-advances' (Marx's 'variable capital'), the rate of profit in his treatment of it was derived from the conditions of the wage-goods sector alone and was identical in this case with the rate of surplus-value.

It is intuitively obvious, I think, that Bortkievicz's demonstration could be extended from three sectors or industries to any larger number of industries. Since his day, a formal proof that it is so extensible to the n-industry case has been afforded by Dr Francis Seton; with the conclusion that this shows the "logical superstructure" of Marx's theory to be "sound enough".* A similar demonstration is also implicit in the equations of Sraffa, whereby prices are derived from conditions of production (in the shape of listed quantities of all the inputs, including labour-power, requisite for producing n outputs) of which we shall presently speak in more detail.†

Discussion of this question, as of the formal structure of his theory generally, has remained, indeed, somewhat restricted, even recondite; and for the most part it has evoked little interest (or even awareness) among Marx-disciples and interpreters. Discussion among the latter has mainly been confined to what Marx had to say on the subject of economic crises – to this and an extension of such ideas to international relations in the shape of export of capital and imperialism. For this reason some mention, at least, of the background of such discussion seems called for here, although it falls outside our (self-imposed) terms of reference.

* F. Seton, 'The Transformation Problem', *Review of Economic Studies*, Vol. 24, 1956–7, pp. 149–60. (This writer at the same time expresses disagreement with the characterisation of profit as fruit of exploitation.) This solution had, indeed, been anticipated by Kenneth May, 'The Structure of Classical Value Theories', *Review of Economic Studies*, Vol. 17, No. 42, 1949–50, pp. 60–9, who speaks of the transformation problem as "merely a formal matter", and at the same time points out that it "is not solvable in terms of aggregates alone" (*e.g.* the three-sector case).   † See pages 259–60.

It is towards the end of his second volume, before he has yet come to the question of price and value, that Marx develops his notion of the two main departments of industry and his analysis of the structural relations between the two. This has attracted considerable attention in connection with the causation of periodical crises, as it has also more recently in connection with the structural relations of economic growth (the Feldman-model and the like). This analysis begins with the case of "simple reproduction" (zero net investment), less for its own sake than as prolegomenon to the study of "expanded reproduction" where a part of surplus-value is devoted to the enlargement of one or other, or both, of the two departments. In the former case the stated condition of equilibrium is that the constant capital of Department II (producing consumers' goods) is equal to both the variable capital (or, rather, total wage-bill of the period in question) and the surplus-value of Department I (producing means of production, or capital goods). The stated condition for expanded reproduction was analogous but less simple (*e.g.* distinction has to be made in each department between the consumed part of surplus-value and the invested part, and in the latter between what is invested as variable capital and as constant).* The statement of these conditions has been taken by some (*e.g.* Tugan-Baranowski) as providing an answer to 'underconsumptionists' like Malthus or Rodbertus, and as implying that there is no crucial obstacle, at least, to continuous capital accumulation, and that if crises occur they must have the character of 'disproportionate' development of the two sectors. Marx evidently thought, however, that any such 'equilibrium', although con-

---

* *Cf.* Marx, *Capital*, Vol. II, pp. 591 *seq.*; also Oskar Lange, *Introduction to Econometrics*, 2nd ed. (Warsaw and London, 1962) pp. 214–18, where the condition is stated as $C_2 + m_2 = V_1 + \overline{m}_1 + m_{1v}$, where the subscript-numbers represent Departments I and II respectively, $\overline{m}$ represents surplus-value consumed and m_v and m_c surplus-value invested in variable and constant capital respectively. Professor Lange emphasises the connection between this schema and that of Leontief, and suggests that "Leontief's analysis ... most likely came into being historically under the influence of the Marxian theory of reproduction and the practice of material balances in the Soviet Union" (*ibid.*, p. 218). (A minor limitation of Marx's arithmetical examples as they stand is, of course, that they are expressed in terms of value not of price.)

ceivable, was unlikely to be achieved in reality save by "an accident";* and pointed to a number of reasons that would preclude such an equilibrium from being achieved, or alternatively cause it periodically to be ruptured. There were, however, those among his disciples, like Rosa Luxemburg, who criticised his treatment of these schema, declaring that this gave too little weight to the problem of "realisation" of surplus-value, in the sense of realisation by sale on a market, and that this represented a chronic threat to the process of 'expanded reproduction' in the absence of the external impetus provided by new (and continually expanding) market-outlets.† Curiously, there is a hint, in some very condensed passages towards the end of Volume II (so condensed as to have little more than the form of notes), that Marx may have envisaged something of this kind. What he says, however, refers (apparently) to expanded reproduction at an *increasing* rate, and not at a constant rate (although if the former is impossible, one could ask how expanded reproduction ever gets started in the first place). In such a case he poses the question as to how the capitalists in the industries producing consumption goods, who previously found a market in consumption out of surplus-value, can dispose of their output; and if they cannot realise their surplus-value in money form, how will they be able to continue the investment-process? If they cannot do so, the demand for means of production will in turn be curtailed (or at least fail to expand as anticipated). The answer to the riddle, which is reserved for the last paragraph of Volume II (where the manuscript apparently breaks off), is that the increase in investment can only occur so far as the now-redundant consumption goods are exported in exchange for new gold from the gold producers.‡ It seems evident that an export-surplus

---

* Marx, *Capital*, Vol. II, p. 578: "These conditions become so many causes of abnormal movements, implying the possibility of crises, since a balance is an accident under the crude conditions of this production."

† *Cf.* in this connection Kalecki's demonstration that Harrodian equilibrium-growth is continually tending to collapse towards zero-growth, referred to on pages 232–3. For his comments on the Tugan-Baranowski *versus* Luxemburg debate *cf.* M. Kalecki, *Selected Essays on the Dynamics of the Capitalist Economy, 1933–1970* (Cambridge, 1971), pp. 146–55.   ‡ *Capital*, Vol. II, pp. 595–6, 610.

financed by export of capital would perform a similar function. But in the absence of either kind of export-surplus an *impasse* of the kind envisaged by Rosa Luxemburg would seem to remain.

In this connection it must be remembered that Marx himself decisively rejected what came to be known as 'Say's Law'; emphasising that the circulation-process of $C-M-C$ (Commodities–Money–Commodities) – or rather, as he substituted for this, $M-C-M'$, where $M' > M$ – was not an automatically continuous flow, but was always liable to be arrested by a hoarding of M instead of reconverting it into C (*i.e.* a temporary increase in saving-propensity, or liquidity). That he was not blind, at any rate, to the 'realisation' aspect is shown by his statement: "The conditions of direct exploitation and those of the realisation of surplus-value are not identical. They are separated logically as well as by time and space. The former are only limited by the productive power of society, the latter by the proportional relations of the various lines of production and by the consuming power of society." To this he adds that "the market must, therefore, be continually extended."*

Volumes II and III, as we have said, were never completed, still less revised and rewritten, during his lifetime, although they had been drafted originally in the middle 1860s (*i.e.* before the completion and publication of Volume I). On his death in 1883 they existed only as unfinished drafts and notes, which Engels faithfully pieced together and published, Volume II in 1885 and Volume III in 1894. In his Preface to Volume II Engels spoke of this material as "fragmentary" and incomplete, "not polished as to language" but composed in "the language in which Marx used to make his outlines, that is to say his style was careless, full of colloquial, often rough and humorous, expressions and phrases . . . The thoughts were jotted down as they developed in the brain of the author . . . At the conclusions of chapters there would be only a few incoherent sentences as milestones of incomplete deductions." "And finally", Engels adds for good measure, "there was the well-known handwriting which Marx himself was sometimes unable to decipher."

* *Capital*, Vol. III, pp. 286–7.

There was also to have been a fourth volume, to consist of all his notes for a critical history of economic thought.* But Engels did not live to complete the editing of it. It was later put together by Karl Kautsky under the title of *Theorien über den Mehrwert* in 1905. Although published in a French translation in eight separate parts in 1924–5, it was not to appear in an English translation during the first half of the present century.† The manuscript of this work was to pass into the hands of the Marx–Engels–Lenin Institute in Moscow, which, critical of Kautsky's editing and arrangement, published its own edition of the work in the course of the 1950s:‡ of this an English translation has been in course of preparation, of which at the time of writing two (out of three) parts have appeared.

* Consisting of an MS of more than 1400 quarto pages, written between August 1861 and June 1863 (according to Engels).

† Certain selected parts of the Kautsky edition (principally on the Physiocrats, Adam Smith and Ricardo), however, appeared in English under the title, *Theories of Surplus Value: Selections,* trans. by G. A. Bonner and Emile Burns (London, 1951).

‡ The first part, published by Dietz Verlag, Berlin, was dated 1956. The English translation is in course of publication in London by Lawrence and Wishart.

7

THE 'JEVONIAN REVOLUTION'

I

Jevons completed that reaction against Ricardo of which we have earlier spoken, as is implied by common association of a revolution in economic thought with his name;* and although Menger could be said to have represented this break with classical tradition even more clearly and completely, Jevons was apparently more conscious of the rôle he was playing in reshunting the "car of economic science" which Ricardo had so perversely directed "onto a wrong line".† The appearance of his work only a few years after the first volume of *Das Kapital* makes it tempting to regard the former as a direct answer to the latter, prompted as much by contemplation of this latter-day progeny of Ricardo‡ as the innovations of the Senior–Longfield school had been by the more jejune conclusions of the 'Ricardian socialists'. But there is no evidence that Jevons had this consciously in mind, or even that he was aware of Marx's work: since the latter was published somewhat obscurely in Hamburg, it is highly unlikely, indeed, that Jevons had come across it, and at any rate Jevons's main ideas were formed at least ten years earlier (probably during his years in Australia) and

* Stigler, not too felicitously, calls him "the forerunner of neo-classical economics", while at the same time estimating Menger's theory as "greatly superior to that of Jevons" (G. J. Stigler, *Production and Distribution Theories* (New York, 1946) pp. 13, 135).

† Preface to the 2nd edition (1879) of his *Theory of Political Economy*. Jevons was particularly averse to Mill, not only to his economics but also to his ideas on logic. Keynes speaks of the "violence of Jevons's aversion to Mill, pursued almost to the point of morbidity". (*Essays in Biography*, New ed. (London, 1951) p. 291.)

‡ *Cf.* John Maurice Clark: "The marginal theories of distribution were developed after Marx; their bearing on the doctrines of Marxian socialism is so striking as to suggest that the challenge of Marxism acted as a stimulus to the search for more satisfactory explanations. They undermine the basis of Marxian surplus value doctrine by basing value on utility instead of on labour cost and furnish a substitute for all forms of exploitation doctrine, Marxian or other, in the theory that all factors of production . . . receive rewards based on their assignable contributions to the joint product" ('Distribution' in *Encyclopaedia of Social Sciences*, 1931; reprinted in *Readings in Income Distribution* (Philadelphia, 1946) pp. 64–5).

embodied in a paper to the British Association in 1862. With the Austrians it was different, especially in the case of Wieser and Böhm-Bawerk, who was not only fully aware of the work of Marx as well as of the social backwash of Lassallean propaganda, but was even in some degree obsessed with its potential appeal. The simultaneity of dates of publication of these new and parallel ideas that were to give a novel character and direction to economic thought in the final quarter of the century has often been remarked upon and is quite striking. Jevons's *Theory of Political Economy* appeared in 1871 and Carl Menger's *Grundsätze* in the same year; Walras's *Éléments* in 1874.* The work of Wieser and Böhm-Bawerk belongs to the ensuing decade of the 1880s. Of their joint innovations Professor Shackle has said: "The 40 years from 1870 saw the creation of a Great Theory or Grand System of Economics, in one sense complete and self-sufficient, able, on its own terms, to answer all questions which those terms allowed . . . In its arresting beauty and completeness this theory . . . seemed to derive from these aesthetic qualities its own stamp of authentication and an independent ascendency over men's minds."†

Speaking at a general level, one can say that this shift in structure and perspective of economic analysis had two main aspects. First, as regards causal influences and determinants, emphasis shifted away from costs incurred in production, and hence rooted in circumstances and conditions of production, towards demand and to final consumption; placing the stress on the capacity of what emerged from the production-line to contribute to the satisfaction of the desires, wants, needs of consumers. From this shift of emphasis derived a certain indi-

* Walras spoke in the Preface to his 4th edition (of 1900) of "the theory of exchange based on the proportionality of prices to intensities of the last wants satisfied" as having been "evolved almost simultaneously by Jevons, Menger and myself" (*Éléments*, p. 44). One should not, of course, omit to mention H. H. Gossen of much earlier date: namely his work of 1854 of which something will be said below. Jevons in the Preface to his own 2nd edition was to acknowledge Gossen handsomely as having "completely anticipated me as regards the general principles and method of the theory of Economics" (2nd ed. London, 1879, p. xxxv); while Walras also paid a tribute to him in an article in the *Journal des Économistes* in 1885.

† G. L. S. Shackle, *The Years of High Theory* (Cambridge, 1967) pp. 4–5.

vidualist or atomistic bias of modern economic thought – preoccupation with micro-analysis of individual market-behaviour and action and the rooting of economic generalisation in such micro-phenomena. It is a familiar fact that this was rendered intellectually possible by discovery (*via* application of the differential calculus) of the notion of marginal increments of utility – Jevons's 'final degree of utility' – which overcame the obstacles that others, wishing to stress the importance of Smithian use-value, had encountered in relating use-value and exchange-value. It was this playing-down of cost and production in favour of the pull of demand and of utility in consumption that has caused the change to be described in terms of a shift to a Subjective Theory of Value.

In a much-quoted passage at the beginning of his work Jevons declared: "Repeated reflection and inquiry have led me to the somewhat novel opinion, that value depends entirely upon utility. Prevailing opinions make labour rather than utility the origin of value ... Labour is found often to determine value, but only in an indirect manner, by varying the degree of utility of the commodity through an increase in supply."* In the Preface he explains that "in this work I have attempted to treat Economy as a Calculus of Pleasure and Pain"; emphasising an analogy with "the science of Statical Mechanics". In his Preface to the second edition (of 1879) he renews his attack on Ricardo with a reference to "the mazy and preposterous assumptions of the Ricardian School"; adding that "our English economists have been living in a fool's paradise". In the concluding paragraph of the work he says: "It is a positive service to break the monotonous repetition of current questionable doctrines, even at the risk of new error."† Keynes speaks of his *Theory* as "the first treatise to present in a finished form the theory of value based on subjective valuations" and "the marginal principle".‡

Secondly and consequentially, what one may call the bound-

---

* *The Theory of Political Economy* (London, 1871) p. 2.
† *Ibid.*, p. 267 (2nd ed. 1879, p. 277).
‡ *Essays in Biography*, 2nd ed. (London, 1951) p. 284. He adds: "The first modern book on economics, it has proved singularly attractive to all bright minds newly attacking the subject."

aries of the subject, as well as its structure of causal links and dependencies, were altered significantly, if to an extent that was little emphasised or commented upon at the time. The system of economic variables and their area of determination was virtually identified with the market, or with the set of interconnected markets that constitutes the sphere of exchange. At first sight this might not seem remarkable, at any rate so far as economic theory consists of value theory, which from the very nature of its subject-matter would seem to be necessarily composed of exchange-relations as its warp and weft. But there is something implied in this affecting the relation between distribution and exchange that is less obvious and has some crucial consequences for the subject as a whole. In the system of determination envisaged by Ricardo, and *a fortiori* and more explicitly as envisaged by Marx, there was a crucial sense in which distribution was *prior* to exchange: namely, that price-relations or exchange-values could only be arrived at *after* the principle affecting distribution of the total product had been postulated. The determinants of distribution, as we have seen, were sited in conditions of production (Ricardo's conditions of production of wage-goods; Marx's 'social relations of production', introduced from outside the market, or as it were from a socio-historical fundament to phenomena of exchange). *Per contra*, the new orientation of economic analysis reduced the problem of distribution to the pricing of requisite inputs by a market process which simultaneously determined the interconnected system of outputs and inputs. Moreover, not only was distribution (what remained of it as a department of economic enquiry) determined from within the market or exchange-process, but in the form of the derived prices of given intermediate goods or productive factors: determination was envisaged as being from the market for final products, and hence ultimately from the structure and intensity of consumers' demand. This was not explicitly developed by Jevons* who only

---

* T. W. Hutchison, *A Review of Economic Doctrines, 1870–1929* (Oxford, 1953) p. 44. As Professor Hutchison points out, Jevons stopped short of applying his marginal concept to producer's goods or factors. *Cf.* also Léon Walras, *Elements of Pure Economics*, trans. W. Jaffé (London, 1954) p. 45.

completed effectively one half of the marginal 'revolution'. But it becomes particularly evident in Menger's treatment of goods of 'first order' and of 'higher order', and his derivation of the prices of the latter from the former by the process of 'imputation' (*zurechnung*), in other words by virtue, in some form, of the marginal productivity of producers' goods in terms of consumers' goods. Even in the Walrasian system this derivation was quite explicit. Walras himself emphasised it when he said: "Though it is true that productive services are bought and sold in their own special markets, nevertheless the prices of these services are determined in the market for products."* It is true, of course, that this appearance of uni-directional determination is because the Austrians (as also Walras in the main) simplified their problem by assuming that one started from *given* supplies of productive factors, whose 'services' entered into the exchange-process by commanding a 'hire price'. This is, indeed, the basis for what was to become the fashionable reduction of the cost-concept to the shadowy and contingent notion of 'opportunity cost' (*i.e.* the cost of foregone productive opportunities for creating utilities). But if this assumption of given factor-supplies is relaxed, the difference that this makes is merely to substitute, in Marshallian fashion, a series of rather vaguely defined and subjectively conceived 'factor-supply schedules' of questionable realism and independence (questionable because dependent on some kind of distribution-relative 'real costs' of 'efforts and sacrifices').† Mutual determination is then achieved by means of a balance of marginal conditions in the supply of productive services or factors as well as on the side of consumers' demand. Such was the wraith of so-called 'Ricardianism' that remained in Marshall's system.

Curiously, however, distribution, to which Ricardo had assigned such prominence, although now demoted if not denuded, continued embarrassingly to claim a certain priority

* *Ibid.*, p. 422.
† 'Sacrifices' was a reference to Senior's 'abstinence', or what Marshall more neutrally termed 'waiting'.

even in the new conceptual scheme. The fact that it did so was very much played down: so much so that one might have thought that its claim had gone unnoticed, although altogether unnoticed it can scarcely have been. This was its priority of influence in shaping the structure of consumers' demand by mediating between utility or want-satisfaction to the individual consumer and the expression of this in purchasing-power on the market, and hence in actual market-pull. As was mentioned in our Chapter 1, some pre-existent income-distribution had, accordingly, to be postulated in order that distribution could be represented as being determined by a pricing-process within the sphere of market-exchange. Once recognised, this certainly spoiled the elegant outlines of the conceptual picture, if not its internal consistency – even if an argument could perhaps be sustained (at best a disputable one) that for practical purposes the difference made by admitting this feed-back influence was not, generally speaking, of major consequence, save in some special cases.

Wieser, for one, was well aware of this intrusion of distribution into the derivation of exchange-value from utility in the manner of the Austrian School. He wrote in his *Natural Value*: "The price of an article never completely expresses the exchange-value it has for its owner. This depends, further, upon the 'personal equation' of money to him . . . The 'personal equation' of money is indispensable in every economy, in order that we may weigh against each other goods estimated according to their exchange value . . . Every separate act of exchange depends upon it." And again: "A second element mingles itself in the formation of exchange value, namely purchasing power. In natural value goods are estimated simply according to their marginal utility; in exchange value according to a combination of marginal utility and purchasing power . . . Exchange value, even when considered as perfect is, if we may so call it, a caricature of natural value: it disturbs its economic symmetry, magnifying the small and reducing the great."* But one cannot say that Wieser followed out the logic of this statement, still

* F. von Wieser, *Natural Value*, ed. W. Smart (1956 edition) pp. 49–50, 62.

less resolved the difficulty that it constituted. By colleagues and followers generally the nettle remained ungrasped.*

An important implication of the new conceptual scheme was that the line which Mill had attempted to draw between the institutional and historico-relative character of distribution, on the one hand, and the 'natural' character of the laws of production, on the other, became blurred once more, even if it did not disappear completely. Institutional differences or change could admittedly modify the pattern of income-distribution between *persons* (*e.g.* by affecting the amount of property owned by various individuals); but the broad pattern of distribution between *factors* (which meant substantially between capital and labour) was not capable of any such influence, given the relation between the relative supplies of factors and their productive *uses*, or their rôle in production and hence the demand for them. Hence economic theory could give no place to any institutional-relative characterisation of, say, property-income, or of the profit–wage ratio: these were purely economic categories in the sense of being dependent on the nature of the prevailing economic situation and the economic problem *per se*.

From an ideological standpoint this was undoubtedly the most important result of the change of orientation: *i.e.* for the picture it offered of the economic system, its problems and imperatives, and hence for judgement as to the rightness or wrongness of current diagnoses of social ills. The change was associated, we have noted, with the drawing of different boundary-lines to the 'economic system', treated as an 'isolated system'; so that questions of property-ownership or class-relations and conflicts were regarded as falling outside the economist's domain, not directly affecting, in major respects at least, the phenomena and relations with which economic analysis was properly concerned, and belonging instead to the province of the economic historian or the sociologist. Such a question as the provenance of surplus, of which we spoke in the

* Sir Erich Roll's comment is: "Although analytically superior to similar attempts ... Wieser's doctrine rests on the assumption common to them all that it is possible to conceive of a subjective social value. Such a concept, it is clear, must be self-contradictory" (*A History of Economic Thought* (London, 1938) p. 402).

previous chapter, could not even be posed within the stated terms of economic analysis. Certainly it was not stated; being dismissed as meaningless or as falling outside the boundaries of the subject.

There were other consequences of the change that were destined to become the subject of ideological debate; but on the whole these were of secondary importance. Jevons's mention of Statical Mechanics, for example, as an appropriate analogy for the methodology of the new economics proved to be prophetic; one result of taking the analogy seriously was that economic analysis became preoccupied with equilibrium-positions under conditions of competition; and in so far as these were positions of *full* equilibrium, the full employment of all productive services or factors of production was virtually assumed.* Thus the possibility of multiple equilibria (*e.g.* at various levels of employment) was neglected, if it was not completely ignored (until the 1930s, *i.e.*). So also did dynamic considerations tend to be ignored; since, although the method of statical mechanics could be adapted to deal with problems of so-called 'comparative statics', it could not deal with the stability or instability of paths of movement, and hence with fluctuations or with change as a process.†

Another result, whether logically consequent or not, was that the shift of focus towards analysis of particular equilibrium led to concentration on what has come to be called 'micro-economics', to the exclusion or neglect of the wider con-catenation of interdependencies and effects that were crucial for the formation of the larger macro-relations, but were too often tucked away behind a *ceteris paribus* clause and forgotten

---

* Since, if there were an unused surplus of any factor, competition would drive its price down towards zero, and if there was any elasticity in the demand the excess would be absorbed.

† *Cf.* Sir John Hicks, *Value and Capital* (Oxford, 1939) pp. 115 *seq.*, 302, with its concluding doubt whether "a stationary state ... is even conceivable as a special case"; also his *Capital and Growth* (Oxford, 1965) pp. 15 *seq.*: "economists are so used to this equilibrium assumption that they are inclined to take it for granted", yet "there are market forms, not necessarily unrealistic or unim-portant, where the mere existence of equilibrium, even in a single market, is doubtful, and perhaps more than doubtful".

in the sequel. (Examples of this were Marshall's ingenious simplifying device of assuming the marginal utility of income to be constant, and any wider effects of what was happening to be capable of being ignored as of 'second order of small quantities'; together with the comparable assumption on the supply-side of given factor-prices, which permitted use of the notion of a long-period supply or cost-curve of an industry.) This undoubtedly represented a serious impoverishment of economics (as it now came to call itself in preference to political economy), which was only seriously challenged in the 1930s or even later with the work of Keynes and the shift of attention after the Second World War from Jevonian statics to the theory of growth.

A particular by-product of the new structure and method-ology that was to yield corollaries of striking ideological *tendenz* was the habit of optimising. This developed as the child of the marriage of utility with the technique of marginal incre-ments and decrements, which itself led directly to the consider-ation of extremal problems. Some have, indeed, virtually identified the change introduced by Jevons with attention to the conditions of 'allocation'* (simultaneously of consumers' expenditure among final products and of productive resources between productive uses *via* entrepreneurial choice and action); the notion of maximising being implicit in the manner of framing the problem. It was not difficult to conclude that the assumed maximising behaviour (of utility on the part of consumers and of profit by *entrepreneurs*) yielded the result that under conditions of competition in all markets the (net) value produced was maximised. By a feat of aggregation this was then translated into the proposition that the social aggregate of utilities was maximised – illicitly so translated since we have seen that the relation between values and utilities, consequently summation of the latter, is conditional on income-distribution (an example, again, of the latter's 'priority' obtruding itself). This was indicated initially by Jevons in stating that "so far as is con-

* *Cf.* Hutchison, *Economic Doctrines*, pp. 42, 44, with its references to "maximising allocation formula".

sistent with the inequality of wealth in every community, all commodities are distributed by exchange so as to produce the maximum of benefit".* Perhaps its best known enunciation at the social level was that of Walras to the effect that, with "production in a market ruled by competition . . . the consequences of free competition . . . may be summed up as the attainment, within certain limits, of maximum utility";† which was followed by the modified and contingent (but no less influential) *optimum* associated with the name of his successor, Pareto. Although subject to criticism at the time by no lesser personages than Marshall and Wicksell (the latter bluntly dismissing Pareto's proposition with the statement: "Pareto's doctrine contributes nothing"‡), this optimising corollary, to which we shall return when we speak later of 'Welfare Economics', was to exert quite unusual influence as justification for a *régime* of perfect competition and the free market.

We have said that the reduction of distribution to the pricing of productive services or factors had the result of excluding the social circumstances of the individuals (or social groups) associated with the supply of these 'services' – even to the extent of dropping from sight the very existence of these individuals. At best they were visible in the background as shadowy and ghostly entities lacking substantial social content or even clear outline. The extreme case was where *given* factor-supplies were postulated, and distribution consisted simply of the pricing of n factor-inputs (in which case not even a uniform rate of profit could be envisaged, since the formation of such a rate implies appropriate changes in the supplies of individual capital-goods). Here the illusion of distribution being integrated completely within the exchange-process was at its greatest. The concept of variable factor supplies, governed by some form of schedule of supply-prices, reintroduced the individuals standing behind the supplies, at least to the extent of linking their actions and motivation with the factor-services. But the link

* Jevons, *Theory of Political Economy*, ed. 1871, p. 134.
† Walras, *Elements of Pure Economics*, pp. 125, 255.
‡ K. Wicksell, *Lectures on Political Economy* (London, 1934) Vol. I, p. 83.

was in fact a spurious one, designed so as to permit some degree of attribution of the value of the services to the individuals. Thus 'abstinence' or the like performed the function of linking (or if not explicitly linking, at least blurring the distinction between) the productive effect of what is owned and of its legal owner. The extreme form of this was J. B. Clark's interpretation of marginal productivity as meaning that each factor, and by implication those responsible for its supply, received the equivalent of what it 'contributed' to production: "the law itself", said Clark, "is universal and hence 'natural'".* Although this in its cruder, Clarkian form was subsequently disowned as untenable,† some implication of attribution (and even more of inevitability) still lingered, even in non-popular textbooks, at any rate to the extent that the factor and its supplier (or owner) were linked by any concept of the type of 'abstinence' or 'waiting'. It was seldom thought necessary to indicate that ownership was first requisite in order to supply, and that in this way once more distribution, and its social determinants, as a prior condition came in by the backdoor.

At the purely formal level there can be little doubt that the new context and methods, with their mathematical analogy if not mathematical form, resulted in enhanced precision and rigour of analysis. In this sense – the sense given prominence by Schumpeter – economic analysis *per se* can be said to have measured an advance. The cutting knives of economic discussion became sharper – whether they were used to cut so deeply is another matter. So far at least as market phenomena were concerned, insight no doubt profited and comprehension of price-formation and of market-price movements (including, later on,

---

* J. B. Clark, *The Distribution of Wealth* (New York, 1899) p. 46. *Cf.* also pp. 7, 47, 323–4n., 325.
† G. J. Stigler, *Production and Distribution Theories* (New York, 1946) p. 297: "he introduced what has been called a 'naive productivity ethics' – his marginal productivity theory contained a prescription as well as an analysis . . . Clark was a made-to-order foil for the diatribes of a Veblen". Clark was not, however, alone in this. As Ian Steedman points out, Jevons also spoke of "natural laws" governing distribution between profits and wages, from which followed the futility of trade unions and an essential harmony between capital and labour ('Jevons's Theory of Capital and Interest', *The Manchester School*, March 1972, pp. 48–9).

that of disequilibrium situations and of fluctuations *about* equilibrium) was refined. Despite the fallacies associated with its use, even the casting of allocation-problems in terms of extremal problems and of maximising was not without importance, or devoid of fruitful application. For one thing, it inspired, if it did not generate, the special technique of linear programming, with its obvious relevance to problems of planning. To say this is not to accept Schumpeter's view that progress in 'pure' analysis was the important feature of the change and its ideological character no more than incidental. Indeed the reverse is true. These formal achievements, moreover, have to be set against the laying of some false scents and, with respect to more fundamental problems, an obscurantist focus on superficial and delusive appearance.

Polemics against the earlier Ricardian tradition, and still more against the Marxian system to which the former was blamed for opening the door, were not confined to Jevons's dismissal in general terms (against which Marshall protested as being too irreverent and iconoclastic).* Most of the arguments used are too familiar to need repeating, having been the commonplace of elementary textbooks for a number of generations (such as the contention that by ignoring the influence of demand, any type of cost-theory is incapable of determining price in conditions where cost varies with the quantity produced). But there is a particular accusation that we touched on above, in Chapter 4, which perhaps deserves to be repeated here because of its apparent sophistication and the fact that it came from no less a person than Walras as well as from Jevons. This was that Ricardo's theory had tried to make "one equation determine two unknowns" by suggesting that price is determined by wages *plus* profits (when rent is excluded) while at the same time treating profit as the surplus or excess of value

---

* *Principles*, App. I, p. 817. Marshall considered Jevons "to have judged both Ricardo and Mill harshly", owing to his "desire to emphasise an aspect of value to which they had given insufficient prominence". Jevons's statement that "value depends solely upon utility" Marshall held to be "no less one-sided and fragmentary, and much more misleading than that into which Ricardo often glided with careless brevity, as to the dependence of value on cost of production".

produced over wages.* This criticism, we have seen, though potentially valid against Smith's 'adding-up-components' theory, rests on a flagrant misconception of Ricardo, as Dmitriev pointed out. Dmitriev in developing the answer to it that we have already quoted, wrote as follows (a passage which we give *in extenso* since the whole matter has for so long been misunderstood):

> A single equation cannot serve to determine two unknowns. Thus we are apparently enclosed in a vicious circle: to define value one must know the size of profit; and profit itself depends upon the size of value. It would seem that there is no other way out than to make the size of value, or of profit, depend on conditions situated outside the sphere of production: it is to such a procedure that A. Smith himself had recourse . . . in placing the level of profits in dependence on the supply and demand for capital. But such a procedure amounts to admitting the inconsistency of the theory of expenses of production itself. The immortal merit of Ricardo consists precisely in his brilliant resolution of this problem which had seemed insoluble.

He then went on to show that Ricardo's originality consisted in his being "the first to show that, among the equations of production, there exists one which affords the possibility of determining r [profit] *directly* (that is to say without resort to other equations). This equation is provided for us by the conditions of production of a [the wage-good], to which in the final analysis expenditures in all products . . . are reducible."†

There is one question raised at this point that will no doubt be in the minds of many, even among those inclined to accept

* *Cf.* Walras, *Elements of Pure Economics*, p. 425. Walras refers specifically to "the English theory" and not to Ricardo by name; but the reference is fairly evident. "It is clear", he says, "that the English economists are completely baffled by the problem of price-determination." Jevons has an identical criticism of the "radically fallacious" attempt to derive "two unknown quantities from one equation", and the reference to Ricardo is clearer (*Theory of Political Economy*, p. 258).

† V. K. Dmitriev, *Essais économiques* (Paris, 1968) pp. 46–7. See above p. 117.

what has been said in criticism of post-Jevonian orthodoxy. Even granted the above-mentioned flaws and deficiencies, does it really follow that nothing at all is being, or can be, said about the structure of exchange-relations, and that nothing of any consequence for economic understanding has been stated amid the semi-mathematical sophistication of the past century since Jevons? There must, surely, be *some* statements about the inter-relationship of prices within the circle of exchange that have general application to *all* types of exchange-society, even if these are incapable of playing the rôle claimed for them of affording a theory of the determination of income-distribution, and hence a satisfactory theory of value and distribution in the classical sense? *Given* a certain pattern of Walrasian *raretés*, is it not true that a certain pattern of prices becomes in some sense 'necessary'; and if so, such a 'necessity' will be supra-institutional?

The question is evidently a pertinent one, and one that cannot be avoided by critics of modern doctrine. If an answer is to be given in general terms, it must be based, it would seem, on a distinction between different *categories* of statement about economic phenomena. When one is talking within what Marx would have called the category of 'market price' (which he himself only reaches towards the middle of his third volume), it is true that there are a number of statements that can be made about supply–demand relations; and because their number is rather limited, as well as their significance in the larger, 'macro', perspective, it does not follow that they may not have importance in certain specialised contexts. The point is that, in order to make such statements a number of things have to be taken as *given* (as – to take the extreme case – in all statements about Marshallian 'short-period', or quasi-short-period, situations): data that are dependent variables at another, and 'deeper', level of analysis. *More* has to be independently postulated in order to explain *less*. This, if one understands him rightly, is equivalent (or analogous) to what Professor Hicks means by a "restricted equilibrium" arrived at by restricting the number of choices that are "open".*

* *Capital and Growth* (Oxford, 1965) pp. 25–6.

Fundamentally it is why supply–demand statements cannot, for reasons that we have considered, include (or reach so far as) a proper theory of distribution; nor is this *genus* of demand-determination theory capable of affording a consistent answer to the classical type of value-problem (for which reason alone the epithet 'neo-classical' as applied to the former is inappropriate if not misleading). So far as distribution is concerned, indeed, we have said that some income-distribution has to be postulated in order to give meaning to 'the pattern of demand', and hence to make any general statement at a global level of a supply–demand type.

One way of illustrating what is meant when one speaks of contexts in which demand-determined exchange-relations are applicable may be the following. One could suppose that all productive inputs were natural objects available at any given date in given nature-determined amounts.* Any exchange-relations in the system would evidently reflect (and be explicable in terms of) diverse and strictly limited commodities *vis-à-vis* the pattern of demand for end-products produced from different input-combinations. But then, of course, the process of production as ordinarily viewed (outside a completely automated world) would be non-existent. One could then modify the supposed conditions to allow labour as an input along with natural objects (*e.g.* labour of collection, adaptation, organisation); and still have the same mode of relationship so far as exchange of natural objects, and between them and final (consumed) products, was concerned: the former would function as *renten-guter*, demanding a price in proportion to the rôle they played in the process of transformation into final products and the relative demand for the products in which they played a major rôle. One could say, indeed, that there was here an analogy with the problems to which the technique of linear programming is applied: the problem of allocating (scarce) natural objects between productive uses and their optimum combination in each use – an optimum that is defined in terms of 'an objective function', commonly interpreted as some suit-

* *E.g.* Marshall's meteoric stones.

ably weighted series of end-uses. In this guise, it could be loosely described as a technique rather than a theoretical explanation of actuality. Indeed, the linear programming analogy is illuminating here precisely because, as is well known, this technique of analysis can be applied to certain problems of a socialist economy, whether at the particular or the general level, as well as to a capitalist economy, and to this extent must refer to aspects or relationships that are supra-institutional. Such an analogy may have at least this advantage: that it presents end-uses as having to be arbitrarily postulated from *outside* the system, whether in the form of some given output-plan (*e.g.* Kantorovitch), or (if based on indicated market-demand) the implicit postulation of a given income-distribution.

To the extent, *per contra*, that human activity is assigned a major rôle in the productive process and reproducible inputs (product of the productive process itself) replace scarce natural objects, the essentials of the economic problem become different, first since the question of the existence and provenance of a value-surplus can now be relevantly posed,* and secondly because the proportion of any given product-value that is assigned to wages (and costed as such), and the mode of distributing the surplus or difference between the two, will be a crucial determinant of the resulting price-structure.

But if a formal mode of determination in terms of scarcity-relations ('scarcity' defined and measured with reference to the set of end-uses) can be constructed, and can convey some information, in a situation of naturally-determined means or inputs, why should it not be able to do so in analogous situations where any set of *n* means or inputs, although not dependent on *natural* limitations, are nonetheless determined as to their supplies in some other way? Moreover, cannot the scarcity-price relations so derived be applied not only to

---

* The reason why such a question would have no place in our previous hypothetical case is, of course, that the 'rents', or scarcity-prices, of naturally-scarce means or inputs would rise towards the price-level of outputs, or should any of these inputs be capable of turning out more of themselves as output than was required as inputs, they would fairly soon cease to be (nature-limited) scarce goods.

products but to these means or inputs themselves? Indeed, this is quite possible; but, as we have seen when speaking of the Austrians, subject to the restrictive condition that the set of n means or inputs is already given as *datum*. The restriction is a large one. It excludes from consideration all situations in which these supplies are likely to change (*i.e.* to change as a 'feedback' effect of their prices), and analysis thus restricted can make no pronouncement as to why and how these changes occur or as to their effects – for which reason we spoke of the situations to which such a theory can apply as 'quasi-short-period situations'. It is obvious that what is essentially a short-period theory cannot be expected to yield answers to 'long-period' problems (*e.g.* concerning equilibrium situations involving a uniform profit-rate).* Escape is sought from this restriction by seeking to group these n means or inputs into larger factor-groups, and to relate supply-changes of the former to the situations of the latter: an escape that has its own special difficulties (consisting in the need to postulate some distinctly odd, indeed metaphysical, entities as generic 'factors') that are to-day becoming familiar and to which we shall return.

It may be noted incidentally that in either of the two latter approaches (and most conspicuously in the second) it is implied that the particular input-combinations, or techniques, chosen are dependent upon (and vary with) the pricing of factors or inputs as derived from the resultant price-relations of the system as a whole. This in turn implies the notion of a 'production-function' or factor-substitution schedule defining all the different combinations of factors or inputs that are capable of yielding the same output (this substitution-curve being 'objective' in the sense of resting solely on technical data in a given state of technical knowledge). In this notion of a 'production-function' there are crucial difficulties, as we shall again see presently when we come to the discussions of recent years. If this approach is abandoned, there is postulated instead a set of n possible production-processes or methods of production for each industry; but although the one chosen at any time will depend

---

* See, however, below, pp. 205, 207.

upon the wage–profit ratio (and the resulting price-structure of products used as inputs), for reasons that will emerge there will not be the obligation that there is in the former case (where factor-groups and their relative supplies played a crucial rôle) to regard these alternative processes as being ordered in a particular way.

II

Prior to Jevons most people would seem to have believed that Adam Smith's 'use-value' could not be quantified. Hence, despite Bentham's reference to degrees of intensity of pleasure and pain, and despite the hints of Say and of others who took after him, there was no systematic attempt to introduce it as a determinant (as distinct from a condition) of exchange-value. The novel element in Jevons that tipped the scales was evidently his singling out of 'the final degree of utility' and his equation of this with exchange-value. This revealed that it was only necessary to treat differences, comparatively small differences, in utility as quantitative to the extent of being comparable in terms of greater or less. Comparison of such differences, declared Jevons, was made by people in their everyday actions, and accordingly one judged the intensities of their feelings from their actions. "It is from the quantitative effects of their feelings that we must estimate their comparative amounts." There was no question of needing to compare *total* utilities. Said Jevons: "We can seldom or never affirm that one pleasure is a multiple of another in quantity, but the reader who carefully criticises the following theory will find that it seldom involves the comparison of quantities of feeling differing much in amount . . . I never attempt to estimate the whole pleasure gained by purchasing a commodity; the theory merely expresses that, when a man has purchased enough, he derives an equal pleasure from the possession of a small quantity more or from the money price of it."* This he has earlier prefaced by stating: "To me it seems that our science must be mathematical simply because it deals with quantities. Whenever the things treated are capable

* Jevons, *Theory of Political Economy* (London, 1871) pp. 13–14, 20.

of being more or less in magnitude, there the laws and relations must be mathematical in nature."*

In his third chapter Jevons develops his theory of value in more detail. Opening this chapter with the statement that "pleasure and pain are undoubtedly the ultimate objects of the Calculus of Economy" he goes on: "To satisfy our wants to the utmost with the least effort . . . in other words, to maximise comfort and pleasure, is the problem of Economy"; he defines Utility (quoting Say and Bentham) as "the abstract quality whereby an object serves our purposes, and becomes entitled to rank as a commodity"; further stating that "utility, though a quality of things, is no inherent quality. It might be more accurately described, perhaps, as *a circumstance of things* arising out of their relation to man's requirements."† He propounds the law of diminishing utility (calling it the Law of Variation of Utility: "utility is not proportional to commodity"), distinguishing between total utility and the utility of an additional increment and drawing a utility-curve of the familiar kind. "The degree of utility" is defined as "the differential coefficient of utility considered as a function of x [the quantity of the commodity in question], and will itself be another function of x"; it being this which decreases as the quantity of a commodity is increased until "satisfaction or satiety" of our appetites is approached.‡ In the following chapter (On Exchange) he posits that "the ratio of exchange of any two commodities will be inversely as the final degrees of utility of the quantities of commodity available for consumption after the exchange is effected".§ Chapters v, vi and vii of the book deal with the Theories of Labour, of Rent and of Capital.

In the second edition he formulated the curious restatement of his theory in abbreviated form‖ upon which Marshall was to comment so adversely:

> Cost of production determines supply
> Supply determines final degree of utility
> Final degree of utility determines value.

* *Ibid.*, p. 4.   † *Ibid.*, pp. 44–5, 52.   ‡ *Ibid.*, pp. 53 *seq.*, 61.
§ *Ibid.*, pp. 95–6.   ‖ *Theory of Political Economy* (London, 1879) p. 165.

On this Marshall, who had reviewed Jevons's book rather ungenerously (Keynes says "grudgingly") in the *Academy* for April 1872, made this comment:* "Now if this series of causation really existed, there could be no great harm in omitting the intermediate stages and saying that cost of production determines value. For if *A* is the cause of *B*, which is the cause of *C*, which is the cause of *D*; then *A* is the cause of *D*. But in fact there is no such series." After propounding his own view of "mutual determination" of "supply price, demand price and amount produced" (which he regards as "the greatest objection of all" to Jevons's presentation), he ends by inverting the order of Jevons's statement ("a catena rather less untrue than his can be made"):

Utility determines the amount that has to be supplied

The amount that has to be supplied determines cost of production

Cost of production determines value,
because it determines the supply price which is required to make the producers keep to their work†

But this question of relative emphasis upon influences on the side of supply and on the side of demand (both being conceived, in the main, subjectively) was really quite secondary to those other characteristics of the shift that were previously discussed. What Marshall was really defending against Jevons was that line of tradition from Smith's 'components of price' to Mill's 'expenses of production' theory of natural value rather than the Ricardian theory in its proper interpretation.

Jevons failed to develop explicitly a general theory of distribution in similar terms (*i.e.* of utility-determination), as we have already seen. He does say, however, with regard to Labour that "its value must be determined by the value of the produce, not the value of the produce by that of the labour", without describing how this is achieved. The problem here, which he does not directly face, is that if factors are jointly

* Marshall, *Principles*, Appendix I, p. 818.   † *Ibid.*, pp. 818–19.

demanded, in the sense of being used in fixed proportions (and proportions that are uniform in various uses), no such derivation of factor-prices from product-prices is possible. Such derivation depends upon the proportions in which factors are used being *variable* (and continuously variable – along a substitution-curve or 'production-function'), or else (as we shall see when we come to the Austrians) on the proportions in which factors are combined, if fixed *in* each use, being *non*-uniform as *between* uses.

The exception (a fairly large one) to what we have said about Jevons and distribution is the case of capital; and it is his Theory of Capital that has aroused an interest second only to his analysis of the relation between increments of utility and price. Here Jevons certainly does introduce what is essentially the notion of marginal productivity, treating this as determinant of the rate of interest. This is introduced in association with his special view of capital as consisting in the advance of subsistence to labourers. Here he is in the classical tradition, and he admits that "on this subject" he is "in fundamental agreement with Ricardo". Such a notion of capital as an 'advance' implies a time-dimension – the period of time over which the advance is made, or 'period of production' as this was to be called. "Capital, as I shall treat it", he says, "consists merely of the *aggregate of those commodities which are required for sustaining labourers of any kind or class engaged in work*". "*The current means of sustenance constitute capital in its free or uninvested form.* The single and all-important function of capital is to enable the labourer to await the result of any long-lasting work – to put an interval between the beginning and the end of an enterprise . . . Capital simply allows us to expend labour in advance."* To enable a lengthening of "the average interval between the moment when labour is exerted and its ultimate result or purpose accomplished" is not only treated as *one* of the functions of capital; it is regarded by Jevons as "the sole use of capital".† Such a lengthening (of which he speaks

* *Theory of Political Economy* (London, 1871) pp. 214 *seq.*
† *Ibid.*, pp. 217, 220.

as an "improvement") increases productivity. It follows that capital has two dimensions: labour and time. First, there is the amount of labour invested: *e.g.* one day's labour on a certain date. Secondly, there is the length of time for which the invested

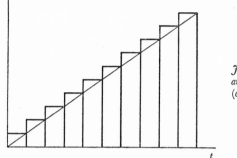

Jevonian diagram of amount of 'investment' (or 'period of production')

labour is 'locked-up' or advanced: *e.g.* for a year or several years or for only a month. The product of these two dimensions he calls "the amount of investment of capital" by contrast with the "amount [of capital] invested". Thus one pound may be invested for five years or five pounds invested for one year; both equalling five pound-years in "amount of investment".* This he illustrates by the famous triangle, in which the horizontal axis represents duration, the vertical line the amount invested by any given date and the total area the total two-dimensional entity, the total 'amount of investment' over the whole period. If £10 is invested during each of ten years, then the 'amount invested' by the end of the ten-year period will be £100, but the (total) 'amount of investment' will be equal to £550 (a figure which approaches £500, or half the total area of *t* × the labour invested over the period, as the intervals between successive acts of investment are shortened and investment becomes virtually a continuous process).

Interest on capital, according to this theory, is "the rate of increase of the produce" resulting from a given increment in this period of advance (or period of production) expressed as a ratio to the whole produce; or, writing *Ft* for the produce of a

* *Ibid.*, pp. 221–8.

given amount of labour advanced for time t and assuming Ft to increase with t:

$$\frac{\mathrm{d}Ft}{\mathrm{d}t} \cdot \frac{1}{Ft}.$$

Thus "the rate of interest varies inversely as the time of investment".* This was equivalent, of course, to determining the rate of return on capital by the marginal productivity of lengthening the period of production.†

Jevons is also remembered, of course, as a vigorous writer on practical questions, such as the changing value of gold, on 'commercial fluctuations', on index-number theory and above all on the Coal Question on which he wrote a best-selling pamphlet in 1865. At the time these attracted more attention than the novelty of his economic theory. He also held strong views about the policy of *laissez-faire* and the wages-question (*vide* his *State in Relation to Labour* of 1882). Unlike his continental contemporaries of whom we shall speak in a moment, his academic influence during his life-time was slight and his theoretical ideas made little headway. His first enunciation of his new theory, in a paper to the British Association in 1862, was ignored; and although appointed to a Chair at Owen's College, Manchester, in 1866, he refrained from lecturing on his own ideas during his ten years at Manchester, preferring to instruct his students instead in the traditional doctrines of Mill. Keynes speaks of him as "a reluctant and unsuccessful lecturer".‡ On publication his book had few reviews and these were cool (including the one by Marshall that we have mentioned, and a hostile one from Cairnes); and only four years

---

* *Ibid.*, pp. 237–8. It will be noted that the increase in the amount of investment = $\mathrm{d}t.Ft$, so that the above expression is equivalent to the increase of produce as a ratio to the increase in amount of investment. On this as a tenable explanation of interest see further below, p. 202.

† Professor Stigler, rather surprisingly, thinks that "Jevons does not depart far from the classical theory. His conception of capital and its rate is basically the same as that incorporated in the wages-fund doctrine"; the main difference being "that the classical doctrine assumes a fixed period of production (one year)" (*Production and Distribution Theories*, p. 29). By "classical theory" is evidently meant here Ricardo as interpreted by Mill.

‡ J. M. Keynes, *Essays in Biography* (new ed., 1951) p. 307.

after succeeding (in 1876) to the Chair at University College, London, he resigned for reasons of ill-health – to be drowned while bathing on the south coast no more than two years later at the early age of 46. Schumpeter remarks that he left few if any personal pupils: "in England he never got his due ... his originality was never recognised as it should have been".* Keynes's comment on him (comparing him with Marshall) was memorable. "It was Jevons's willingness to spill his ideas, to flick them at the world, that won him his great personal position and his unrivalled power of stimulating other minds. Every one of Jevons's contributions to Economics was in the nature of a pamphlet."†

III

In his book of the same year as Jevons's Carl Menger (a civil servant who two years later was appointed to one of the two Chairs of Political Economy at the University of Vienna) produced a closely parallel theory in more general form, but without Jevons's mathematics (what Professor Stigler has called his "repellant mathematical formulation").‡ Like Jevons he expounded a subjective theory of value, starting from the consumers' end, with consumers' goods ("goods of first order") deriving their value from their power of satisfying human wants. As we have seen, he proceeds to derive the value of producers' goods ("goods of higher order") from the contribution these make to the production of goods that cater directly for human wants; this derivation being by a process that came to be known as 'imputation' (*zurechnung*) to each input of the difference which its presence (or absence) makes to production. The fulcrum of such imputation is the so-called Loss Principle: the value of a horse to a farmer is that of which he is deprived if he

---

* Schumpeter, *History of Economic Analysis*, p. 826. He also speaks of Jevons as "without doubt one of the most genuinely original economists", although "his performance was not up to his vision". Prof. Lionel Robbins said of him in an appreciation: "Since his death he has been recognised universally as one of the most outstanding figures in the history of economic thought"; adding that: "He formed no school. He created no system" ('The Place of Jevons in the History of Economic Thought', *Manchester School*, Vol. VII, No. 1, 1936, p. 1).

† *Essays in Biography* (London, 1933) p. 211 (new ed., 1951, p. 174).

‡ Stigler, *Production and Distribution Theories*, p. 135.

is without it. This can be seen to be substantially the notion of marginal productivity, although without using the term as such and without entering into the quasi-mathematical refinements that were to become associated therewith. Menger was careful, however, to distinguish between the cases of fixed and of variable proportions of inputs or factors in production. For the first case (fixed proportions) he enunciated the principle that the value of an input or factor withdrawn was equal to the total resulting loss of product *minus* the product resulting from the use of the complementary inputs or factors in alternative employments for them. In the second case (variable proportions) this value was equal to the difference made to the product by the withdrawal of one unit of the input or factor, after what remained of this and of other factors had been suitably rearranged and combined to the best advantage. Such a solution, as will appear in a moment, left open a number of questions and can even be said, as it stood, to involve a contradiction.

Reverting to 'goods of the first order': Menger stressed that wants approach satiation as more of a good is available, and that a consumer maximises his satisfaction at any time by so distributing his income as to make the want just satisfied at the margin equal in all directions ("the most important of all those concrete wants which are not satisfied are of the same significance for all types of wants and accordingly all concrete wants are satisfied to an equal level of importance"). The general sense of this proposition is, of course, fairly clear. But it is not enunciated at all precisely, since it does not make clear what is the unit in terms of which wants just satisfied (or left unsatisfied) are measured and equalised. It will manifestly make all the difference to the sense or nonsense of the statement whether the equalisation is assumed to take place in terms of physical units of each commodity (bushels of corn, yards of cloth and bottles of whisky) or of units of money income spent on these various commodities. The latter interpretation becomes equivalent, then, to speaking, *not* of equalising the want satisfaction, or marginal utility, of *commodities*, but of making their marginal utility (in terms of some physical unit of each commodity) proportional to their prices. Clarity about this interpretation is not just pedantry, but is relevant to the question as to whether any such statement can be extended or aggregated so as to apply to a group as distinct from separate individuals. If money incomes are unequal (so that the marginal utilities of those individual money incomes are unequal) any attempt so to extend it is plainly fallacious – although the fallacy is far from unknown.* When extended beyond individuals to a group, we find, yet again, that this proposition only has unambiguous meaning after some assumption about income-distribution has been imported.

It should, perhaps, be explained that a feature of Menger's approach, and of his school as a whole, was that with reference to wants as well as to 'higher order' goods used as inputs in production, the fact of complementarity was stressed, as well as the fact that one had to deal with finite units (*Teilquantität*), not with infinitesimals (an emphasis associated with their antipathy to the 'mathematising' of theory in the manner of Jevons and Walras). The significance of this emerges in the particular way in which they interpreted 'imputed value' or marginal productivity.

Menger (who was to live until after the First World War) has been called the father of the Austrian School, since the best known representatives of this School, Wieser and Böhm-Bawerk, who were to develop his theory, especially on the side of 'imputation' as a theory of distribution and of the theory of capital, were his personal disciples. Menger, indeed, was in every way more successful than Jevons in achieving recognition and influence within his lifetime; although it can be doubted whether he would have done so, especially against the latent opposition of the powerful German Historical School (with whom in later life he was engaged in extensive polemics), without the aid and literary activity of his two leading pupils, who attracted attention to Menger's doctrines by their own work in the course of the ensuing decade. But before we deal with their contributions (in some ways more interesting than their master's) a word

* See below, pp. 243–4.

deserves to be said about that German forerunner of whom neither Jevons nor Menger were aware, apparently, when they wrote their respective works in 1871, but whom Jevons, as we have seen, was to acknowledge when his book came to a second edition. As early as 1854 Hermann Heinrich Gossen had published a book with the title of 'Development of the Laws of Human Action and of the consequent Principles of Human Commerce' (*Entwicklung der Gesetze des menschlichen Verkehrs und der daraus fliessenden Regeln für menschliches Handeln*), in which a semi-mathematical theory of pleasure and pain was presented, with the notion of satiability of wants or diminishing utility (his 'first law') and the principle that the attempt to maximise enjoyment will result at any one time in making the final increments of all enjoyments equal (or more correctly, as we have seen, of the final increments of money income expended in acquiring various enjoyments). This principle by analogy was extended to goods used in production (which he called "goods of the third class") and to labour; and since labour involved disutility, equilibrium in production involved a balancing of the disutility of additional labour against the additional enjoyment resulting from the fruit of that labour. Value depends entirely on the relation between the object and the subject.*

Gossen, however, treated utility as bearing a linear relation to quantity, so that the demand-curves in his diagrams are all straight lines. What is remarkable, but perhaps not altogether surprising, is that Gossen's work should have remained almost unknown and without influence, until it was publicly acknowledged by Jevons in 1879.

It was Friedrich von Wieser who, in addition to trying to develop a theory of exchange-value from a theory of prices (or 'natural value') arising in the context of individual exchange or barter between trading partners or groups, sought to develop Menger's Loss Principle more rigorously as a general theory (the word *zurechnung* is in fact his); while E. von Böhm-Bawerk is known for his theory of capital and interest along Jevonian

* *Cf.* on Gossen, Erich Roll, *History of Economic Thought* (London, 1938) pp. 371–3.

lines. The latter was expressly designed as an answer to Marx's theory of surplus-value. Indeed, preoccupation with criticism of socialist doctrines was prominent in most of the representatives of the Austrian School (as also with Pareto of whom we shall presently speak); and the theory of imputation was developed by Wieser as an answer to the socialist claim (derived, as he thought, from the Labour Theory of Value) that income on property represented 'exploitation' of labour. They, in company with Pareto, could well be called conscious apologists of the existing system – and Schumpeter, indeed, dubbed Böhm-Bawerk "the bourgeois Marx".*

Wieser's two best-known works were published in the 1880s: the first of them, *Über den Ursprung und die Hauptgesetze des wirthschaftlichen Werthes* (Origin and Law of Economic Values) in 1884, and the second, *Der Natürlichen Wert* (translated by C. A. Malloch and edited by William Smart in 1893 as *Natural Value*) in 1889. Menger's Loss Principle for imputing or deriving the values of producers' goods from the values of consumers' goods is developed in the direction of a theory of marginal productivity, if in a special version of his own – Schumpeter's "marginal productivity with a difference".† As such it rested on the equality of the price of a producers' good (under conditions of competition) with what he called its 'productive contribution' (he also spoke of this as 'marginal contribution' or 'marginal product').

We have noted the Austrian use of finite units and their emphasis upon complementarity. This was not accidental: it arose from their rejection of any broad classification of factors of production, in favour of treating each distinguishable type of input as a separate producers' good to be priced by the imputation-process; and these latter goods had to be handled in terms each of its own physical unit, which could involve, especially in the case of fixed capital, large indivisible units and significant elements of complementarity. Wieser starts by showing that Menger's Loss Principle when applied to such cases of complementarity would result in the values of all the com-

* Schumpeter, *History of Economic Analysis*, p. 846.   † *Ibid.*, p. 915.

plementary factors exceeding the value of the production* (*i.e.* when the former are valued in the way that Menger suggested as equal to the total product of the 'best' combination less the product of the other factors in the combination when put to an alternative, second-best use). While Wieser allows that proportions can commonly vary and are by no means always fixed, he takes it for granted that any such (finite) variations away from the combination yielding 'the greatest attainable return' are bound to affect the product adversely; and he accordingly offers a solution designed to be the 'strongest' case where proportions are absolutely fixed (a consideration that Professor Stigler seems to miss in his curt dismissal of Wieser's answer). This alternative principle of imputation propounded by Wieser required, however, the assumption that, while factors or inputs are combined in fixed proportions in each use, these proportions are *different* as between various uses. The prices of the inputs are then derived from the differences in technical coefficients and differences in product-prices in the system as a whole.

This was illustrated, in a simplified 3-factor, 3-product case, in the following way. Writing x, y, z for the unit-values of the three factors or inputs, two of which are used in each industry, and putting the values of the products (assumed to be predetermined in the market for consumers' goods) on the right-

---

* In England it was P. H. Wicksteed who considered this so-called 'adding-up problem' and sought to prove it with the aid of Euler's Theorem, subject to the proviso that the production-function was "homogeneous and of the first degree" (or linear): in other words, that constant returns to scale, or constant costs, prevailed (*Coordination of the Laws of Production and Distribution*, London, 1894). Wicksell (also Walras) supported Wicksteed's conclusion on the ground that, even though there might be *ranges* of output (of a firm) over which increasing or diminishing returns to scale might prevail, the assumption of competitive equilibrium required the firm in competitive equilibrium to be producing at minimum cost (and hence in the immediate neighbourhood of the equilibrium point at constant cost). This would seem to leave 'external economies' out of the picture. Prof. Joan Robinson, however, showed that the question at issue was purely formal, since even when external economies existed (and the *industry* was subject for this reason to increasing returns to scale) it was the marginal product to the *firm* (and not to the industry) to which the price of a factor was equated in competitive equilibrium (Joan Robinson, 'Euler's Theorem and the Problems of Distribution', *The Economic Journal*, September 1934, pp. 398 *seq.*; reprinted in *Collected Economic Papers* (Oxford, 1951) pp. 1–18).

hand side of each equation, he presented the three equations for the three products as follows:

$$x + y = 100,$$
$$2x + 3z = 290,$$
$$4y + 5z = 590.$$

"Instead of the one equation $x + y = 10$", we now have three equations and three unknowns, and the value of x, y and z can be found by solving the equations (in this case they can be found to be respectively 40, 60 and 70). "The productive contribution, then, is that portion of return in which is contained the work of the individual productive element in the total return of production. The sum of all the productive contributions exactly exhausts the value of the total return."*

This ingenious solution involved, however, several limitations. First, there have to be at least as many end-products as there are separate producers' goods whose prices have to be determined. This would not be at all serious as a limiting condition if one were dealing with factors of production grouped in a few main classes or groups in the classical manner. But when physically-distinguishable producers' goods – each different metal, fuel or machine-tool or grade of labour or of land – has to be priced separately, this could be a much more serious limitation. Secondly, some critics (e.g. Stigler) have pointed out that, since product-prices are taken as given, this implies that final demands are infinitely elastic, so that product-prices remain unaffected by output adjustments. This objection, again, may not be so insuperable as at first might appear, provided that an appropriate equilibrium-condition (e.g. equality of costs and revenue) can be postulated to allow for some mutual adjustment of product-prices and output and prices of producers' goods in the course of reaching equilibrium. Wieser was, indeed, responsible for the notion that was to become known as alternative or opportunity-cost – that the usefulness of an input in any one use affected its availability and hence cost of obtaining it for alternative and rival uses –

* *Natural Value*, ed. W. Smart (London, 1893) p. 88.

so that he can hardly be accused of completely ignoring the reaction of producers' goods prices on output and hence product-prices.

Thirdly, there is a difficulty of more fundamental consequence: what one may call a dilemma concerning the assumption to be made about factor-supplies – what on the supply-side is to be taken as *given*?* We are back at a crucial difficulty that we touched on, in a preliminary manner, in the first section of this chapter: a difficulty which must confront any theory of demand-determination that operates with separate capital goods or inputs. If the assumption is made that what is given (and treated as constant) is the supply of various individual producers' goods, then we have no more than what in Marshallian terms could be called a short-period (or quasi-short period) theory. The value of a durable producers' good such as a piece of machinery is derived as a 'quasi-rent', and will be different for different types of fixed capital. As we said, no uniform rate of profit on the diverse components of fixed capital will emerge. If, on the other hand, the assumption of constancy is made to refer only to some broader grouping of factors (*e.g.* to capital) within which the relative supplies of particular items can be allowed to vary subject only to constancy in quantity of the *genus* as a whole, then one runs into the now-familiar problem of how to give an independent quantitative meaning to capital – a difficulty that we shall meet again (in a slightly different perspective) in the case of Walras and shall examine in more detail in relation to modern discussion and critique.

It should, perhaps, be noted incidentally that if one deals with infinitesimal increments and continuous variation, as was later to become fashionable, Wieser's solution and Menger's Loss Principle can be shown to come to the same thing even in the fixed proportions case. There is, however, some loss of realism in so doing since all problems connected with indi-

* Strictly speaking, if one has fixed coefficients, relative factor-supplies cannot affect the result (*cf.* Stigler, *Production and Distribution Theories*, p. 178). But if one regards this as the 'strong case' only, and allows the possibility of some variation in practice, then as soon as the latter is introduced, factor-supplies become relevant and some postulate about them is necessary.

visibilities* are *ipso facto* excluded. In terms of continuous variation the position can be summed up as follows. In the case of fixed proportions the value of a factor or input is determined by its utility in alternative uses. In the case of *variable* proportions (*i.e.* variable *in* each industry) such quantities of the different factors or inputs as can be substituted for each other in order to obtain the same additional quantity of the product must be of equal value (*i.e.* their prices = the ratio of their marginal products).

To fill the gap in Menger–Wieser 'imputation' so far as a theory of profits was concerned was the task of the well-known theory of interest on capital that was the special contribution of Eugen von Böhm-Bawerk to the work of the Austrian School. This was along Jevonian lines, and, worked-out and presented with Teutonic thoroughness, it concentrated on the notion of a period of production as the quantitative essence of 'capital' as a productive factor. His two-volume work *Kapital und Kapital-zins* also appeared in the 1880s; his first and historical volume *Geschichte und Kritik* in 1884, and the second *Positive Theorie* in 1889.† His intention of revising this work systematically in the light of discussion and criticism was prevented by fifteen years of preoccupation with Parliamentary affairs, during which he was three times Minister of Finance; until in 1905 he returned to academic work as Professor at Vienna (in the interval he had been no more than Professor Honorarius, holding an occasional seminar but no more). This revision of his work and reply to criticism was scarcely completed on his death nine years later in 1914. His well-known (and for a number of decades highly influential) critique of Karl Marx was written during his Parliamentary period in 1896.‡

We have said that his theory of capital, which was to constitute the Austrian theory of capital as we know it, had major affinity with that of Jevons. In treating the concept of a period

* *E.g.* an important category of external economies concerned with economies in the supply of subsidiary products or increased specialisation, with marginal cost accordingly diverging from average cost.

† The English edition, under the editorship of W. Smart, appeared in 1890 and 1891 respectively.   ‡ See above, p. 141.

of production as the essence of capital, it emphasised the potentially enhanced productivity of labour when associated with 'longer' or 'more roundabout' processes of production; the rate of interest being derived from the additional productivity from lengthening this time period. "That roundabout methods lead to greater results than direct methods is one of the most important and fundamental propositions in the whole theory of production." His theory also had affinity with Jevons in regarding capital as consisting essentially of advances of subsistence to labourers: that is, as being reducible basically to a subsistence fund. Increase of productivity with lengthening of the period of production would generally be in decreasing proportion to the lengthening: in other words, the marginal productivity of lengthening tended to fall. With a given quantity of labour, any increase of capital must necessarily result in extending this period (a longer period, *ceteris paribus*, requiring more capital because of the extension of the time-dimension). It followed, according to familiar reasoning, that with a given rate of wages and a given supply of capital, a certain length of production-period was possible on the average; and competition would ensure (competition, that is, of *entrepreneurs* seeking capital with which to extend the period) that the rate of interest would equal the ratio of the additional product gained by lengthening the period to the additional capital required thereby (Jevons's 'amount of investment of capital'). Alternatively, one could express it in this form: given the supply of labourers competing in the market for employment (bartering their labour for subsistence) and also the supply of capital seeking investment, the level of wages, the length of the period of production and the rate of interest were mutually and simultaneously determined. "In a community interest will be high in proportion as the national subsistence fund is low, as the number of labourers employed by the same is great, and as the surplus returns connected with any further extension of the production period continue high."*

But what determines the amount of capital seeking invest-

* *The Positive Theory of Capital*, trans. W. Smart (London, 1891) p. 401.

ment? If this were unlimited, there would be no upper limit upon the period of production and no lower limit to the rate of interest which would fall towards zero. Here it is that Böhm-Bawerk places his theory of capital within the framework of the Subjective Theory of Value by enunciating his famous 'subjective undervaluation of future goods compared with present goods'. From this notion all subsequent explanations of interest in terms of 'time-preference' or 'time-discount' (*e.g.* Irving Fisher's) derive. It is this which can be said to provide the supply-side of the Austrian theory, so far as the supply of 'savings' is concerned, and hence the supply of capital seeking investment at any given date. For this 'subjective under-valuation of future goods' he provides 'three grounds', which have been the subject of much (some of it tedious) discussion – discussion into which we may perhaps be excused for not entering.

The first ground was stated as follows: "The first great cause of difference in valuation of present and future goods consists in the different circumstances of want and provision in present and future." In other words, the future is likely to be better provided for and have a higher real income than the present; this applying at any rate to the community as a whole, even if as between individuals the comparative prospect for the present and the future may vary (some individuals expecting a fall in income while others anticipate a rise).

Secondly, "to goods which are destined to meet the wants of the future we ascribe a value which is really less than the true intensity of their future marginal utility", due to defective imagination which underestimates future needs or to defective will-power to resist the attraction of present needs, reinforced by the shortness of human life. This is obviously an irrational difference of valuation over time, and its prevalence has been denied by some.*

---

* "Present goods must have an agio, as legitimate consequence of the constant fact that present goods are more useful and more desired, than future goods, and that they are never present and offered in unlimited abundance. This agio is thus organically necessary' (*ibid.*, p. 336). "If exchange is to take place between present and future commodities, the existence of some gain is an entirely normal phenomenon, is indeed economically necessary" (*ibid.*, p. 361).

Thirdly, the alleged "technical superiority of present over future goods", for the reason that present goods are available to be invested in more productive roundabout methods of production. It has been persuasively argued that this is not really a reason independently of the first ground, and is in fact the basis for the expectation of a higher income in the future on which this first reason for discounting future income compared with present income depends.*

In summary, Böhm-Bawerk explains: "I attempt to show that the technical facts of production, which I describe as the greater productivity of time-consuming methods of production, provide a partial ground for the higher valuation of present goods, the possession of which permits the use of those more productive time-consuming methods. From this point of view the technical and psychological facts are coordinated from the start."† And drawing together the various elements of his theory, he concludes: "The relation between want and provision for want in present and future, the undervaluation of future pleasures and pains, and the technical advantage residing in present goods, have the effect that, to the overwhelming majority of men, the subjective use-value of present goods is higher than that of similar future goods." This relation of subjective valuation is then reflected in the market in "a higher objective exchange value and market price for present goods".‡

During the next three decades there were few issues that divided economic theorists more sharply than this particular way of viewing capital and of determining the rate of interest. The theory had its devoted admirers as well as its critics. Of the former Knut Wicksell can be counted as one, though not uncritical: with some emendations and additions of his own, he certainly accepted the period of production and declared that "in this theory for the first time a real substitute is provided for the obsolete wage fund theory".§ *Über Wert, Kapital und Rente*

---

* For the 'Three Grounds' see *ibid.*, Book v, Chs. ii, iii, iv, pp. 249 *seq.*
† *Geschichte* (4th ed.) pp. 301–2; *cit.* T. W. Hutchison, *A Review of Economic Doctrines, 1870–1929* (Oxford, 1953) p. 169.
‡ *Positive Theory*, trans. W. Smart (London, 1891) p. 281.
§ K. Wicksell *Value, Capital and Rent*, trans. S. H. Frowein (London, 1954) p. 145.

of 1893 was his own restatement and defence of Austrian doctrine.

Among criticisms perhaps the commonest has been the denial that the notion of a period of production corresponds to anything actual in the rôle of capital in production (in which case it would seem that the classical notion of capital as 'advances to labour', however interpreted, is also denied to have relevance to the problem). It has been argued, for example, that in static equilibrium, in the absence of investment, production and consumption are always simultaneous. With a constant stock of capital-goods (of constant age-composition) a certain proportion of this stock is being replaced each year by currently applied labour; and one can regard current output as being produced by the labour currently employed in producing these capital-goods for replacement, without resorting to a notion of labour applied at past dates in producing originally the various items in the existing stock of capital-goods in use. This would seem to be a valid contention when one is within the context of static equilibrium. What it overlooks, *qua* criticism of a theory of capital formation, is that, as soon as net investment is introduced into the picture and changes in the stock of capital, the consideration that enlargement of the stock inevitably takes *time* cannot be excluded; and such a consideration is immediately relevant when one poses such a question as why the existing stock of capital is what it is and could not be so large relatively to labour and natural factors as to reach 'capital saturation' and reduce the marginal productivity of capital to zero.* Would not something at least resembling the notion of a period of production then reappear and the notion of *additions* to final output as being produced wholly by current labour no longer suffice?

More serious, as well as apparently more fundamental, is the criticism of the 'period of production' that it cannot be given any clear quantitative significance. If it cannot, one can give

---

* *Cf.* Schumpeter's statement (echoing Böhm-Bawerk): "if physical capital is to yield not only returns but also net returns, something must prevent it from being produced up to the point at which its earnings would no more than repay its cost" (*History of Economic Analysis*, p. 926).

no meaning either to its constancy (*e.g.* when calculating the marginal productivity of some other factor than capital), or to one period being larger than another, and hence give un-ambiguous meaning to an increase in the period and accordingly in the quantity of capital. When some critics argued that the notion involved one inevitably in infinite regress, Böhm-Bawerk retorted (with justification) that after a certain point in the regress the relevant labour-inputs become so small as to be negligible even when multiplied by the time intervening; and he was content to measure (and compare) his 'average' period as the simple arithmetic mean of the labour-inputs of various dates multiplied by the intervening time.* But the real difficulty goes deeper. One cannot rest content with a simple arithmetic average, since this would not be consistent (when translated into value-terms) with different investments obtaining the same *rate* of profit (which competitive equilibrium, with long-run mobility of capital requires). So soon, however, as compound interest is employed in the weighting of labour-inputs of various dates, it becomes evident that one period of production with a particular time-pattern of labour inputs may appear 'longer' than another (with a different time-pattern) at one rate of interest and 'shorter' at some other rate. In other words, as the rate of interest changes, different time-patterns of labour-inputs may change places as regards the order in which they stand in the ranking of 'periods of production' according to their respective 'lengths'.† To this problem in its fuller implications we shall return in the context of discussion and criticism of so-called 'neo-classical' doctrine in recent decades.

Finally, there is the third stream of innovation associated with Léon Walras and what is sometimes described as the Lausanne School (alternatively the Mathematical School, in distinction

---

* *Positive Theory of Capital*, trans. W. Smart (London, 1891) pp. 88–9.

† For an analogous critique of Jevons's notions of 'amount of investment' and 'average time of investment' (with his assertion that the interest-rate is inversely related to the average period of investment) *cf.* Ian Steedman, 'Jevons's Theory of Capital and Interest', *The Manchester School*, March 1972, pp. 31 *seq.*, where it is cogently argued that "Jevons's theory provides no explanation of the rate of interest".

from the Austrians). Walras, who was mentioned by Marshall no more than three times in his *Principles*, and then only incidentally, is described by Schumpeter as being "in my opinion the greatest of all economists". The reason given for this accolade is that "his system of economic equilibrium, uniting as it does the quality of 'revolutionary' creativeness with the quality of classic synthesis, is the only work by an economist that will stand comparison with the achievements of theoretical physics".* Yet "his professional contemporaries were mostly indifferent or hostile".† Synthesis of various aspects of the new approach into a mathematical system of mutual dependence is certainly his main achievement – this rather than novelty of emphasis or of exposition. But despite preoccupation with mathematical formalism, we have seen that he was quite well aware that the economic interpretation and causal implications of his system were in essentials similar to Jevons or Menger:‡ namely the derivation of product-prices from consumers' wants and of the value of the services of capital-goods and factors from their productive use in the creation of consumers' goods. As Walras said in his *Éléments d'Économie Politique* of 1874: "In the last analysis the utility curves and the quantities possessed constitute the necessary and sufficient data

* Schumpeter, *History of Economic Analysis*, p. 827.
† *Ibid.*, p. 829.
‡ In his Preface to the fourth edition of *Éléments* Walras speaks of "the theory of exchange based on the proportionality of prices to *intensities of the last wants satisfied*" as having been "evolved almost simultaneously by Jevons, Menger and myself" (*Elements of Pure Economics*, ed. W. Jaffé (London, 1954) p. 44). He also speaks of "the Austrian economists" as having "established exactly the same relation between the value of *Produkte* and the value of *Produktivmittel* that I established" (*ibid.*, p. 45). That he was certainly not averse to causal interpretation of his equations is shown by such statements as: "if it is certain that *rareté* and value in exchange are two concomitant and proportional phenomena, it is equally certain that *rareté* is the cause of value in exchange" (*ibid.*, p. 145), or his reference to "underlying price determinants" (*ibid.*, p. 146, and *cf.* p. 307). Pareto was, however, to dissent from Walras's statement on the ground that mutual determination (by a system of simultaneous equations) was to be contrasted with simple causation: "One can declare that any economist who seeks the *cause* of value shows that he has not understood anything of the synthetic phenomenon of economic equilibrium"; it is this "mutual dependence of economic phenomena which renders indispensable the use of mathematics; ordinary logic can serve well enough to study relations of cause and effect" (*Manuel* (Paris, 1909) pp. 246–7).

for the establishment of current or equilibrium prices." "Value comes from scarcity." This standpoint he opposes to that of Smith and Ricardo: "the theory which traces the origin of value to labour is a theory that is devoid of meaning rather than too narrow, an assertion that is gratuitous rather than inacceptable".* And again: "Equilibrium prices are equal to the ratios of the *raretés*", which are defined as "the intensities of the last wants satisfied for holders of the commodities".† The principle that prices in final equilibrium must equal cost of production, together with the principle of marginal productivity, yields a simultaneous determination of prices of products and prices of the productive services (*i.e.* of producers' goods or factors). Entering into such determination are the Walrasian 'technical coefficients' defining the inputs needed to produce a unit-quantity of a given product, which he at first assumed, for simplicity, to be *fixed* coefficients, thereby demonstrating that his general equilibrium solution was possible with this assumption. But subsequently (in his third edition of 1896) he extended the solution to the case of variable coefficients by treating the coefficients chosen as functions of the prices of productive services on the assumption that the least-cost method of production at any given set of prices of productive services was chosen.

As with Menger and Wieser, however, the Walrasian system was confronted with the question as to what to take as 'given' on the side of supply. So far as the conditions of static equilibrium were concerned, specific capital goods were assumed to be present in certain quantities as part of the data of the historical situation; the respective productive services of these being valued in the usual way, in conjunction with the technical coefficients and the prices of products. Durable capital goods then derived a value by the process of capitalising the market valuation of their respective productive services per unit-period. But no theory of profit could arise from this: the latter were determined as Marshallian quasi-rents, and there was no

---

* Walras, *Elements of Pure Economics*, pp. 143, 202.
† *Ibid.*, pp. 143, 145. He adds that "value in exchange, like weight, is a *relative* phenomenon; while *rareté*, like mass, is an absolute phenomenon" (p. 145).

reason why the valuation of particular durable goods should bear any close relation at all to their reproduction-cost. To surmount this difficulty, Walras had resort, in a less static context, to a market for savings, which directed these towards investment in new capital goods that had a relatively high valuation compared with their cost. In this way, in the course of a change in the amounts (and hence *raretés*) of diverse capital goods, a tendency was established towards a uniform rate of return (*via* the value of their productive services as a ratio to their own value and cost).* In terms of the controversies of the 1930s, this has been called a 'loanable funds' theory.† But since the rate of profit has first of all to be assumed in order to give the value and cost of capital goods a meaning, this would seem to be a questionable procedure for establishing, not merely a tendency towards *uniformity* of rates of return, but a determinate unique *level* of this rate of return on capital in long-term equilibrium.‡ Indeed, as a way of constructing a theory of profit, this resort to a market in 'savings' becomes more curious and more questionable the more one examines it.

One could carry criticism of this approach further in terms such as these. If the situation is handled in terms of concrete capital-goods (dispensing with the *genus* of 'capital' as a supposedly scarce factor), then if these goods are reproducible there should be no reason for any positive rate of profit at all in

---

* *Ibid.*, pp. 267–306.
† F. A. Lutz, *The Theory of Interest* (Dordrecht, 1967) p. 81.
‡ *Cf.* P. Garegnani, *Il Capitale nelle Teorie della Distribuzione* (Milano, 1960) pp. 112–21. Wicksell regarded Walras's theory on this point as "certainly incorrect" and as resting "upon incorrect assumptions", hence it "cannot be regarded as definitive" (because lacking the Jevons–Böhm-Bawerk concept of a period of production and the marginal productivity of lengthening this) (*Value, Capital and Rent* (London, 1954) p. 167). He later pointed out that "it is futile to attempt – with Walras and his followers – to derive the value of capital goods from their own cost of production or reproduction; for in fact these costs of production include *capital* and interest ... We should, therefore, be arguing in a circle" (*Lectures on Political Economy*, trans. E. Classen (London, 1934) Vol. I, p. 149). In the same context he drew attention to the crucial consideration (although without developing its implications, save for a minor anomaly) that "whereas labour and land are measured each in terms of its own *technical* unit ... capital, on the other hand ... is reckoned, in common parlance, as a sum of *exchange value* ... In other words, each particular capital-good is measured by a unit extraneous to itself" (*ibid.*, p. 149).

strictly static conditions.* If all inputs other than labour are produced inputs, whence the specific 'scarcity' from which profit is supposed to arise? If assumptions of full static equilibrium are consistently adhered to, then production in the capital-goods sector of the economy will tend to be enlarged until the output of these goods is severally adapted to the need for them; this need consisting of current replacement of the existing (equilibrium) stock of machines, etc. in industries producing for the consumer (on a scale determined by final demand) and in the capital-goods sector itself. With the supply of them fully adapted to the demand for them for purposes of current replacement, there will no longer be any ground for their prices to be above the (prime) cost of their own current replacement (or depreciation).† At any rate, this will be the case in static equilibrium with fixed coefficients: *i.e.* with a single available technique in each industry.

But will not this cease to be the case if the assumption of fixed coefficients is dropped? Then each industry will be confronted with a whole set of alternative techniques (Professor Joan Robinson's 'spectrum'); and as profit (or interest) falls, increasingly costly, more capital-intensive equipment will become economically viable. In face of these (possibly infinite) possibilities of 'deepening' will not the 'scarcity' of capital-goods re-emerge, since existing productive resources will set a limit to the possibility of extending the 'deepening' process further, and hence to the extent to which resort can be had to the more attractive, yet costly, capital-intensive types of equipment? Accordingly a positive rate of profit reflecting this scarcity at

* In this connection *cf.* Keynes's judgement: "I feel sure that the demand for capital is strictly limited in the sense that it would not be difficult to increase the stock of capital up to a point where ... the aggregate return from durable goods in the course of their life would ... just cover their labour-costs of production *plus* an allowance for risk and the costs of skill and supervision" (*General Theory* (London, 1936) p. 375).

† In the mind of Walras this possibility might have been excluded by the assumption that saving would have fallen to zero before this position was reached – in other words, the assumption of a positive supply-price of saving. But this seems a precarious assumption on which to rest a theory of profit-determination, especially in modern conditions of large-scale collective saving in the form of company reserves.

any given date will emerge. But what we should have here would be no longer a stationary state with zero net investment: so long as the 'deepening' process continued, there would be a progressively changing situation characterised by positive investment and growth. Its long-period outcome, however, would be again a stationary equilibrium with zero profit, even if the period be an exceptionally long one. In the absence of technical progress, the 'deepening' process would then be complete.

A possible way-out could be (one might call it, perhaps, neo-Walrasian) to appeal to some or all of Böhm-Bawerk's 'three grounds' and to make willingness to augment stocks of capital-goods dependent upon the subjective discounting of future goods compared with present goods. This subjective time-discount would form the basis of a positive rate of return which all the several capital-goods would need to earn in order to be produced initially, or retained in use in certain quantities, and hence of a positive (and uniform) equilibrium-rate of interest. One need hardly add, perhaps, that such a subjective explanation, if it avoided the difficulties associated with the notion of capital as a factor of production,* would share the inherent defect of any theory that starts from the preferences or behaviour-reactions of individuals: namely, in abstracting from all social influences over individual desires and behaviour and in ignoring the distribution-relative nature of any aggregation of such individual preferences or actions. It is well to remember, moreover, that in equilibrium-systems of this kind one may be presented with a set of identities with little or no explanatory value.†

Whatever may be the logic of stationary states, the majority of economists may well feel impatient with attempts at exploring them, and refuse to contemplate anything more abstract than a Marshallian long-period equilibrium with positive net in-

---

* One may well ask whether it would, indeed, escape the type of criticism levelled by Dr L. Pasinetti against the Fisherian explanation (in *Economic Journal*, Sept. 1969, pp. 508–29), seeing that the values of the capital goods would themselves change with changes in the rate of profit (notably when several distinct capital goods were combined in one line of production).

† See above pages 11–12.

vestment and 'secular growth'. With a 'moving equilibrium' of this kind, Walrasian 'scarcity', as applied to capital-goods in general, might seem to be relevant – otherwise continuing capital accumulation would have no point. But so far as explaining profit in terms of Walrasian 'scarcity' is concerned, one is now on another horn of dilemma. Mengerian-type imputation is at least plausible to the extent that production has the form of a straight-line process of given inputs maturing into final outputs. But once continuing net investment and growth are introduced, a significant part of the productive process must have the form, instead, of a circular loop, with outputs ploughed back as fresh inputs* before they have had a chance to emerge as final consumers' goods. It is hard to see how and why in these circumstances income-distribution should be determined by the pattern of consumers' demand rather than by characteristics of the growth-process (and the pattern of production appropriate thereto). According to a now-well-known theoretical growth-model of von Neumann, with a constant (given) real-wage, growth is maximised when prices are such as to make the profit-rate equal to the growth-rate.† The profit-rate is here independent both of the pattern of final consumption‡ *and* of the existing stock of capital; and if it is independent of the latter

* Part of these, it is true, will appear as wage-goods for additionally employed labour – so far as employment is expanding – but a part of them (output of the capital goods sector) will represent raw materials and components and new machines etc. to equip new production processes that are being started.

† J. von Neumann, 'A Model of General Equilibrium', *Review of Economic Studies*, Vol. XIII, No. 1, 1945–6, pp. 1–9. If there be consumption out of profit, the rate of profit, on the assumptions of the Neumann-model, will exceed the growth-rate; the latter will be equivalently lower than its potential maximum (in face of the given real wage level) and the share of profit in total output will be equivalently larger. In other words, capitalist extravagance in consumption benefits capitalists as a class but harms the economy (contrary to the Lauderdale–Malthus thesis). See below, pp. 222–3.

‡ Be it noted that this refers to the pattern of relative demand for various goods (and the degree of their satisfaction), and not to *total* demand for output. It stands to reason that profit can only be realised on output that is *sold*, and must in *this* sense be limited by total demand (investment *plus* non-wage-earner spending). Nor is this inconsistent with the ratio of profit to wages being equal to the ratio of surplus to necessary labour-time (provided the latter is interpreted to mean the labour spent on producing wage-goods). But either of these statements is quite different from a Walrasian-type derivation of relative factor-prices from demand.

as well as of the former, any kind of explanation in terms of factor-proportions or relative factor-scarcity manifestly fails in relevance.*

Walras's successor in the Chair at Lausanne, Vilfredo Pareto, was to develop the theory of consumers' demand in terms of Edgeworthian 'indifference curves', exhibiting demand-curves as derivations of these. In the course of doing so he summarised the problem of general equilibrium in a much-quoted phrase as being the outcome of conflict between tastes and the obstacles to their satisfaction (*i.e.* obstacles arising from circumstances of production and the limitation of factor supplies).† This he did in two main works, the *Cours d'Économie politique* of 1896 and the *Manuel* of 1909. He is usually taken as being the first explicitly to divorce the theory of demand from its roots in Hedonism and Utilitarianism: defining as he did Utility (or *Ophelimité* as he preferred to call it) simply as 'Desiredness' – the quality of being desired by a consumer, irrespective of whether it is capable of giving real satisfaction and contributing to the consumer's welfare. As such he treated it as a purely ordinal magnitude, and moreover as something that was not comparable as between individuals, and hence not capable of being *added* together in order to form a total for a group or for society. Beyond this and an emphasis on the greater realism of assuming fixed coefficients for dealing with problems of production and the determination of factor-prices ("coefficients are partly constant or almost constant and partly variable"),‡ and some excursions into applied problems, he did little more than trans-

---

* Professor Sir John Hicks has suggested the possibility of a compromise (and apparently pragmatic) position: "I would not now maintain that *the* theory of factor distribution is that which runs in terms of production functions and elasticities of substitution, but I would not abandon that theory altogether. The light that it casts upon the practical problem may not be a very bright light, but neither is that which is cast by the Growth Equilibrium theory. We need, at the least both of these approaches" (*Capital and Growth* (Oxford, 1965) p. 172). This conclusion seems to rest on the presumption that it is possible to have a plurality of partial truths and that to admit this is pragmatically justified. But it scarcely seems possible to go far in this manner without becoming involved in uncertainty and contradiction (unless the implication be that the two theories are reconcilable).

† *Cf. Manuel d'Économie Politique*, (trans. A. Bonnet, Paris, 1909) pp. 150 *seq.*

‡ *Ibid.*, p. 636.

late the Walrasian system into a more accessible form. In later years his interest was to shift towards sociology on which he was to write a treatise.

The contrast, and opposition, between the mathematical 'interdependence' of the Walrasian system and what has been called the 'causal-genetic' approach of the Austrians (*i.e.* the latters' emphasis on simpler straight-line linkages of cause and effect) was specially emphasised by Pareto; this bearing some analogy with Marshall's attitude towards Jevons (although in the main Marshall eschewed mathematical methods, outside appendices, and favoured a 'partial equilibrium' approach). In this respect Pareto managed to be *plus royaliste que le roi*, and even expressed disapproval of certain statements of his predecessor which he thought yielded too much to the 'causal' view.* In this exclusive emphasis on mutual dependence he seems to have been as crudely one-sided as Jevons or the Austrians sometimes were in the opposite sense of depicting situations or processes in too simple uni-directional causal chains. To some extent, no doubt, the contrast can be explained by concern with different levels of abstraction. But enough has perhaps been said in our first chapter to suggest that the dichotomy is an unreal one, so far at least as the subject-matter of economics is concerned, and that once a system like the Walrasian is given an economic interpretation – and *a fortiori* economic application – a *determination* of some factors by others necessarily emerges. This is, indeed, how the master himself seems to have regarded it; and in such an interpretation any *substantial* difference between his approach and that of the Austrians or of Jevons surely disappears.

---

* *E.g.* the passage to which we have already referred in *Éléments*, pp. 307–8, and Pareto's comment in *Manuel*, p. 246n.

REKINDLING OF DEBATE

I

According to Professor Shackle the 1920s saw the opening of an "Age of Turmoil", succeeding "the Age of Tranquillity . . . across the great divide of the 1914–18 war."* To most economists of the time the major theoretical innovations since then would appear to have been the so-called 'Keynesian revolution' (eclipsing the 'Jevonian') and the attempt of Growth Theories from the 1940s onwards to supply something by way of an economic dynamics to redress previous concentration upon static equilibrium. These developments are commonly and alternatively described as a shift of focus back again from 'microscopic' phenomena to 'macroscopic', with which the classics were more largely concerned – to a concern with aggregates and with aggregate relations instead of with particular products and their individual prices. The two events following in fairly quick succession, the one upon the other, were clearly not unconnected, since interest in the wider horizon was implied in Keynesian preoccupation with levels of aggregate output and employment; and it was an easy and rather obvious passage from examining the determinants of the level of output in macroscopic perspective to examining the reasons why the level of output *changed*.

To these two developments some would no doubt feel inclined to add two others as being worthy of comparable emphasis. First, the new theory of 'imperfect competition' and 'monopolistic competition' (associated especially with the names of Joan Robinson and Edward Chamberlin)† deserves to be

* G. L. S. Shackle, *The Years of High Theory* (Cambridge, 1967) p. 289.
† Henry Sidgwick, in listing his "qualifications and exceptions" to *laissez-faire*, had drawn attention to the quite common case under competition where "each producer thinks himself likely to gain more on the whole by keeping up the price of his services rather than lowering it to attract custom"; associating this with retail trade and "established goodwill or business connection" and with the "social waste" of advertising (*The Principles of Political Economy*, 2nd ed. (London,

regarded as an outstanding landmark on the horizon of the inter-war decades. A landmark it certainly was so far as the interest it aroused among academic economists at the time and the attention devoted to it.* Its story has been very fully told by Professor Shackle† and it would be pointless to duplicate his admirable account. It can be said, however, of this development, important as it no doubt was in its own right, that it affected relatively little the general corpus of economic theory as an analytical and conceptual framework. In one respect, namely for the policy-implications of theory, it was quite devastating: namely, in dealing a fatal blow to the doctrine of *laissez-faire* so far as this rested on the alleged 'optimising' character of a *régime* of competitive pricing – for which reason many stoutly resisted the conclusion that the resulting prices in an 'imperfect' market were likely to diverge significantly from those of perfect competition.‡ Perhaps one of the most unsettling conclusions that emerged (from Chamberlin's treatment of selling-expenditures, to which the level and elasticity of demand were related) was that once advertising and salesmanship were admitted as a market influence, very little could be definitely said about price-determination, let alone about 'normal prices', since demand had so largely become the creature of the 'adman' and the so-called 'hidden persuaders'. At first attention was focussed on imperfect competition as a theory of pricing at the microscopic level of particular industries and product-markets. Little attention was paid§ to its signifi-

1887) p. 411). One might regard the theory of imperfect competition as a working out and generalising of this case.

* It could be said to have developed largely out of a discussion in the 1920s about increasing returns, both privately in Cambridge and in the pages of *The Economic Journal* – a discussion sometimes referred to as 'empty economic boxes'. This discussion raised the question: how is the existence of economies of scale, if internal to the firm, consistent with the existence of (apparent) competition? *Cf.* R. F. Harrod, 'Theory of Imperfect Competition Revisited', *Economic Essays* (London, 1952) p. 174: "The 'Law of Increasing Returns' played an important part in the origins of thought about imperfect competition."

† Shackle, *Years of High Theory*, Chs. 3–6. This author very justly begins the story, and dates the discussion, from the famous Sraffa-article in *The Economic Journal* of 1926, which he dubs "the Sraffa Manifesto of 1926" (*ibid.*, p. 12).

‡ *Cf.* Harrod, *Economic Essays*, pp. 139 *seq.*

§ The exception was Joan Robinson's chapter, 'A World of Monopolies' in Book x of *The Economics of Imperfect Competition* (London, 1933).

cance on a macroscopic scale. So far as its significance for the theory of distribution was concerned, this was left for Kalecki to develop as a distinctive contribution; and to this we shall revert when we come to him in another context.

Secondly, much discussion (to judge *e.g.* by space in journals) was devoted to the development of what came to be called 'welfare economics' (even 'the *new* welfare economics')* as a special application, if not a special branch, of economic analysis. Such discussion was stimulated particularly by a neo-Paretian vogue for denying the possibility of inter-personal comparisons of mental states, and hence of utility or welfare, and for purging normative economics of considerations concerning income-distribution. For economics in its relevance to policy-making this new branch of normative (or 'optimising') applications has at least potential importance that makes it deserving of some attention.

Economists who (like Schumpeter) attach special value to the perfecting of formal techniques of analysis would doubtless wish also to emphasise the rapidly growing vogue of mathematical economics and econometrics since the Second World War. This vogue was stimulated in part by Leontief's pioneering work in input–output analysis; but it could also be regarded as reviving and extending the tradition of a pioneer such as Cournot, of Jevons, the little- (or less-) known Auspitz and Lieben and Dmitriev and above all of Walras. Perhaps this development might have come sooner but for the weight of Marshallian influence (in English-speaking countries, at least) in playing down mathematical formulation as unsuitable in the main to the problems with which economics had to deal. To this day opinion has varied quite sharply on how far it is at best mere formal refinement and how far a substantial contribution to economic understanding – or, in Wicksteed's phrase, a "reagent that will precipitate the assumptions held in solution in the verbiage of our ordinary disquisitions".†

---

* *Cf.* G. J. Stigler, 'The New Welfare Economics', *American Economic Review*, Vol. XXXIII, No. 2, June 1943, p. 355.

† P. H. Wicksteed, *An Essay on the Coordination of the Laws of Distribution* (London, 1894) p. 4.

Finally (and chronologically most recently) there has been a growing critique of economic theory in its post-Jevonian dimensions and conceptual framework, particularly as a theory of distribution, to which we shall devote exclusive attention in the next and final chapter. This critique has gathered momentum in recent years, and especially since 1960. To those outside the range of this critique, or unconvinced by it (and these may well include the great majority of transatlantic economists), the attention here given to it may seem excessive. But this attention at least accords with the interpretation that we have adopted of earlier (especially classical) doctrinal trends; and consistency in this respect must be (in part at least) its justification or excuse.

The 'Keynesian Revolution' can scarcely be put on a level with the Jevonian, despite its author's statement that "the matters at issue are of an importance that cannot be exaggerated".* For one thing, its effect upon the general conceptual framework of economic theory went less deep, whatever the significance of its policy-implications for the conduct of a modern capitalist economy may have been. More evidently and directly than in the case of that earlier event, it reflected contemporary events and problems: namely, the deflation, wage-reductions and unemployment of the 1920s and the world economic crisis and accentuated unemployment of 1929–32. What the doctrinal change illustrates particularly well is the strength with which existing theory that has hardened into a dogma can exert a paralysing effect upon the human mind and vision, blinding it to the most obvious truths thrown up by experience and inhibiting the capacity for even asking the right questions (*vide* the well-known reference in the Preface to the *General Theory* to the author's "long struggle of escape – a struggle of escape from habitual modes of thought and expression", *i.e.* escape from old ideas "which ramify, for those brought up as most of us have been, into every corner of our minds").

---

* J. M. Keynes, *General Theory of Employment, Interest and Money* (London, 1936) p. vi. He himself did not claim that his book would revolutionise economic *theory*, but he did that it would "largely revolutionise . . . the way the world thinks about economic problems" (Letter to Bernard Shaw, *cit*. in R. F. Harrod, *Life of J. M. Keynes* (London, 1951) p. 462).

The ideas involved in this arresting change were admittedly extremely simple, even though they exercised something like a shock-effect on minds reared in traditional habits of thought. They did nothing to challenge or disturb the existing (post-Jevons) theory of value and distribution, and may be said to have moved within it as a general framework. They challenged traditional doctrine only at one crucial point: namely, its assumption of a unique position of static equilibrium, with full employment of all available productive resources as a necessary condition.* Although in practice various frictions might impede the attainment of such an equilibrium at any one time, the system was supposed to have an inherent tendency towards it; with the implied corollary that policy should be directed to-wards modifying or removing the frictions rather than to any other kind of intervention. The reason for the assumption was that in any other position than the unique one relative prices in the system (including factor-prices) would tend to move, and such movement, whether large or small, would suffice to shift output and employment towards equilibrium:† whence the corollary that if there were signs of permanent unemployment, this must be evidence that wages were too high (a corollary of Pigou's theory that Keynes was especially concerned to attack). As against this contention, the new theory asserted the possibility of equilibrium being attained at *any* level of output and employment (*i.e.* employment of labour *and* of productive equipment); with either no necessary tendency in such a situation for relative prices to shift or in the event of such a shift no appropriate response on the part of output and employment.

This was, of course, harking back to the controversy between Ricardo and Malthus about 'gluts' and the traditional interpretation of 'Say's Law' as meaning that a state of general over-

* Keynes interpreted this to imply that "the utility of the wage ... is equal to the marginal disutility" of labour at a given level of employment, and the wage simultaneously "equal to the marginal product of labour", thus excluding the possibility of "involuntary unemployment" in his sense of the term (*General Theory*, pp. 5 *seq.*).

† It was this assumption that Oskar Lange was concerned to examine critically in his important (but at the time too-neglected) study, *Price Flexibility and Employment* (Bloomington, Indiana, 1944).

production was impossible because in general "supply always creates its own demand".* Keynes himself recognised that he was retracing the steps of this old controversy, and sought to rehabilitate Malthus (also other heretics of like *tendenz* such as J. A. Hobson) as one who had seen the truth and championed it against Say and Ricardo (which had the incidental disadvantage of causing him to identify the traditional view that he was opposing with the 'classical school'). This reference to Say's Law and its specific corollaries might lead one to assign the new doctrine to the pigeon-hole of 'trade-cycle theory', as a special explanation of how depression can become chronic – even in Schumpeter's phrase a new type of "breakdown theory" ("though Keynes' 'breakdown theory' is quite different from Marx's, it has an important feature in common with the latter: in both theories, the breakdown is motivated by causes inherent in the working of the economic engine, not by the action of factors external to it").† But to relegate it to a specialised department of the subject in this way would be to belittle its generality and its significance as a critique of accepted theory of market-equilibrium at a macro-level.

The justification of the contention that 'supply creates its own demand' is that all income is either consumed or invested, and hence in one way or the other is spent as demand for output either in the market for consumers' goods or in the market for capital goods (or for labour). This was the sense of Ricardo's assertion: "I deny that the wants of the consumers generally are diminished by parsimony – they are transferred with the power to consume to another set of consumers."‡ It was equivalent to saying that investment always equalled saving: that if the latter increased or decreased, it would in some esoteric manner bring about a change in investment in the same direction and of equivalent amount; and this irrespective of whether

---

* *Cf.*: "The gist of this Keynesian criticism [of orthodox economics] can be summed up simply as a flat rejection of what has come to be known as Say's Law of Markets" (Paul Sweezy in *Science and Society* (Fall, 1946) reprinted in Seymour Harris (ed.), *The New Economics* (New York and London, 1947–8) p. 104).

† In Seymour Harris (ed.), *New Economics*, p. 94.

‡ *Notes on Malthus*, Vol. II of *Works and Correspondence*, ed. Sraffa, p. 309.

those who did the saving and those who initiated investment were identical people (*e.g.* some early Victorian captain of industry) or quite different persons. To the ears of common-sense this was a strange, if not monstrous, assertion. Was income never 'hoarded'? Did individual thrift never take the form of holding money or adding to bank deposits? Everyday observation suggested that this was certainly a common case. Whose magic wand decreed that every increase of bank or savings deposits would be forthwith matched by increased investment by businesses? The economists' answer to this, sometimes but not always made explicitly, was that interest-rates were the equilibrating mechanism. Like any other price in a market, interest could be represented as varying as the intersection of a supply-schedule of savings and a demand-schedule; the latter depending on the desire or willingness of business *entrepreneurs* to borrow funds to finance investment. If the will to save increased in face of any given interest-rate, this was equivalent to a shift in the supply-schedule to the right. With demand for borrowing unchanged, this would involve a point of intersection at a lower interest-rate: in other words, interest-rates would fall until more borrowing was encouraged and hence more investment. Equality of saving and investment, if not true at each moment of time, existed as a continual and fairly quickly-operating equilibrium-tendency in the presence of a developed capital- and credit-market.

It was this very pivot of Say's Law that became the central point of Keynes's attack against what he chose to call the 'classical' doctrine. He denied that the rate of interest could be regarded as determined by the supply and demand for savings, or that the interest-rate could be regarded as a mechanism whereby changes in the desire to save exerted a causal influence, in the requisite sense, upon the level of investment. It could not be so regarded because the amount saved was a function, not only of thriftiness, the distribution of income and the rate of interest, but *also* of the level of total income; and the latter could not be regarded as independent of the amount of invest-ment (and hence of the level of output and employment). If

8

the two equations defining respectively the supply- and demand-schedules were not independent, the traditional view of the determination of interest-rates was fallacious.*

This denial of the crucial role of the interest-rate as equilibrator of saving and investment led directly to the Keynesian theory of employment-determinants. Given the 'propensity to consume', and hence the proportion of any given income that will be spent by individual consumers (on which the size of R. F. Kahn's 'Multiplier' depends), the level of output and employment will be a function of investment. According to the level at which investment (also consumption) stands, the level of output and employment may be almost anything between zero and full-capacity output. There is at any rate no longer any unique level to which the system is necessarily tending. So far as investment consists of private investment, it will remain governed by the 'marginal efficiency of capital' (anticipated profitability), modified, on the one hand, by 'expectations' (powerfully swayed by 'business mood' and the like), and on the other hand by the cost of borrowing, namely the prevailing rate of interest. So far as it was public investment by government bodies, such considerations might well not enter in, and its volume would simply be postulated as an independent variable. Thus was the causal emphasis of theory reversed: instead of any change in saving being translated into an equivalent shift of investment, investment became the independent and (*via* income-changes) the volume of savings the dependent variable.†

---

* *Cf.* R. F. Harrod in Seymour Harris (ed.) *New Economics*, pp. 593–4: "I suggest that the most important single point in Keynes' analysis is the view that it is illegitimate to assume that the level of income in the community is independent of the amount of investment decided upon. No results achieved by the short-cut of such an assumption can be of any value."

† In the *Treatise on Money* of six years earlier something of this kind was already hinted at. There the excess or deficiency of investment compared with saving was depicted as playing the crucial rôle in determining business profits and movements in the price-level. In the *General Theory*, however, saving and investment were so defined as to be always instantaneously equal (the former being the difference between individual and company incomes and what was spent on consumption; the latter the difference between total output and consumption goods sold; changes in stocks being automatically included in investment). Hence changes in investment effected a change in output and income 'until' saving had changed by an equivalent amount (the higher the saving *propensity*, the lower the investment-multiplier and conversely).

What then of the rate of interest: *if* it had lost its rôle of balancing saving and investment, where did it fit in and how was it determined? Here came the second arresting novelty. Interest was converted virtually into a *money* rate – something influenced on the one hand by monetary policy (affecting the supply of money available) and on the other hand by the current attitude towards it as something worth holding (*qua* bank-deposit, *e.g.*) in preference to other assets (*e.g.* bonds). This latter constituted the famous 'liquidity-preference' – a preference powerfully influenced by expectations (or uncertainty) about *future* movements of interest-rates (and hence of bond-prices: *e.g.* if bonds were held, there could be consequential capital gains or losses, the effect of which might swamp that of interest accruing as yield on the bonds). Lest this should open the door to the purely 'monetary theorists' of trade depression and trade cycles, it was emphasised that there was an important limit to the power of monetary policy *per se* to influence the interest-rate in a downward direction: the famous 'liquidity trap' when the preference-schedule for liquidity became highly (in the limit infinitely) elastic. Thereby emphasis was thrown upon the direct stimulation of investment, including extension of government investment, as the policy-specific for curing depression and unemployment.

It may be remarked that while this constituted a theory of depression, precisely fitting the context of discussion within which Malthus and all underconsumptionists had written, it also held out the possibility of chronic or secular stagnation as the spur to private investment weakened. This was an aspect of the matter (the so-called Stagnation Thesis – fiercely contested by many)* that was developed in particular by Alvin Hansen in the U.S.A., with the circumstances of the 1920s and 1930s in mind; and it was this that provoked Schumpeter's reference that we have quoted to a certain affinity with the explanation of crises by Marxian writers. With either the social implications or the details of the latter Keynes himself, of course, would have

---

* An outstanding, but far from solitary, example in America was Professor T. McCord Wright.

had scant sympathy: despite an inclination *épater les bourgeois* and to patronise heretics, he went no further than the position of an interventionist liberal, alive to the needs of his time; and his aversion to socialist ideas hardened rather than abated as the decade of the 1930s advanced. The policy-implication to which his new theory led was, as he himself saw it, the need for (and the viability of) a concerted 'full employment' policy by government through the instrument of State spending or investment, and fiscal or budgetary policy; the precise admixture of which was for practical experience, illuminated by the new concepts, to decide. Others may have seen the theory as pointing further; but it can hardly be decided on simple *a priori* grounds whether they were right or he.

What of the pre-Keynesian contention that 'wage-flexibility' (meaning in practice wage-reductions) would always suffice to lessen unemployment, by widening profit-margins and stimulating increased output and investment? Keynes's answer was again a contemptuous, iconoclastic denial. How could it be assumed that the price-level would not fall if wage-cost fell? In all probability prices would fall *pari passu* with wages, in which case the alleged stimulating effect would be *nil*. This probability could be held to rest, either on the conception of competition in a buyers' market in the short-period quickly aligning prices with (marginal) prime costs,* or upon the assumption of non-wage-earners' demand being fairly inelastic† in the short run, so that any response that this demand might make to an initial price-fall would involve a time-lag, during which (unless the propensity to consume generally had risen) non-wage incomes‡ would very soon have fallen by as much as had the price-level. About the only concession he was willing to make to his critics was that there might possibly be some positive influence on investment through the small backdoor

---

* Or, in the case of imperfect competition or monopoly, equating marginal revenue and marginal cost, with price still bearing the same proportionate relation to the latter as it did before.

† Kalecki, whom we mention immediately below, explicitly assumed that "the personal consumption of capitalists is relatively inelastic" (*Studies in the Theory of Business Cycles 1933–39* (Warsaw and Oxford, 1966) p. 3).

‡ At any rate those of profit-receivers.

of the transaction-demand for holding money and hence on interest-rates (but if so, why not achieve a like result simply by expanding the supply of money?).

When we come to Michal Kalecki, whose criticism of previously accepted doctrine ran on closely similar lines, we meet categories of thought that are much more reminiscent of Marxist discussion of the so-called 'realisation problem'. His work could, indeed, be regarded as a formalisation of that 'realisation problem'; and, except for his starkly formal and mathematical presentation, Marxists could find themselves in a familiar world. One source of inspiration for him is clearly Rosa Luxemburg;* and since his first enunciation of his theory anticipated (quite independently) the *General Theory* by three years, economists could have spoken (and some have) of the 'Kaleckian revolution'. But since his early writings were mainly in Polish,† they made no immediate impact upon Anglo-Saxon or even continental discussion.‡

The position from which Kalecki started was a remarkably simple one, even if the conclusions to which it led had the air of sharp paradox. He used a simplified two-class model of wage-earners and capitalists (the former spending all their earnings and the latter doing all the investing), in which such profits (gross) as capitalists as a class are able to realise in a closed system depend upon the amount that this class itself spends on consumption and gross investment. ($P = C + A$, where C stands for goods consumed by capitalists and A for gross accumulation of capital – it was as simple as that!)§ Applying this to the mechanism of business cycles, he assumed that accumulation or investment would vary with the expected rate of profit on capital: a rate (and hence motivation to further investment) that would vary positively with investment itself, but negatively with the existing stock of capital, whose rate of change itself

* This he acknowledges in his Foreword to *ibid.*, p. 1, where he speaks of "a certain affinity" with the theories of Rosa Luxemburg.
† Save one article in *Revue d'Economie Politique*, March–April 1935.
‡ They only began to do so after the publication in English in 1939 of his *Essays in the Theory of Economic Fluctuations*.
§ He then divides C into a constant part B_0 and a part proportional to gross profits, which he writes as λP, so that $P = B_0 + \lambda P + A$.

depended (subject to a short time-lag) on investment-activity in the recent past (or in a slump on *dis*investment). In a business-upswing, after a certain time, the second influence – increase in amount of capital equipment – starts to put a brake on "the rate at which investment activity is increasing, and at a later stage causes a decline in investment orders". Hence the upswing or boom is destined to be no more than short-lived. Once declining investment has reached the point where it no longer covers current replacement, the stock of capital also starts to decline, the mechanism goes into reverse and a cumulative depression sets in until decline in the rate of profit is halted. As he was to put it later: "The tragedy of investment is that it causes crisis because it is useful. Doubtless many people will consider this paradoxical. But it is not the theory which is paradoxical, but its subject – the capitalist economy."*

In his 1933 booklet in Polish he explained this mechanism as follows: "An increase in investment orders calls forth an increase in the production of investment goods which is equal to the gross accumulation. This in turn causes a further increase in investment activity . . . However, after an interval of time . . . has elapsed from the time when investment orders have exceeded the level of replacement requirements, the volume of capital equipment starts to increase. Initially this restrains the rate at which investment activity is increasing, and at a later stage causes a decline in investment orders."†

Later in the same essay he writes as follows, to meet possible doubts about his general approach: "The conclusion that the increase in capitalists' consumption increases in turn their profits, contradicts the common conviction, that the more is consumed the less is saved. This approach which is correct with regard to a single capitalist, does not apply to the capitalist class as a whole. If some capitalists spend money, either on investment or consumer goods, their money passes to other capitalists in the form of profits. Investment or consumption of some

* *Essays in the Theory of Economic Fluctuations* (London, 1939) p. 149.
† *Studies in the Theory of Business Cycles 1933–1939* (Warsaw and Oxford, 1966) pp. 10–11.

capitalists creates profits for others. Capitalists as a class gain exactly as much as they invest or consume, and if – in a closed system – they ceased to construct and consume they could not make any money at all. Thus capitalists as a whole determine their own profits by the extent of their investment and personal consumption. In a way they are 'masters of their fate'; but how they 'master' it is determined by objective factors, so that fluctuations of profit appear after all to be unavoidable."*

He was later to develop in analogous terms a highly ingenious (if again simplified) monopoly-theory of distribution,† according to which the *ratio* of profit to wages depended on the 'degree of monopoly' in the system as a whole (this determining the possible gross-profit mark-up on prime costs that capitalists could exact), and *total* output, employment and profit were dependent upon the aforementioned demand-factors. One thing that went a long way to achieve simplicity in this analysis was that he operated with an inverted-L-shaped short-period cost-curve. This he defended as being the most realistic in any situation of given technical equipment in any firm or industry. (This very treatment of under-capacity working of equipment as a normal situation could again be regarded as a supposition appropriate to an age of monopoly.) It followed that up to the point of full-capacity working, one was operating subject to constant (prime) cost; output being determined by the intersection of the (negatively inclined) marginal revenue curve (relevant to any partial monopolist) with this horizontal cost-curve, and the price determined by the equivalent demand-price for that level of output. As an extension of this Kalecki developed (and quite early, in 1939) an analogous answer to that of Keynes concerning the effect of wage-reductions on employment. Since prices were determined in the manner we

---

* *Ibid.*, p. 14.

† Of monopoly he says: "Monopoly seems to be deeply rooted in the nature of the capitalist system: free competition, as an assumption, may be useful in the first stage of certain investigations, but as a description of the normal state of capitalist economy it is merely a myth" (*Essays in the Theory of Economic Fluctuation* (London, 1939) p. 41).

have just described, as a mark-up on prime costs according to the size of the prevailing degree of monopoly, prices would always fall in the same proportion as wages.* Not only will output and employment have no tendency to increase, they may even possibly *fall* if the degree of monopoly rises (as he suggested there was a tendency for it to do in a slump). He held the constancy of real-wages and of the share of wages in total output in the course of the trade cycle (as well as over longer periods) to be strong empirical support for his theory.

It is clear that monopoly, and monopolistic price-policy, is a factor of which account must be taken in any explanation of distribution that is to fit the modern capitalist world. Some have found ground for criticism in the fact that Kalecki's use of the notion of monopoly-power is represented as the downward slope of the demand-curve facing the seller (and hence of its derived marginal revenue curve). Admittedly, this is a considerable simplification, omitting (or else in some manner subsuming) such aspects as so-called 'monopsony' and sheer bargaining-power in factor-markets, in particular the labour market. On the other hand, is it possible to deal with monopoly and monopoly-price-fixation *except* in terms of market-conditions and hence of the state of demand? Is one not inevitably here within the category of 'market price'? If so, it can hardly be valid ground for criticism that the matter should be handled in such terms. How far it can form a sufficient basis for a general theory of distribution and employment, as distinct from a particular *ad hoc* theory (*e.g.* of the realisation

---

* This conclusion stood in contradiction to the classical contention (*e.g.* of Ricardo – and repeated by Marx in his well-known defence of trade-union action to raise wages in his *Value, Price and Profit*) that if wages rose profits would fall, the average level of prices remaining the same. This was, of course, because they were assuming a commodity-money standard, *i.e.* a gold standard (see above, Chapter 3, page 76–7). In Keynesian language, it *was* possible in these circumstances for workers by bargaining over money wages to determine, or influence, their real wages. Once a commodity-money system is abandoned, however, the price-level is no longer dictated by (and pegged down to) the value of gold relatively to that of commodities other than gold: it is free to vary according to a number of factors, including monetary or credit policy and the price-policies of monopolists. When money-wages rise, monopolist firms are in a position (at least, if demand is favourable) to pass this on in higher monopoly prices.

problem and investment fluctuations), is another question. But then it may well be that, as some have held,* no general determinate theory of monopoly is possible, especially of situations approximating to 'oligopoly'.

The Keynesian formulation of employment-determinants has sometimes provoked criticism because it is couched in terms of psychological 'propensities'; this looking more tenuous, perhaps, in the case of influences affecting entrepreneurial investment than in the case of personal consumption (where it is merely a way of stating a relationship between consumption and income, or its reciprocal the 'savings gap').† Certainly these do not afford any theory of distribution: indeed they do not claim to do so – unless the profit–wage ratio is supposed to depend upon the shape of a short-period supply-schedule (or cost-curve) of output (and hence on the relation between average and marginal cost); in which case it would be purely a short-period and not a long-period theory. It could be said in mitigation that this had no relevance to the immediate issue in hand. The notion of marginal efficiency of investment as an investment-determinant, related as this was to a current *rate* of investment as well as to future expectations, might suggest, indeed, that traditional profit theory, as a theory of stationary equilibrium, was not being called in question or refashioned. Yet this very aspect of the *General Theory* remains, in all probability, its most vulnerable point.

II

There was some discussion in the years following the *General Theory* as to whether the theory as there presented was truly dynamic or still moved within the limits of static assumptions. Some argued that the place accorded to expectations in the determination of equilibrium took it outside the limits of the

* *Cf.* Paul M. Sweezy, *The Theory of Capitalist Development* (New York, 1942) pp. 270–1: "No reasonably general laws of monopoly price have been discovered because none exist . . . Monopolistic price theory rapidly turns into a catalogue of special cases, each with its own particular solution."

† *Cf.*: "All the important Keynesian results are derived from schedules of economic behaviour and not from defined relations among observables" (Lawrence R. Klein, *The Keynesian Revolution*, 2nd ed. (New York, 1966) p. 131).

latter.* Harrod, however, considered this "not enough to make a theory dynamic" since dynamic theory essentially deals with rates of growth of output and income as unknown variables.† Be that as it may, discussion of the issues raised by the *General Theory* about changing output-levels soon directed attention towards rates of growth and their determination, their stability or instability. What undoubtedly clinched the matter, reinforcing the shift of focus, was the growing importance attached to the comparative growth-rates of different countries in the post-war period and the reasons for them.

Already in 1939 Harrod in what was to prove a path-breaking article‡ advanced his Fundamental Equation of what he was to call 'warranted growth' – an equation of "extreme simplicity" (as he was later to call it) and one that was "truistic" in the sense of being "necessarily true" by definition of its terms. What was more important was that he proceeded to pose a number of significant questions, including the question of its stability or instability and of its relation to what he, by contrast, called the "natural rate of growth".

Inspired by discussion of trade-cycle theories, the Harrod-equation drew jointly upon what was coming to be called the 'acceleration principle' and the Keynesian relation called the 'multiplier', and was admittedly inspired by the notion first advanced in Keynes's *Treatise on Money* of 1930 that the relation between the amount saved out of income and the amount devoted (by *entrepreneurs*) to investment in additions to real capital (both treated *ex ante*, according to the terminology of

* Professor J. R. Hicks has defined dynamics as a study "where every quantity must be dated" (*Value and Capital* (Oxford, 1939) p. 115). If outputs and/or prices at future dates needed always to be postulated in order to determine equilibrium, it would seem that this condition was fulfilled.

† Roy Harrod in *Econometrica*, January 1937, reprinted in Seymour Harris (ed.), *New Economics*, pp. 604–5; *cf.* also pp. 41–2, 162, 238–9. *Cf.* also Paul Samuelson: a "dynamical system" is "any set of functional equations which together with initial conditions (in the most general sense) determine as solutions certain unknowns in function of time" (*Collected Economic Papers of Paul A. Samuelson*, ed. J. E. Stiglitz (Cambridge, Mass.) Vol. I, p. 565).

‡ In *The Economic Journal*, March 1939, pp. 14–33. This was restated after the war in some lectures reprinted as *Towards a Dynamic Economics* (London, 1948) Lecture Three, pp. 63 *seq.*

the Stockholm School) was the prime cause of tendencies to expansion or contraction in the economy (*via* the effect of this relation upon prices and profits). The "warranted rate of growth" was defined as "that rate of growth which, if it occurs, will leave all parties satisfied that they have produced neither more nor less than the right amount", or, in other words, "put them into a frame of mind which will cause them to give such orders as will maintain the same rate of growth".* Its equation was $G_w = s/C$, where s represented the proportion of income saved, while C represented the capital–output ratio, or "the value of capital goods required for the production of a unit increment of output". Thus it was "determined jointly by the propensity to save and the quantity of capital required by technological and other considerations per unit increment of output".†

What gave this notion its arresting appeal (involving something of a "mental revolution" as its author claimed) was the assertion that a growth-path defined by this equation was highly unstable, in the sense that any departure from it, on the contrary to being 'self-correcting', would set up a cumulative tendency (at least within limits) to further departure in the same direction. "Thus in the dynamic field we have a condition opposite to that which holds in the static field. A departure from equilibrium, instead of being self-righting, will be self-aggravating. G_w represents a moving equilibrium, but a highly unstable one."‡ The simple essentials of this are easily seen if we conceive of C entirely in terms of working capital; which means that the situation can be expressed in terms of changes in stocks of raw materials and goods-in-process and of the reaction of such changes upon production. Any deviation of the actual

---

* *The Economic Journal*, March 1939, p. 16.
† *Ibid.*, p. 23. If we introduce investment and income explicitly (writing I for investment, S for total saving and Y for income), the above equation can be seen to be equivalent to:

$$\frac{\Delta Y}{Y} \cdot \frac{I}{\Delta Y} = \frac{S}{Y},$$

which amounts to the Keynesian equality of investment and saving *ex post*.
‡ *Ibid.*, p. 22.

growth-rate above G_w will result in a depletion of stocks below normal: this will stimulate fresh orders down the line in an attempt to replenish stocks, which will accordingly stimulate further growth of output. Conversely, a deviation below G_w will cause stocks to be involuntarily accumulated above normal, which will tend to depress production in the following period owing to a decline in replacement-demand by businesses. Thus self-reinforcing "overproduction is a consequence of production below the warranted level."*

The "natural rate of growth" (or G_n) was defined *per contra* as "the maximum rate of growth allowed by the increase of population, accumulation of capital, technological improvement".† The crucial significance of the relationship between G_w and G_n was this: if the former exceeded the latter (*e.g.* owing to a high rate of saving), there would be a persistent tendency to depression with chronic unemployment. Thus a string was provided for the underconsumptionist's bow and a vista opened of chronic stagnation as a quite possible (and understandable) state of the economy. Conversely, if the warranted stood below the natural rate, deviations in an upward direction were likely to result in a series of inflationary situations and booms. At any rate, "there is no inherent tendency for these rates to coincide".‡

About the same time as Harrod's post-war lectures (although subsequently to his pre-war article) Professor Domar, in the *American Economic Review* of May 1947, was expressing substantially the same relationship in what might look superficially a different form. The essence and implications of the two, at any rate, were closely similar; and for this reason many have come to speak of the Harrod–Domar formula as a conjoint product.

---

* *Ibid.*, p. 24.   † *Ibid.*, p. 30.

‡ *Ibid.*, p. 30. It was on this conception that Professor J. R. Hicks was to build his theory of the trade cycle, based on 'explosive' tendencies in the system towards expansion and contraction (depending on the value of a crucial coefficient, which he calls "the Investment coefficient – the ratio of the induced investment to the change in output which called it forth"), contained within a 'floor' and the 'ceiling'. Expansion reaching the ceiling was retarded; this retardation starting a process that carried it down into depression. The (rising) 'floor' consisted of so-called 'autonomous investment' that tended to increase over time (*The Trade Cycle* (Oxford, 1950)).

What Domar was particularly concerned to stress was what he called the "dual character of investment": it both generated increased income (*via* the multiplier-effect) and on the other hand increased productive capacity. The former represented the demand-side and the latter the supply-side (or the potential supply). Given the propensity to save, there was only one rate of growth that would be self-maintaining in the sense that the new capacity brought into being was balanced by an equivalent growth of demand. His formula can be written as:

$$\Delta I . \frac{1}{\alpha} = I\sigma,$$

or alternatively as

$$\frac{\Delta I}{I} = \alpha\sigma,$$

where α is the propensity to save (and hence $1/\alpha$ the Keynesian 'multiplier'); σ is the productivity of investment, the inverse of Harrod's capital–output ratio; and I stands for investment. He adds: "It shows that it is not sufficient, in Keynesian terms, that savings of yesterday be invested to-day, or, as is often expressed, that investment offset savings. Investment of to-day must always exceed savings of yesterday. A mere absence of hoarding will not do ... The economy must continuously expand." Again he says: "In a private capitalist society where α cannot be readily changed, a higher level of income and employment at any given time can be achieved only through increased investment. But investment, as an employment-creating instrument, is a mixed blessing because of its σ effect. The economy finds itself in a serious dilemma: if sufficient investment is not forthcoming to-day, unemployment will be here to-day. But if enough is invested to-day, still more will be needed to-morrow ... As far as unemployment is concerned, investment is at the same time a cure for the disease and the cause of even greater ills in the future."[*]

The ideological implication of a theory that defined an equilibrium growth-path only to emphasise that this was

[*] Evsey D. Domar, *Essays in the Theory of Growth* (New York, 1957) pp. 92, 101.

characterised by a 'knife-edged instability' is quite clear; and for this reason it is scarcely surprising that many economists, especially American economists, were at considerable pains to blunt (at least) its damaging implications. This was achieved mainly by demonstrating (as was done by Robert Solow in the U.S.A. and Trevor Swan in Australia)* that the alleged instability was dependent upon the assumption of a constant C (capital–output ratio). The model could be given greater stability, it was argued, if a more traditional assumption were to be substituted about the flexibility of technical methods (and hence in the value of C) in face of changes in factor-prices, in particular in the ratio of profit to wages. This was equivalent to reintroducing the notion of a 'production-function', which had played a crucial part in the theory of marginal productivity, and of which we shall say more in the next chapter. If refashioned in this way, Harrod's 'warranted rate' would have a long-run tendency (at least) to converge upon his 'natural rate', or ceiling rate; and for the system to grow thereafter at the maximum possible rate consistent with population-growth and technical progress. A high or low savings-ratio (Harrod's s) would then make no difference to the growth-rate, paradoxical as this may seem at first sight: it would affect merely the level of output and of consumption at any date, making this respectively high or low. The mechanism by which this result was obtained was as follows. Let us take the case where Harrod's warranted rate, G_w, is above his natural rate, G_n. Then the high level of the former, by creating labour scarcity, will raise wages, and higher wages will provoke a transition to more capital intensive techniques (and consequently a higher level of output per man employed). This shift in technique will accordingly *lower* G_w by raising the C of Harrod's formula. It is also possible that the income-distribution shift from profit to

* *Cf.* R. Solow, 'A Contribution to the Theory of Economic Growth', *Quarterly Journal of Economics*, Feb. 1956; T. W. Swan, 'Economic Growth and Capital Accumulation', *The Economic Record*, Nov. 1956. Said Professor Solow: If the assumption of "fixed proportions ... is abandoned, the knife-edge notion of unstable balance seems to go with it. Indeed it is hardly surprising that such a gross rigidity in one part of the system should entail lack of flexibility in another" (*loc. cit.*, pp. 65–6).

wages will lower the average savings-ratio, s,* and that this would make a further contribution to lowering G_w. A converse series of changes would occur in the opposite case where G_w was below G_n: mounting unemployment would lower real-wages, which would encourage a shift to less capital-intensive techniques, thus lowering the C of the Harrodian formula.

This attack on the instability-thesis turns out, however, to be less convincing than when first launched it appeared to be. It is open to a rather simple objection. The series of adaptations in question (shift in factor prices and the reaction of these upon the techniques in operation) represents a long-period effect (or series of effects). For them to ensue, it would be necessary for actual growth to persist at the warranted rate for an appreciable length of time. But if the actual growth-path of the economy is highly unstable in the way that Harrod's argument depicts, it is unlikely to stay at G_w for very long, and once it diverges from the latter for any reason it will move further away. In the situation where $G_w > G_n$ it will be prevented from being as high as G_w for more than a very short period, and will accordingly have a pronounced tendency to diverge in a *downward* direction into stagnation with unemployment. Once this has occurred, this downward movement will have precisely the *opposite* effect to what the allegedly-stabilising mechanism requires.†

* This effect was emphasised particularly in Professor Kaldor's theory, and allowed for, as we shall see, in Professor Joan Robinson's (although her emphasis was rather on the effect of income-distribution-shifts directly on investment).

† *Cf.* M. Dobb 'Modern Western Theories of Economic Growth', *Acta Oeconomica* (Akadémiai Kiadó, Budapest) 1966, *Tom* 1, *Fasc.* 3–4, p. 382; also A. K. Sen, 'Interest, Investment and Growth', *Growth Economics*, ed. Amartya Sen (London, 1970) pp. 227–31: "If growth theory is to have any relevance to policy, it cannot do without an investment function, and once this is given a fair play, it is easy to recognise that anything that reduces the 'knife-edge' balance between G_n and G_w will tend to highlight the 'knife-edge' balance between G and G_w ... The difficulty is usually concealed by doing without an independent investment function in the growth models. It is a dodge ..." Sometimes the concept of 'normalcy' is introduced to reduce the *short-run* instability of G_w (*i.e.*, the expectation that G_w will continue because it has come to be regarded as 'normal'). But Professor Sen shows that this can least of all be assumed when G_w is *changing* (as it must be doing if it is allegedly moving towards G_n). "The absurdity of the assumption of G being continuously equal to G_w" can be seen when it is realised that a necessary implication is that "a *rise* in the interest rate *stimulates* growth and a fall discourages it" (*ibid.*, p. 229).

In connection with Harrod's model and its implications one should not omit to mention another criticism of it from a very different (indeed, opposite) angle: namely a little-noticed critique by Kalecki in *The Economic Journal* for March 1962. By contrast with the Solow–Swan criticism that Harrod had exaggerated the instability of growth, Kalecki's sought to show that the Harrodian model was insufficiently dynamic: that the trend-rate of growth it *appeared* to yield was no more than ephemeral and was tending always to relapse into a static position of zero growth, unless a steady stream of innovations was postulated to endow the system with buoyancy. In one sense this might be regarded as a pessimistic extension of Harrod's 'instability' argument, in the shape of the contention that instability in a *downward* direction is more likely than the converse, and that once declining growth has started there is no halting place short of zero. This emphasis is due to Kalecki's view, already expounded in his earlier works, including his *Studies in Economic Dynamics* of 1943,* of the dependence of investment-decisions on current profit, which was in turn dependent upon the investment undertaken (*plus* capitalist consumption) in the immediate past. Since investment had the result (after a certain time-lag) of expanding productive capacity, there would only be sufficient demand to keep this capacity occupied (and to enable profit on it to be realised) if investment continually expanded (thus keeping demand in step with growing productive capacity). Without the intervention of some special 'boost' factor, there was, accordingly, a chronic tendency for new investment to slacken for want of inducement, and once slackened to decline cumulatively towards zero. Thereafter his cycle-mechanism of which we have already spoken would operate around a zero-growth trend-line.

Said Kalecki: "The 'Harrodian rate of growth' is ephemeral

---

* *Cf.*: "Although growth of population or increasing productivity are a necessary condition for the long-run expansion of output if no large reserves of labour are available, these factors seem not to play an important rôle in *inducing* the trend movement. It follows that growing population and increasing productivity of labour may well cause long-run unemployment without setting to work forces which would absorb it" (*Studies in Economic Dynamics* (London, 1943) pp. 88–9).

in the sense that any deviation from the path determined by it renders the system stationary – *i.e.* subject to cyclical fluctuations but no trend . . . The system cannot break the *impasse* of fluctuations around a static position unless economic growth is generated by the impact of semi-exogenous factors such as the effect of innovations upon investment . . . Semi-exogenous factors, such as innovations, enable the capitalist system to break the *impasse* of the stationary state and to expand at a rate dependent on the importance of these factors."*

Inspired by Harrod, but exercising a comparable degree of influence of its own upon subsequent discussion, was the work of Professor Joan Robinson in the middle-1950s, *The Accumulation of Capital.* Her intention also was to propound the conditions for steady growth at a constant rate (what she termed 'golden age' conditions); but like Harrod she stressed the *in*-stability attending such a steady advance, and specified with greater particularity the various snags and obstacles which cause the system, operated according to what she called "the capitalist rules of the game", to run downhill into depression, unemployment and chronic stagnation, or alternatively to explode into cumulative inflation. Despite this general emphasis however, her analysis does include one or two potential stabilising mechanisms that are lacking in the pure Harrod-model: in particular, the tendency of changes in real-wages to effect shifts in "the spectrum of techniques". Thus if the labour-supply increases less fast than capital accumulates, this may lead to a rise in real-wages and thereby encourage a shift towards more labour-saving techniques; and conversely in the case where the labour-supply grows faster than capital accumulates. Alternatively a change in real-wages may react on the rate of accumulation itself: if, for example, increase in labour-supply outruns productive capacity, the resulting fall in money

* 'Observations on the Theory of Growth', *The Economic Journal*, March 1962, pp. 134, 150. Kalecki added this comment: "Several attempts have been made to lend stability to the 'Harrodian' trend movement by introducing additional specific assumptions. These assumptions appear to me highly artificial and unrealistic. In fact, they obscure the problem which was so acutely posed by Harrod instead of solving it" (p. 134).

wage-rates may "make the reproduction cost of capital goods less than their historic cost and so induce some extra investment".* But although the possibility of such equilibrating reactions is indicated, it is also shown that there is no necessity that these should be the result. The actual result may vary with circumstances and in particular with the manner in which the investment-plans of firms react to changes in money-wages. It is to be noted that in Professor Joan Robinson's model profits (and along with them *real*-wages) are primarily determined by the rate of investment (as with Kalecki); and accordingly profit and real-wages cannot be affected unless the rate of investment is affected (or else what is termed *rentier*-consumption).

While this approach has clearly been influenced, as we have said, by Harrod, the ideas bear resemblance in a number of respects to those of Rosa Luxemburg. The resemblance, indeed, both to Rosa Luxemburg and to Marx is more apparent in an article she wrote for *The Economic Journal* of March 1952, entitled 'The Model of an Expanding Economy', than in her book of four years later where she refrains from mentioning either. In this article she wrote as follows: "The meaning of a proposition depends very much upon what it denies. In this respect the model is two sided. On the one hand, it shows that there is no inherent logical impossibility in conceiving of a capitalist system enjoying continuous expansion – it contradicts the view that there is an inescapable necessity for capitalism to run down. On the other hand, the model shows that certain special conditions are required for continuous expansion, and so it contradicts the view that there is, in general, an automatic tendency for capitalism to keep going."†

---

* *Accumulation of Capital* (London, 1956) p. 197. It is pointed out, however, that "a downward drift in money-wages due to a long-run surplus of labour takes the form of falls in wages during periods of buyer's markets, not offset by rises during seller's markets. The impact of a fall in wages is therefore felt at times when it does least good as a stimulus to investment, and the mechanism which tends to adjust capacity to available labour is much weaker when the economy is subject to fluctuations in demand than it would be in golden-age conditions. This strongly reinforces the conclusion that a deficiency of demand for labour relatively to supply is much less likely to be self-correcting than a deficiency of supply relatively to demand" (*ibid.*, p. 197).

† *The Economic Journal*, March 1952, pp. 42–3.

In the same line of descent, though *sui generis*, was a model of stable growth propounded by Professor N. Kaldor in the first place in *The Economic Journal* for December 1957, later reprinted in that author's *Essays on Economic Stability and Growth* of 1960 (and subsequently brought out in a new version some years later).* This model can be regarded as answering in the main a different type of question from the other theories we have mentioned. While it emphasises convergence and stability, it is concerned not so much with stability in the rate of growth as in certain features of the growth-process, especially with the alleged stability over the long period in the capital–output ratio and the share of profit in national income (of which it is claimed that there is strong empirical evidence). But in general implication it falls within the category of those that reconcile the 'warranted' and the 'natural' rates of growth by demonstrating a long-term tendency for the two to converge: in this case by mutual interaction between the two.

According to this theory, growth is a joint product of two tendencies: that of *entrepreneurs* to innovate, thereby raising productivity, and their tendency to accumulate or invest. The capital–output ratio will depend upon the respective rôles played by these two tendencies: *i.e.* upon the respective strengths of productivity-raising technical innovation and of increase of capital. If one of these two tendencies outruns the other, there will be forces at work serving to accelerate, or alternatively to retard, investment; and it is *via* such a 'compensating' mechanism that the long-term tendency towards a stable capital–output ratio operates.

This is represented in a now-familiar diagram, of which the two axes consist of the rate of increase of capital per worker per unit of time $\left(\frac{1}{C_t} \cdot \frac{dC}{dt} \right)$, measured along the abscissa, and the rate of increase of output per worker per unit of time $\left(\frac{1}{O_t} \cdot \frac{dO}{dt} \right)$ in consequence of improvements, this latter being measured

---

* N. Kaldor and J. A. Mirrlees, 'A New Model of Economic Growth', *The Review of Economic Studies*, Vol. XXIX, No. 3, pp. 174–92.

along the ordinate of the diagram. The state of the economy at any one date as regards the rate of growth of output will depend primarily on the 'technical dynamism' of its *entrepreneurs* – their will and capacity for innovating, which is

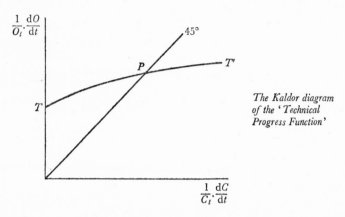

The Kaldor diagram
of the 'Technical
Progress Function'

expressed in the diagram by a curve ($T...T'$) termed 'the technical progress function'. According as this curve is high or low, the growth-rate will be high or low. Investment, on the other hand (as represented by a movement towards the right on the diagram) will depend on the prevailing level of profit and on the prevailing relationship between business turnover, or output, and the productive capacity of existing equipment. Thus if one of the two main tendencies outruns the other, there will be forces set to work to accelerate or to retard (as the case may be) the rate of investment, until the conjoint growth-process converges on the 45-degree line, representing a constant ratio of output-growth to capital-growth, and hence a constant capital–output ratio.

Let us suppose, for example, that one happens to be in a position on the $T...T'$ curve to the *left* of the diagram: in this position output will be growing relatively to existing productive capacity, and there will accordingly be an inducement to increase the rate of investment, or in other words to move along the $T...T'$ curve to the *right*. This inducement will be reinforced by the rise of profit that results from a higher rate of investment;* and the rightward movement along the $T...T'$ curve will continue until point P is reached, where the curve crosses the 45-degree line through the origin and the rates of increase of output and of capital are equal. A converse movement would be set in train if one happened to be at any point to the *right* of P: in this case a movement towards a lower rate of investment (since productive capacity was growing faster than output), and with it a decline in profit, reinforcing the decline in investment.

It may have been noticed that, unlike the Harrod–Domar model, this one does not really explain the growth-rate itself – or, in so far as it may be held to do so, explains this in another and quite different sense,† and is not concerned with its stability or instability. The actual level of the $T...T'$ curve in the diagram and hence the growth-rate depends on what is termed the "technical dynamism" of the economy – something that is not much further explained. Unlike Harrod, Kaldor does not make growth dependent on the savings-ratio: this latter affects primarily the level of profit (which varies inversely with savings) and only indirectly the rate of growth (*via* the effect of profit upon investment). As he expresses it: "The prime mover in the process of economic growth is the readiness to absorb technical change combined with the willingness to invest capital in business ventures."‡ Regarding the relation of his own model to that of Harrod, he has written as follows: "The implications of our model in terms of Mr Harrod's terminology could be summed up by saying that the system tends towards

* In Kaldor's model the share of profit in total income is a function of investment, given the savings-propensities out of profits; as he himself writes, "the rate of return on capital depends solely on the rate of economic growth and the division of capitalists' incomes between consumption and savings and is independent of everything else" (*Essays on Economic Stability and Growth* (London, 1960) p. 287). Wages are a residual, depending on productivity (this because profits are regarded as being adjusted to demand *via* changes in prices, with money-wages passive in face of such changes).

† Thus, whereas alternative theories make growth dependent on what are regarded as statistically measurable entities such as the volume of investment, its capital-intensity and the savings-ratio, this theory explains it by a vaguer and less tangible quality of the system – its 'propensity to innovate' or to enhance productivity by improved technique or rationalised methods of work.

‡ *Essays on Economic Stability and Growth*, p. 270.

an equilibrium rate of growth at which the 'natural' and the 'warranted' rates are equal, since any divergence between the two will set up forces tending to eliminate the difference; and these forces act partly through an adjustment of the 'natural' rate and partly through an adjustment of the 'warranted' rate".*

In its emphasis on the 'technical dynamism' of the *entrepreneur*, the Kaldor-theory can be observed to show some affinity with Schumpeter (who made the capitalist *entrepreneur* the centre-piece of development as the innovator *par excellence*). This apparently gives it a conservative implication (so far as least as *entrepreneur* is implicitly identified with capitalist firms). On the other hand, by denying any meaning to the traditional assumption of 'constant technical knowledge' in static theory (and hence to the notion of a 'production function'), he proclaims himself an iconoclast so far as the traditional Marginal Productivity Theory of Distribution is concerned. In his later article on 'A New Model of Economic Growth' (written with J. A. Mirrlees) he writes: "The model is Keynesian in its mode of operation (entrepreneurial expenditures are primary; incomes, etc., are secondary) and severely *non*-neo-classical in that technological factors (marginal productivities or marginal substitution ratios) play no rôle in the determination of wages and profits. A 'production function' in the sense of a single-valued relationship between *some* measure of capital, K_t, the labour force N_t and of output Y_t (all at time t) clearly does not exist. Everything depends on past history, on how the collection of equipment goods that comprise K_t has been built up."†

A novel and intriguing theorem spawned by the literature of growth-models, but having an evident bearing upon concepts of value and distribution, may be worth mention before abandoning our present subject. Perhaps one should speak of

---

* *Ibid.*, p. 285. He further remarks that in his own model "the assumption of given savings propensities...does not define a unique warranted rôle, but is consistent with any number of warranted rates, depending on the distribution of income".

† *Review of Economic Studies*, Vol. xxix, No. 3, p. 188.

two distinct but not unrelated theorems. Of these the first, and perhaps less striking at first glance, known as the Non-Substitution Theorem, is attributable to Professor Paul Samuelson. This states that, with one scarce factor, labour, and all other inputs reproducible inputs, the optimum technique (or set of techniques in various industries) is independent of demand (and hence of the comparative outputs of different products).* In other words, there is in these circumstances one most efficient method of producing each product and a unique level of cost independently of the scale of output: as Professor Hicks has explained its implications, "the Leontief system produces under constant cost, even if methods are (in principle) variable" and "choice of method [is] independent of demand".† The second theorem, christened the 'Golden Rule' or 'Neo-Neo-Classical Theorem', enunciated that under dynamic conditions only when *all* profit is invested, and none devoted to consumption, will the set of techniques be chosen which maximises total production in the sense of permitting consumption to be at a maximum for any given growth-rate (or *vice versa*).‡ This theorem can be seen to derive from two postulates of modern growth-theory: (*a*) that a condition for maximum (balanced) growth is that the profit-rate should be equal to the growth-rate; (*b*) that total profit is equal to the sum of investment *plus* capitalist consumption (from which it follows that, since growth is a function of the former, the profit-rate will exceed the growth-rate in the degree that consumption out of profits is positive). Dr D. M. Nuti has pointedly used this to postulate a second and "more subtle form of exploitation" under Capitalism: "the lower average level of consumption per

---

* P. Samuelson, 'A New Theorem on Nonsubstitution', *Collected Papers of Paul A. Samuelson*, ed. J. E. Stiglitz (Cambridge, Mass., 1966) Vol. i, p. 520. *Cf.* also R. M. Goodwin, *Elementary Economics from the Higher Standpoint* (Cambridge, 1970) pp. 28, 81. As we shall see later, the same applies to prices, since the existence of so-called 'constant returns to scale' is implied in the one-scarce-factor assumption (all other inputs, since they are freely reproducible, being costed and priced in terms of this factor).

† J. R. Hicks, 'Linear Theory', *The Economic Journal*, December 1960, p. 703.

‡ Joan Robinson, 'A Neo-Classical Theorem', *Review of Economic Studies*, Vol. xxix, No. 3, June 1962, pp. 210–14. *Cf.* also Goodwin, *Elementary Economics from the Higher Standpoint*, pp. 80–1: "This result ... has come to be called the Golden

head associated with a sub-optimal technical choice, whenever consumption out of profit prevents the fulfilment of the golden rule".*

III

Treatment of innovations in the field of Welfare Economics (under the flag of the self-styled 'New Welfare Economics') would hardly be justified, perhaps, by our general terms of reference were it not for the unusually strong ideological connotation that this 'normative' branch of economic theory holds. These innovations are relatively remote from the theory of value and distribution as we have treated this hitherto; and although spawning an extensive literature of its own, Welfare Economics to-day is usually assigned (in textbooks and lecture-programmes) no more than a specialised sector or chapter. Yet the space occupied by discussion of it in modern literature is certainly evidence to the increasing prominence given to 'optimising' conclusions in economic theory at large, and may be held to justify some (if only cursory) attention to it here.

In this case the watershed between 'old' and 'new' turned on the so-called 'denial of the possibility of interpersonal comparisons'. Yet this was not so very novel, being an echo, indeed, not merely of Pareto, but also of Jevons of sixty years before. In the 1930s, however, such denial became the fashion with quite remarkable rapidity, especially in America; and was sometimes justified by the desire finally to close the door upon nineteenth-century Utilitarianism. A not-unimportant additional reason, possibly the main one, is not, however, far to seek: namely, that older (Pigouvian) writing about Welfare had derived from the 'Law of Diminishing Utility' the principle that the less unequally a given national product was distributed, *ceteris paribus*, the greater the resulting total sum of utility or welfare would be.† Such pronounced egalitarian conclusions,

Rule because it makes consumption as great as possible subject to the growth rate. It is a direct consequence of von Neumann's analysis with the difference that, whereas he took consumption as given and maximised growth rate, here the growth is given and consumption is maximised."

* 'Capitalism, Socialism and Steady Growth', *The Economic Journal*, March 1970, p. 54.

† This constituted the second of the two main propositions, or principles, of Pigouvian economies of welfare. The first was to the effect that the utility

constituting one of two main Pigouvian propositions in *The Economics of Welfare*, were manifestly unwelcome and embarrassing in certain quarters. It seemed a relief to have a system of welfare economics from which awkward questions about distribution could be excluded; and the 'New' Welfare Economics (priding itself on its rigorous positivism) proceeded to refashion itself in such a way as to make the intrusion of such questions irrelevant and unnecessary. Yet this very unwillingness, or inability, of the New Welfare Economics to pronounce on income-distribution, at first sight so simplifying, was to turn out to be its Achilles heel.

The danger threatening this new approach was that in refusing to compare or aggregate individual utilities, it might jettison the possibility of comparing one product-total with another (something that was evidently required if one wished to talk about maximising a production-total and sought to propound conditions of economic 'efficiency' in such terms). It was to meet this difficulty and to restore the distinction between questions of distribution (which was jettisoned) and questions of production (which could be retained) that Professor Kaldor produced his Compensation Principle. It was always possible, surely, to say, at any rate in principle, in the case of any economic change, such as the repeal of the Corn Laws, whether the gainers from the change could or could not compensate the losers from it and still be better-off than they were originally. If this could be done, the result of the change could be deemed to represent an increase in total production or national income, and conversely. Thus the possibility of compensation as defined was made to constitute the definition of an increase in total output, without resort to any adding-up of individual utilities.* Unfortunately for this as a solution of the theoretical difficulty (as distinct from serving as a practical

derived from a given volume of national income would be maximised if resources were so distributed as to equalise the *social* marginal net product of resources in all uses.

* All that was needed was to define compensation as leaving every individual among the losers 'on the same indifference curve' as before the change, and the amount needed to do this could be calculated in terms of money payments or income.

test applicable no doubt in many actual cases) this Compensation Principle turned out to involve certain rather crucial contradictions.*

Having adopted Pareto's non-comparability of individuals' utilities, the new welfare economists proceeded to employ his notion of an optimum that has come to be known as the 'Pareto-optimum'. At first sight this notion has great attractions. It was defined as a position where, with the money income available to everyone taken as given, no individual could be made any better off without making some other individual (or individuals) worse off. (This was, in fact not a unique position – there was a multitude of such positions, one for each different distribution of money income.)† What better could one hope for as a policy-objective, definable in purely objective economic terms that were independent of distribution, and hence capable of being used as a positivist, *wertfrei* criterion of economic efficiency? As such it was widely, if not quite universally, adopted by writers of economic textbooks. Those who still had a conscience about unequal distribution would take the trouble to point out to their readers that this was to say nothing about 'equity', which was another question worth considering in its own terms and its own right; while at the same time they displayed satisfaction at the opportunity afforded to them by this Paretian concept of confining themselves *qua* economists to questions of economic efficiency pure and simple.

This so far as it went was satisfactory enough and might have been above criticism had it not been for the trap it laid for those unable or unwilling to distinguish between a necessary condition and a sufficient condition for an optimum. As defining a condition (or conditions) needing to be fulfilled for any full optimum to be obtained (*e.g.* the tangency of the price-line to an indifference-curve of each and every consumer, or equality

---

* *Cf.* N. Kaldor, 'Welfare Propositions and Interpersonal Comparisons of Utility', *The Economic Journal*, Sept. 1939, pp. 549–52; reprinted in his *Essays on Value and Distribution* (London, 1960) pp. 143–6. The problems involved and the subsequent debate are discussed in the present writer's *Welfare Economics and the Economics of Socialism* (Cambridge, 1969) Chs. 5 and 6.

† All points along Edgeworth's 'Contract Curve' (points of tangency of indifference-curves) were Pareto-optima.

of rates of factor-substitution in all lines of production) it evidently has an interest and importance for any optimising theory. But so also has some postulate about the way in which income is distributed between individuals as a necessary condition; and in its absence (and we have seen that it has been deliberately excluded by the 'new' welfare economics), these other, so-called Pareto-conditions are quite *insufficient* to characterise a position as optimum. A situation in which they are fulfilled may well be *inferior* to a number of other situations where they are not fulfilled. All economists presumably recognise this when they are confronted with it explicitly (indeed, they are then apt to retort that they have known this all the time). Nonetheless it is a truth that is apt to be forgotten surprisingly often by many, and by no means only by lesser luminaries in the firmament, as two examples below will bear witness.

The trouble seems to start as soon as a Pareto-optimum is identified with an equilibrium reached under perfect competition or free trading; and at once fallacy and confusion seem to intrude. The commonest example is reasoning of the following kind. If consumers are rational and can spend their money-incomes freely, they will severally distribute this expenditure between different commodities so that the ratio of the marginal rates of substitution (or ratio of marginal utilities) is equal to the ratio of their prices (this is the tangency of price-line to indifference-curve of which a Pareto-optimum, when applied to the consumers' retail market, consists). This amounts to saying that consumers in general are in a position where no consumer can improve his own situation further *given* the prices confronting him and his own money-income – which is saying *some*thing, but obviously not very much. It is tempting to conclude from this* that, when combined with the condition that the price-ratio is equal also to the ratio of marginal costs in production, the amounts of any two commodities *A* and *B* being produced are such as to maximise *social* welfare. Yet it is

---

* Since it means that each consumer is indifferent whether a little more of one of the two commodities, say commodity *A*, or more of the other commodity *B*, is produced *at that same price*, since a shillingsworth of both *A* and *B* is of equal utility at the margin of expenditure.

fallacious to conclude this, since the above-mentioned condition, while fulfilled for each consumer severally, can*not* be aggregated. Any such aggregation (*e.g.* into some collective indifference-curve) depends on the distribution of money income, in the sense that the marginal utility of expenditure (or the m.u. of income) will differ between individuals with differences in their incomes, and any process of aggregation will involve a weighting of the various individuals according to these differences.*

Yet it is precisely such a fallacy into which 'new welfare economists' have fallen in attempting to demonstrate the optimal nature of the results of perfect competition in a free market system. Since some may find this hard to believe, we may give two far-from-negligible examples. Professor R. Dorfman in a book on *Prices and Markets* has provided the following demonstration of the virtue of so-called consumers' sovereignty on a 'free market': "Since all consumers purchase at the same (or at least similar) prices, all consumers will have the same marginal rate of substitution between every pair of commodities. We are, therefore, justified in saying that there is a community marginal rate of substitution between every pair of commodities, and that it is equal to the ratio of their price . . . [Hence] we see that in competitive equilibrium every productive resource is being used in such a way that if it were shifted to a different commodity it would not produce goods that consumers valued more highly than the ones it currently produces; every resource is being used as consumers want it to be."† The conclusion, needless to say, is a complete *non sequitur*.‡

---

* Or – if the logic of denial of interpersonal comparisons forbids one to speak of such differences – one must be altogether silent about such aggregation.

† R. Dorfman, *Prices and Markets* (New Jersey, 1967) p. 91.

‡ Sometimes this kind of conclusion is defended on the ground that the author is supposedly assuming some political mechanism, or *deus ex machina*, under the name of 'lump-sum transfers' of money income, whereby income-distribution is made (and maintained in face of price-adjustments) 'ideal'; which seems to be equivalent to suggesting that there is some conceivable Land of Cathay in which competitive equilibrium could be optimal. This conjuring device is then used to enable the writer in question to conclude that there is virtue in making (if not an obligation to make), *e.g.*, price-ratios equal to ratios of marginal cost even in situations where it is patent that distribution is far from 'ideal'.

The same applies to a contention in a widely used textbook in the joint editing of which the same author has played a rôle (along with Professors Samuelson and Solow).* Here reference is made to the double proposition to the effect that "every competitive equilibrium is a Pareto optimum" and "every Pareto optimum is a competitive equilibrium" as constituting "the fundamental theorem" and "the backbone of welfare economics"; from which the conclusion is drawn that a competitive equilibrium is always superior to a non-competitive one.† This is again manifestly guilty of making the concept of a Pareto-optimum carry much more than, as a necessary but not a sufficient condition, it can logically be made to bear.

Apart from these more general issues of welfare-optimising (or some would prefer to say 'improvement'), into which ideological issues necessarily and most obviously enter, exploration of this subject has also involved discussion of a number of more specific questions. These have included the discussion of certain 'exceptions' to the case for *laissez-faire* (independently, *i.e.* of the question of distribution): notably the discussion of increasing returns industries in the 1920s, arising out of the well-known chapters on this subject in Pigou's classic *Economics of Welfare*. Included also was the well-known (and more ideologically charged) debate of the inter-war period about the possibility of economic calculation in a socialist economy, deriving largely from a much-quoted article and book by the Austrian von Mises in the early 1920s (who denied such a possibility), but conducted, so far as English-speaking economists were concerned, mainly in the 1930s. It was in the context of the latter that much of the subsequent discussion of average *versus* marginal cost as a basis for pricing developed (or at least originated); and since the former discussion of the 1920s raised the rôle of 'indivisibilities' in occasioning diver-

---

* R. Dorfman, P. Samuelson and R. Solow, *Linear Programming and Economic Analysis* (New York, 1958).
† *Ibid.*, pp. 409–12. The words used here are that this theorem "provides the fundamental welfare argument against monopoly, against indirect taxes and against tariffs". *Cf.* comment on this in the present writer, *Welfare Economics and the Economics of Socialism*, p. 6on. *passim.*

gence between marginal and average cost, these two seminal debates can be assigned joint responsibility for a series of further analyses of particular cases (e.g. transport, electricity) where the existence of indivisibility entailed special problems involving conflict in some form between 'total benefit' and the attempt to cover total cost in the price charged. But to pursue such specialised excursions into the realm of applied economics would be inappropriate here and the temptation to do so must be resisted.

9

A DECADE OF HIGH CRITICISM

I

It is always difficult to date the birth of a particular set of ideas or trend of thought, and perhaps even harder when this represents a critical reaction against traditional doctrine and an integrated system of related concepts. Any doctrinal innovation has its precursors, its unknown and at the time neglected forerunners, as we have seen to have been the case with the 'Jevonian revolution'. Commonly the crucial moment in the theoretical process comes as a synthesis, 'mediation' or 'overcoming' of previous, more partial criticism, or of 'false starts' and incomplete attempts to explore some new perspective and angle of approach. The real novelty may well be the posing of a new question, or of old questions in a novel way, quite as much as finding the convincing answer. The crucial turning-point, however, is not difficult as a rule to identify in retrospect, even if at the time its significance may have passed unnoticed.

Revival of interest in the classical economists of the Ricardian age may well have had a joint parentage in the shift of focus towards 'macroscopic' questions of which we have already spoken and the new light on Ricardian doctrine represented by Piero Sraffa's edition of the *Works and Correspondence of David Ricardo* of the early 1950s (especially the novel interpretations of Ricardo's theory of profit and of his search for an invariable measure of value, modestly embodied in the editor's General Introduction).* Explicit criticism of post-Jevonian and post-Austrian theory of distribution in terms of marginal productivity or derived demand began to be heard about the same time (*i.e.* the 1950s) from the voice and pen of Professor Joan Robinson in questioning the concept of Capital as a magnitude

---

* *Works and Correspondence of David Ricardo*, ed. P. Sraffa, Vol. I (Cambridge, 1951) pp. xiii–lxii.

independent of the income on concrete capital-goods that the aggregate concept was used to explain. This line of criticism culminated in her *Accumulation of Capital* of 1956 of which we have already spoken in the context of theories of growth, and in which that author abandoned the notion of a continuous 'production function' (in favour of that of a 'spectrum of techniques') along with capital as a magnitude.* This author proceeded to employ the term 'neo-classical' to refer to ortho-dox distribution-theory deriving from Jevons and the Austrians,† and to become a leading critic of that doctrine (of which 'counter-classical' might be a description more consonant with our interpretation in previous chapters). It was, indeed, in response to this challenge that Professor James Meade com-posed his *Neo-Classical Theory of Growth* in 1961.

The true watershed in critical discussion, dividing the older and newer climates of opinion, was undoubtedly the appearance (in 1960) of Piero Sraffa's slender but classic volume called *Production of Commodities by Means of Commodities*; since not only did this launch something of a school among the younger generation of economists – with a *tendenz* that could be described as 'back to the study of Ricardo and of Marx' – but it also provoked a famous, if recondite, discussion of the mid-1960s, commonly referred to as the 'multiple-switching of techniques'

* *Cf.* esp. Ch. 11, 'The Evaluation of Capital.' Here it is pointed out that whereas in the conditions of any given 'golden age', with a given wage-rate and rate of profit, "the value of capital in terms of commodities has an unambiguous mean-ing", "it is by no means obvious how stocks of capital should be compared which belong to golden-age economies in which the rates of profit, or the techniques of production, or both, are different". In this case "the evaluation of a stock of capital goods is insoluble in principle" (*ibid.*, pp. 114–17). Moreover, comparison of the productivity of different techniques or kinds of combination of capital goods, and hence an ordering of degrees of mechanisation, "has an exact mean-ing only for economies in a state of zero net investment" (*ibid.*, p. 119). *Cf.* also Joan Robinson, 'The Production Function and the Theory of Capital', *Review of Economic Studies*, Vol. XXI, No. 2, 1953–4, pp. 81–106, reprinted in *Collected Economic Papers*, Vol. 2 (Oxford, 1960) (the production function "has been a powerful instrument of miseducation", *ibid.*, p. 114); and 'Accumulation and the Production Function', *The Economic Journal*, Sept. 1959, pp. 433–42.

† In the 1953–4 article the term was used apparently in a Keynesian context: "The neo-classical system is based on the postulate that, in the long run, the rate of real wages tends to be such that all available labour is employed" (*Collected Economic Papers*, Vol. 2, p. 126). It had also been used some years before this by other writers, *e.g.* Stigler (1946), *cit.* above p. 166.

debate. The sub-title of this book was, significantly enough, 'Prelude to a Critique of Economic Theory.' One commentator on modern controversy about capital theory has spoken of it as leading ("in spirit anyway") the attack on the marginal theory and method.* Professor Meek, reviewing the book a year after publication, said that it could be alternatively regarded "simply as an unorthodox theoretical model . . . designed to solve the traditional problem of value in a new way", "as an implicit attack on modern marginal analysis", or "as a sort of magnificent rehabilitation of the Classical (and up to a point Marxian) approach to certain crucial problems relating to value and distribution".†

Allusion has already been made to the problem of conceiving of Capital as a magnitude for purpose of the theory of marginal productivity. No more need, perhaps, be said about it than the following brief extension-*cum*-recapitulation. The notion of a production-function is a familiar feature of the traditional theory of the pricing of factors of production. This is commonly represented by a curve depicting the diverse combinations of factors that are available to be chosen from in a given state of technical knowledge; each point on this curve representing a given technical method of production with its appropriate factor combination. One cannot, indeed, conceive of adding an additional unit of one factor to a constant quantity of another (or of others) without changing the proportion in which factors are combined and moving from a point on one 'isoquant' to an adjacent point on another. At any point on the curve the ratio of factor-substitution (or its inverse, the ratio of marginal productivities) must in competitive equilibrium be equal to the inverse of the ratio of factor-prices, since only then will it be the most profitable combination for an *entrepreneur* or firm to choose. It follows that, if relative factor-prices change, the most profitable, or least-cost, technique will change accordingly;

---

* G. C. Harcourt, 'Some Cambridge Controversies on the Theory of Capital', *Journal of Economic Literature*, Vol. VII, No. 3, June 1969, p. 386.

† 'Mr. Sraffa's Rehabilitation of Classical Economics', *Scottish Journal of Political Economy*, June 1961; reprinted in R. L. Meek, *Economics and Ideology and Other Essays* (London, 1967) p. 161.

and in any well-ordered production-function, as wages rise and profits fall, technique will tend to shift in a more 'capital-intensive' direction towards a factor-combination that utilises more capital and less labour.

Unless heterogeneous capital goods are reducible to a single quantity of Capital, it is hard to see how any meaning can be given to an ordered series of Capital–Labour proportions of this kind (or, what comes to the same thing, to the statement that one technical method represents a larger amount of capital per man-hour in production than another method). This can always be done, of course, by valuing individual capital-goods at their current prices; but such valuation, as we have several times seen,* assumes a rate of profit or interest, since the valuation of durable plant or equipment is normally arrived at by capitalisation of its expected returns (or 'yield') at the pre-vailing rate of interest. One's ordering of various technical methods may accordingly be affected by changes in the rate of interest or profit itself. It was to avoid this difficulty (of which he was well aware) that Böhm-Bawerk introduced his 'period of production' as an entity compounded of labour and time. But this did not really surmount the difficulty, save in the straightforward case where inputs of labour were uniform throughout the period:† in other and more complex cases the ordering of different periods, we have again seen, may be different with one rate of interest from what it is with another.

Defenders of the theory of marginal productivity have adopted various devices for giving plausibility if not reality to the notion of Capital as a measurable entity. Sometimes this has taken the form of an 'as if' assumption: the postulation of some primary substance as forming the substratum or origin of all capital goods. This has been variously described in terms of meccano sets, malleable clay, putty and the like: it has been called "the

---

* Above, pages 196, 204–5 and 205n.

† *Cf.* Böhm-Bawerk's reference to "methods of production where the expenditure in original powers is distributed equally over the whole period" (and the "absolute length" and the "average" yield the same result when used as measures) in *Positive Theory of Capital*, ed. W. Smart, p. 90.

malleability assumption".* Such an assumption, needless to say, is quite arbitrary, and the intention in making it is by no means always serious. Professor Joan Robinson has referred to 'ectoplasm' in order to stress the metaphysical character of any such postulated substance.† With more serious intent Professor Samuelson introduced the parable of a 'Surrogate Production Function', to which we shall refer again later. Professor Solow has sought to by-pass the difficulty by claiming that the main propositions of the theory can be stated in a way that makes them independent of any measurement of capital. This took the form of defining 'the social rate of return' on investment in a socialist system in a particular way‡ and demonstrating that this must be equal to the rate of interest. "An important property of the interest rate has been over-looked: . . . however the rate of interest is actually determined, so long as full employment and competitive pricing prevail, the interest rate is an accurate measure of the social rate of return on saving."§

An obvious property of the kind of production-function, or factor-substitution relationship, that we have described is that,

---

* *E.g.* Prof. J. E. Meade's "assumption of perfect malleability of machinery" ("all machines are alike (they are simply a ton of steel)" (*A Neo-Classical Theory of Economic Growth* (London, 1961) pp. 5–6).

† It is not uncommon for statements in economics to have forerunners. This one could be regarded as a late-echo of Piercy Ravenstone's "it [capital] has none but a metaphysical existence . . . it is like the subtle ether of the older philosophers . . . It is not less useful to our economists than that was to the philosophers. It serves to account for whatsoever cannot be accounted for in any other way" (*A Few Doubts as to the Correctness of some opinions generally entertained on the subjects of Population and Political Economy* (London, 1821) p. 293).

‡ This was the ratio of the additional (future) consumption per annum resulting from the investment to the initial and once-for-all amount of consumption foregone in order to make this investment possible; both being valued at the set of prices relative to a given interest-rate (and hence simultaneously determined with the latter).

§ R. Solow, 'The Interest Rate and Transition between Techniques', C. Feinstein (ed.) *Socialism, Capitalism and Economic Growth* (Cambridge, 1967) pp. 30–9. To this the reply was made that to devise a definition and to make what is defined equal to something is to say nothing about how the latter (in this case the rate of interest) is *determined*. *Cf.* A. Bhaduri, 'On the Significance of Recent Controversies on Capital Theory: a Marxian View', *The Economic Journal*, September 1969; L. L. Pasinetti, 'Switches of Technique and the "Rate of Return" in Capital Theory', *The Economic Journal*, September 1969.

as the rate of interest falls, the amount of capital per man used in production must rise: in other words, more 'capital-intensive' techniques must be uniformly substituted for more 'labour-intensive'. If this does not happen uniformly, and throughout the whole range of technical choice represented by the substitution-curve, there is evidently something seriously wrong with the whole notion of a 'production-function' – and, again, with the notion of capital as an independent quantitative entity that can be substituted in defined amounts for other factors of production. It was precisely this crucial property that was called in question as a result of Mr Sraffa's *Production of Commodities by Means of Commodities*. Of the general character of the system that this work constituted, and in particular its relation to the classical, we shall have something more to say in a moment. In a sense, its rigorous demonstration of the possibility of what came to be called the 'double-switching of techniques' with changes in the ratio of factor-prices, came as an incidental corollary of that work. But it represented, perhaps, its most important single contribution to 'a Critique of Economic Theory', and occasioned a debate that will one day, no doubt, become celebrated.

What this possibility of 'switching' amounts to is that, as wages rise and profits fall, a certain relatively labour-intensive technique, A, which is at first in use may be replaced by a more capital-intensive one, B; but at a still higher wage-level (with a correspondingly lower profit-rate) A may once again come into favour as the lower-cost technique and be substituted for B accordingly. To anyone reared in the modern tradition the possibility of such an occurrence appears as an unbelievable paradox. Accustomed as a modern economist is to think of income-distribution as being derived from the price-relations of final products, the idea that price-relations are themselves relative in any large degree to income-distribution, changing with every change in the profit–wage ratio, is apt to sound strange if not alien. Yet it is precisely such a relativity of prices to income-distribution that this possibility of 'switching', previously unnoticed, serves to illustrate. For this reason it should not, perhaps, seem so obscure or surprising to anyone familiar with Marx (or even with Ricardo); since it amounts to changing relative deviations of Marxian 'prices of production' from 'values' – in particular, the prices of inputs and of inputs into those outputs – as wages change and with them the rate of surplus value (or the profit–wage ratio).

To clarify the reasons for this apparent paradox further, one may represent the production-situation in this way. The cost and final price of a commodity can be conceived as the summation of a vertical series of stages of production spread out backwards in time, each consisting of a labour-input *plus* commodity-inputs (machines, raw materials, components) that are products of some earlier stage; each with its labour-input having its attached date in the vertical series. This is what Mr Sraffa has called 'Reduction to Dated Labour'. Manifestly everything will depend, so far as the effect of changes of interest-rates on prices is concerned, upon the manner in which these labour-terms are distributed in time. Let us first take the case of two commodities, one with larger total labour-inputs but these bunched at *recent* dates, and the other with smaller total labour-inputs bunched at *distant* dates. With low wages and high interest the first may come out cheaper despite its larger wage-bill. As wages rise and interest falls, the second will at some stage have the advantage because of its lower wage-bill: an advantage that one would expect it to retain however high wages rose and interest fell. This is the orthodox case to which an ordinary production-function can be fitted. Secondly, one can suppose a case where one commodity has all or most of its labour-inputs applied at some *intermediate* date, the other having some labour at a very distant date but the bulk of it at a quite recent date. It is now quite possible for the second of the pair to have the price-advantage at intermediate levels of interest and wages, but the first one to be preferred (because cheaper) *both* at very high levels of interest (with low wages) *and* at very low levels of interest (with equivalently high wages). The reason is, of course, the possibility of differences in the compounding-effect of interest-rate changes on the comparative cost of inputs of very distant and of intermediate dates. Sraffa's example of this is that of wine and the old oak chest.*

A concise way of expressing it would be to say that in this latter case the result depends on widely different proportions of labour and other inputs at different 'layers' in the vertical production-process. Mr Sraffa has explained the situation as follows. "The relative price-movements of two products came to depend, not only on the 'proportions' of labour to means of production by which they are respectively produced, but also on the 'proportions' by which those means have themselves been produced, and also on the 'proportions' by which those means have themselves been produced, and also on the 'proportions' by which the means of production of those means of production have been produced, and so on. The result is that the relative price of two products may move, with the fall in wages, in the opposite direction to what we might have expected on the basis of their respective 'proportions'; besides, the prices of their respective means of production may move in such a way as to reverse the order of the two products as to higher and lower proportions."†

The relevance of this to the quantity-of-capital issue was immediately underlined: namely, its "bearing on the attempts that have been made to find in the 'period of production' an independent measure of the quantity of capital which could be used, without arguing in a circle, for the determination of prices and of the shares in distribution". The possibility of the type of case we have considered "seems conclusive in showing the impossibility of aggregating the 'periods' belonging to the several quantities of labour into a single magnitude which could be regarded as representing the quantity of capital. The reversals in the direction of the movement of relative prices [as wages change], in the face of unchanged methods of production, cannot be reconciled with *any* notion of capital as a measurable quantity independent of distribution and prices."‡

The debate that followed this was opened by an attempt made

---

* Sraffa, *Production of Commodities by means of Commodities*, p. 37.
† *Ibid.*, p. 15.   ‡ *Ibid.*, p. 38.

from Harvard to demonstrate that it is impossible for 'reswitch-ing' to occur in a whole 'system of production' (*i.e.* where *n* commodities are produced by a number of alternative methods), as distinct from in a single industry.* This 'impossibility' was soon disproved, and shown to involve a mathematical error, by L. Pasinetti and also by P. Garegnani.† In the course of his reply in the *Quarterly Journal of Economics* the latter generalised the question at issue in the following way: "Capital, to be the factor the price of whose service is the rate of interest, must be conceived ultimately as the value, in some unit, of capital-goods; and the value of any capital-good, like the value of any other product, changes with distribution." It follows that "the very possibility of ordering the techniques according to the proportions of capital to labour slips from our hands; that order may change as prices and distribution change". Putting a finer point on it, he then shows that it is not even possible to claim when there is a switch-point between two techniques "that the technique we switch to, as interest falls, is always the one which – when the capital goods of both techniques are evaluated at the prices of the switch point – shows the higher value of capital per man. This claim would be groundless. As the rate of interest falls, the switch can be in favour of the technique requiring capital goods of a smaller, and not a larger value per man."‡ He concluded that "the consequence of admitting this is far-reaching". From "the rise of the proportion of capital to labour in the economy as interest falls, there has been deduced 'demand functions' for 'capital' (*i.e.* 'saving') and for labour . . . Hence, in particular, the explanation of interest (profits) by the scarcity of 'capital' and as the reward for 'waiting'. It is hard to see how this elaborate structure can stand, when its premise is found wanting."§

* D. Levhari, 'A Nonsubstitution Theorem and Switching of Techniques', *The Quarterly Journal of Economics*, Vol. LXXIX, February 1965.
† L. Pasinetti, 'Changes in the Rate of Profit and Switches of Techniques', *Quarterly Journal of Economics*, Vol. LXXX, No. 4, 1966, pp. 503 *seq.*; P. Garegnani, 'Switching of Techniques', *Quarterly Journal of Economics*, Vol. LXXX, No. 4, November 1966, pp. 554 *seq.*   ‡ Garegnani, *ibid.*, pp. 562, 564.
§ *Ibid.*, p. 565. Professor Garegnani had earlier taken a similar general line of criticism against Böhm-Bawerk, Wicksell and Walras in his *Il capitale nelle teorie*

It may well be asked whether this alleged difficulty in the theory of capital cannot be surmounted by Professor Paul Samuelson's invention of a so-called 'Surrogate Production Function', since it was presumably advanced with this intention in mind.* The answer is that this ingenious 'parable' only shows the results claimed for it on a restrictive assumption, which *ipso facto* excludes situations where the kind of shifts in relative prices that create the phenomenon of 'reswitching' is possible. It is intriguing to find, indeed, that this implicit assumption turns out to be precisely that which in Marx's system renders 'prices of production' equal to 'values' and suffices to preclude any divergence between the two: namely 'equal compositions of capital' between industries, or uniform ratios of means of production to direct labour in all lines of production. It has again been demonstrated by Professor Garegnani, first that the curve representing all the possible relationships between the rate of interest and (maximum possible) wages for all possible techniques (called by Samuelson a 'Factor–Price Frontier') can in reality be concave as well as convex to the origin, and in case of concavity it could not be a production function of the accepted type;† secondly that the Samuelsonian production function can exist in reality only when all the individual frontiers, each relative to a particular technique, are straight lines,‡ which implies that the proportion of capital-goods to labour is the same in the relevant industries "so that the relative values" of the commodities in question "is constant as the division of the product between wages and

della distribuzione (Milano, 1960). *Cf.* the reference to "a third revolution ... initiated a few years ago by the 'Cambridge School'" and to Garegnani's demonstration of the untenability of marginal theory in Paolo Leon, *Structural Change and Growth in Capitalism* (Baltimore, 1967) pp. 4–6: "It is impossible to establish what is the technical marginal productivity of the aggregate factor capital unless it is expressed in terms of value, or at given prices."

* P. A. Samuelson, 'Parable and Realism in Capital Theory: the Surrogate Production Function', *Review of Economic Studies*, Vol. XXXIX, No. 3, June 1962, pp. 193–206; reprinted in *The Collected Papers of Paul A. Samuelson*, ed. J. E. Stiglitz (Cambridge, Mass., 1966) Vol. I, p. 325.

† Since it would depict the marginal product of capital as *rising* with a rise of capital per man.

‡ The convexity of the 'envelope' curve is implied in this stricter condition applying to the individual curves.

interest changes". His conclusion is that "Samuelson's 'surrogate production function' is thus nothing more than the production function whose existence in such an economy no critic has ever doubted."*

II

Apart from its special corollaries, what is particularly striking (some might say revolutionary) about the Sraffa-system viewed as a whole is its rehabilitation of the Ricardo–Marx approach to problems of value and of distribution from the side of production; with the consequential result that relative prices are independent of the pattern of consumption and of demand. Indeed, it was "ignoring the influence of the commodity-mix that consumers wish to have" and its "neglect of the composition of consumer demand" that puzzled Sir Roy Harrod in his review of the work, and which he considered unjustified.† We have already remarked that the failure of demand to appear as a determinant was also a characteristic of the von Neumann model; and there was similar bewilderment at this feature of the model when it first appeared. The peculiarity in this latter case was commonly, if wrongly, attributed to the fact that it was a growth-model and that all outputs were inputs, including wage-goods which were implicitly treated (as by Marx) as

---

* P. Garegnani, 'Heterogeneous Capital, the Production Function and the Theory of Distribution', *The Review of Economic Studies*, Vol. xxxvii, No. 3, July 1970, pp. 407 *seq. Cf.* also Joan Robinson and K. A. Naqvi, 'The Badly Behaved Production Function', *Quarterly Journal of Economics*, Vol. lxxxi, No. 4, 1967, pp. 579 *seq.* Professor G. C. Harcourt had this comment: "The neo-classical tradition, like the Christian, believes that profound truths can be told by way of parable. The neo-classical parables are intended to enlighten believers and non-believers concerning the forces which determine the distribution of income between profit-earners and wage-earners ... and the choice of techniques of production associated with these developments". Then referring to the Samuelsonian type of parable in the light of discussion, he concludes: "Even as parables, they must be expunged from the Bible proper ... though no doubt they will continue to be told in the commentaries and Sunday School lessons for a long time to come" (*loc. cit.*, pp. 387–8; and *cf.* more generally for a lucid summary and comment on the debate pp. 389–93).

† *The Economic Journal*, December 1961, pp. 784, 785. In the following June Mr Sraffa had a Note in the same journal to show that the criticism rested on a misunderstanding: not in the sense that demand *did* play a rôle in the Sraffa-system, but that the allegation made by Sir Roy was mistaken, to the effect that a shift in the quantities produced would affect prices in terms of Sraffa's own theory (*Economic Journal*, June 1962, pp. 477–9).

simple replacement of labour used-up in the production-process (profits being wholly ploughed-back as new investment). There was accordingly no capitalist consumption and no discriminating luxury-demand. It has been not uncommon since then for mathematical models, without these specific restrictions, to exhibit the same general characteristics of prices derived directly from conditions of production and unaffected by the pattern of consumption. Thus a year after the appearance of *Production of Commodities by Means of Commodities* a formal system was presented by an American economist which resulted in the conclusion: "We are led to conclude that price-ratios are determined by the technological conditions of production; in particular, no considerable rôle seems to be left for the 'supply and demand' considerations which are so central to the customary economic theory of price ... We emphasise once more ... that, considering the almost vanishing rôle played by consumer preference in the above analysis,* we have before us very strong presumptive evidence against the marginal utility theory (or more precisely, against its special significance)."† Later on the same writer summarised "the proper conclusion at this point" as being "that the rate of profit ρ is not successfully determined by the Walrasian theories from consideration of production coefficients, utility functions and so forth. What our analysis shows, in fact, is that the determination of the rate of profit is not purely a question of economics at all, but is rather a social–political question ... Thus an initial scepticism about classical equilibrium analysis is justified ... The Walrasian determination of this rate is questionable."‡

Already in earlier chapters,§ in connection with Dmitriev's defence of Ricardo's system, we have referred to his demonstration that profits and hence relative prices can be immediately determined once the real-wage and the conditions of

* *I.e.* of price and profit-determination.

† Jacob T. Schwartz, *Lectures on the Mathematical Method in Analytical Economics* (New York, 1961) pp. 26, 34.

‡ *Ibid.*, pp. 196–7. *Cf.* also the method and analogous results of Dr R. M. Goodwin, *Elementary Economics from the Higher Standpoint* (Cambridge, 1970) (and esp. the additional Chapter added to the French and Italian editions of that work).

§ Above, Chapters 4 and 7.

production (labour expenditures and their dating in time) are known. It was also mentioned that, while conditions of production can be expressed in terms of dated labour (thereby giving a time-pattern to production), they can also be expressed in terms of simultaneous production by means of a set of input–output equations, with labour as one of the inputs (thereby avoiding any problem of infinite regress).

This in essentials can be said to be the method adopted by Sraffa. If in the Dmitriev-equation* one were to substitute for the labour terms (the N's) the quantities of the wage-good (A) needed in the course of producing each good, one would certainly have the nucleus of the Sraffa-system. The price-equations in Chapter II of *Production of Commodities by Means of Commodities* provide for a series of products that are also inputs, some of them in the form of subsistence for workers; the price-equation for each product consisting of the sum of the various input-quantities multiplied by their several prices, with the addition of the rate of profit times that sum. These equations accordingly have this form:†

$$(A_a p_a + B_a p_b + \ldots K_a p_k) \quad (1 + r) = A p_a$$
$$(A_b p_a + B_b p_b + \ldots K_b p_k) \quad (1 + r) = B p_b$$
$$\cdot \qquad \cdot \qquad \qquad \cdot$$
$$(A_k p_a + B_k p_b + \ldots K_k p_k) \quad (1 + r) = K p_k$$

There are k equations for the k products, all of which appear both as inputs in some or other products and as outputs; and the k independent equations suffice to determine the $k-1$ price-relations and the rate of profit. These products he calls 'basics'; and it is emphasised that *only* the conditions of production of 'basics' play a part in determining prices and the rate of profit. If there are products that do *not* play a productive rôle as inputs (they are called 'non-basics' or 'luxuries'), then "these products have no part in the determination of the system. Their rôle is purely passive. If an invention were to reduce by half the quantity of the means of production which are required

---

* Above, page 117.
† Sraffa, *Production of Commodities by Means of Commodities*, p. 6.

to produce a unit of a luxury commodity of this type, the commodity itself would be halved in price, but there would be no further consequences; the price-relations of the other products and the rate of profit would remain unaffected."[*]

In a later chapter it is explained that each of the price-equations of which we have been speaking could be replaced by a series of labour-terms each with its appropriate date. This is called "Reduction to dated quantities of labour"; and the two formulations are essentially equivalent expressions for the same production-situation, looked at from different angles or in different perspectives, as it were. The reduction-equation for each commodity then consists of a series of labour-terms, each multiplied by the wage, with the addition to this of the rate of profit for the period intervening between the date of the labour-input in question and the emergence of the final product. The price-equation for product A would then have this form:

$$L_a w + L_{a_1} w (1 + r) + \ldots L_{a_n} w (1 + r)^n + \ldots = A p_a.$$

What this amounts to is that there are two main ways in which prices can be derived from production-conditions: two ways, as we have just said, that are substantially equivalent. First, prices can be derived by describing production in terms of labour expenditures per unit of output, with a time-period attached to these expenditures.[†] Secondly, they can be derived by describing the situation in terms of total commodity-inputs per unit of output; in which case *both* the rate of profit *and* the prices are simultaneously determined as resultants. In the first case the level of real-wages has to be explicitly postulated, in terms of cost in labour or of product, and in the second case this has to be included as one of the commodity-inputs. It should be added that with durable fixed capital in the picture the first alternative cannot be used without some *ex cathedra* postulation of a depreciation principle, since outputs of different

---

[*] *Ibid.*, pp. 7–8.
[†] This latter is, of course, necessary since the *rate* of profit is involved in price-determination.

time-periods, or dates, are *joint products* of the durable equipment in question.*

The fact that the level of wages has to be independently postulated as a *datum* in this mode of price-determination ("regarded as consisting of specified necessities determined by physiological or social conditions which are independent of prices or the rate of profits")† means that we are back at the methodology and approach of the (truly) classical system. No attempt is made to derive a theory of distribution from *within* the circle of exchange; and in the abandonment of this attempt we witness a reversion to the pre-Jevonian order or pattern of determination: prices are derived from (or in part dependent upon) conditions of distribution rather than distribution being derived from the structure of prices treated as being in turn a resultant of demand. True, when handling an equational system, one is dealing with a case of mutual determination; but this, as we have seen, does not negate or exclude direction-pointers to the determination in any substantial theory; and what is of substantial importance here is that among the given conditions of the problem, or postulated data, a *social datum* is introduced from *outside* (or, as some might prefer to express it, *beneath*) the market process.‡ Thus the boundaries of economics as a subject are *ipso facto* drawn differently and more widely: they are drawn so as to include social, and moreover institutional and historically-relative, changing and changeable, conditions that were excluded from Economics as viewed in the post-Jevonian tradition. The ideological implications of such a difference are evidently extensive and quite crucial; and we have already commented on them in an earlier chapter.

It is in this light that we should, I believe, view an aspect of

---

* It is for this reason – that he needs in the case of fixed capital to deduce a consequential depreciation principle for the system of determination to be complete – that Mr Sraffa adopts the former of the two ways of deriving prices. Without fixed capital (*i.e.* in the pure 'working capital' case) the two methods can be used indifferently and can be used as equivalent alternatives.

† *Ibid.*, p. 33.

‡ *Cf. ibid.*: "The rate of profit, as a ratio, has a significance which is independent of any prices, and can well be 'given' before prices are fixed. It is accordingly susceptible of being determined from outside the system of production . . ."

Sraffa's system – or perhaps one should say of his mode of exposition of it – that some readers appear to find puzzling. Initially labour is treated on a par with material inputs, valued *qua* input at a subsistence wage, "on the same footing as the fuel for engines or feed for cattle". Surplus then has the same significance as Marx's surplus-value or Ricardian net revenue. Afterwards, to allow for the possibility that wages "may include a share of the surplus product", he adopts the device of "treating the whole wage as variable", excluding it from among the inputs and treating wage-goods consequentially not as 'basics' but as 'non-basics'. Net income then conforms to the conventional definition of national income as including *both* wages *and* profits. The wage, however, is still explicitly stated in the equations of price-determination, being introduced there along with the quantities of labour used in the various industries (instead of appearing in the guise of inputs of necessary subsistence). Actually this change is made for reasons of formal convenience, as making it easier to define maximum profit for purpose of the Standard Commodity and demonstrating the effect of a changing wage–profit ratio upon relative prices; and nothing in principle is involved in the change. (As he himself says, translation of things into "the more appropriate, if unconventional, interpretation of the wage" can easily be made at the cost of some additional circumlocution.) But it could be regarded as a device for handling situations in which collective bargaining had grown to be a significant influence in the labour market and trade unions were able to encroach upon surplus-value in the interest of higher wages. If one were to seek a Marxian analogy, it might be this. Marx's concept of the value of labour-power could be regarded as being within the context of 'pure' Capitalism, with labour-power sold competitively by individual bidding. Collective bargaining, as soon as it developed, introduced a new element into the situation; and as a result the price of labour-power need no longer correspond with its value but could rise at the expense of surplus-value. For theoretical purposes one will now have to adopt as *datum* the degree and market-influence of labour-organisation, since this determines how much of what in the 'pure' case was surplus-value is now included in the wage.*

A central place is occupied in the Sraffa system by a concept that is devised to solve what we have seen to have been a crucial (and unsolved) problem for Ricardo: that of finding an 'invariable standard', or measure of value, which will be invariable to changes in the ratio of profit to wages. Ricardo sought this in Labour as his Absolute Value; but found that there were difficulties in using this *simpliste*, to the extent that the proportions of capital (Marx's 'organic composition of capital') differed as between industries. Sraffa's unique contribution has been to solve this problem by means of his so-called 'Standard Commodity':† namely by selecting (hypothetically) a commodity, or set of commodities, that have the required properties, so that if this were to be selected as money, or as *numéraire*, measurement in terms of it would be invariant to distribution-shifts in two crucial respects. First, if wages are defined in terms of it, there is a linear relationship between changes in wages and resulting (and inverse) changes in profit. This is, indeed, the case whether profit is expressed in terms of the standard system or alternatively in terms of the actual system. Secondly, and consequentially, "the ratio of the net product to the means of production would remain the same whatever variations occurred in the division of the net product between wages and profits".‡

In loose and popular language this standard measure consists of a commodity produced under some kind of average-type conditions of production. But what *kind* of average? On close inspection definition of such a type is less simple than at first might appear for reasons with which practitioners of input–output analysis are familiar. If one were to look for an actual individual commodity, the qualities it would need to possess for the purpose are explained as follows:

---

* See below Note to Section II of Chapter 9.
† It may be noted that this is described as "a purely auxiliary construction". "It should therefore be possible to present the essential elements of the mechanism under consideration without having recourse to it." (*ibid.*, p. 31.)
‡ *Ibid.*, p. 21.

The key to the movement of relative prices consequent upon a change in the wage lies in the inequality of proportions in which labour and means of production are employed in the various industries. It is clear that if the proportion were the same in all industries no price-changes could ensue, however great was the diversity of the commodity-composition of the means of production in different industries. For in each industry an equal deduction from the wages would yield just as much as was required for paying the profits on its means of production at a uniform rate without need to disturb the existing prices.*

What one accordingly needs to look for is a "critical proportion" of labour to means of production, such that, *if* it were possible to find a commodity that was produced with this proportion, its price would be invariant to a change in wages, since any wage-change yielded just that addition to, or subtraction from, profit as was needed to yield the new uniform rate of profit. This 'critical proportion', be it noted, would need to apply to each 'layer' in its vertical chain of production: to the production of the means of production themselves *and* to that of the means of production in turn used to produce the former, and so on.

Definition of this crucial proportion is then reduced to two alternative " 'pure' ratios between homogeneous quantities . . . namely the quantity-ratio of direct to indirect labour employed, and the value-ratio of net product to means of production". A standard "composite commodity" is then defined as a set so chosen from existing ones that "the various commodities are represented among its aggregate means of production *in the same proportions* as they are among its products"; or alternatively a set of commodities arranged "in such proportions that the commodity composition of the aggregate means of production and that of the aggregate product are identical".† Reflection should make clear that the ratio of net product, or surplus, to

* *Ibid.*, pp. 12–13.   † *Ibid.*, pp. 16–17, 26.

means of production, or inputs, of this system has a unique meaning – a meaning capable of expression in product-terms as much as in Ricardo's simple product-case of Corn as both input and output.

The relation between this and Ricardo's 'Absolute Value'* is then most ingeniously shown by taking a quantity of labour as an alternative but equivalent standard. "A more tangible measure for prices of commodities . . . is 'the quantity of labour that can be purchased by the Standard net product'." This quantity is given "as soon as we have fixed the rate of profits, and without need of knowing the prices of commodities, a parity is established between the Standard net product and a quantity of labour which depends only on the rate of profits; and the resulting prices of commodities indifferently regarded as being expressed either in the Standard net product or in the quantity of labour which at the given level of the rate of profits is known to be equivalent to it". As wages change, and with them (inversely) profits, this quantity of labour serving as standard likewise changes. The conclusion is that "all the properties of 'an invariable standard of value' . . . are found in a variable quantity of labour, which, however, varies according to a simple rule which is independent of prices". This quantity of labour serving as a unit of measurement "increases in magnitude with the fall of the wage, that is to say with the rise of the rate of profits, so that, from being equal to the annual labour of the system when the rate of profit is zero, it increases without limit as the rate of profit approaches its maximum value".†

Thus what was conceived to be a central problem of classical political economy in Ricardo's day has been solved a century and a half later. In the absence of a solution there could be no way of distinguishing in the case "of any particular price

* But also, and curiously, with Malthus's measure, 'Labour commanded'.
† *Ibid.*, p. 32. The quantity of labour in question varies as the equation

$$\frac{1}{w} = \frac{R'}{R'-r},$$

where R' is the maximum possible rate of profit (when the wage is zero) and r the actual rate.

fluctuation whether it arises from the peculiarities of the commodity which is being measured or from those of the measuring standard".* But there is a reflection occasioned by this signal achievement that may appear to many as of even more general interest than the details of the solution itself. This is that for so long this problem should have been entirely misconceived, even to the extent of denying its existence as a real problem, and the reason for this misconception and neglect. The reason evidently was the same as for blindness to the possibility of 'reswitching' of productive methods: the inability of post-Ricardian economists to appreciate the dependence of the price-structure on distribution, in their preoccupation (at any rate since Jevons and the Austrians) with the converse dependence of distribution upon a demand-determined price-structure. In this we seem to have yet further illustration (if it be needed) of the bias imparted to thought by the given conceptual framework of one's subject, whether this is inherited or acquired – a framework or 'picture' which at the outset we suggested was ideologically permeated if not prompted and inspired.

What the sequel to all this will be it is too early to say with any assurance; and to remain silent is better than to indulge in speculation that is lacking in sure foundation. But whatever the future course of discussion and analysis, little but clarification can result from the animated critique of the past decade, whether its main significance is destined to be primarily negation and overcoming or mediation and transcendence in some novel synthesis. Whatever the particular outcome, one can say that the discussion of the 1960s was manifestly a turning-point. If only because what had been widely accepted as an orthodoxy of the textbooks has been shaken, and an older, discarded tradition revived, nothing can ever be quite the same again as it was before.

* *Ibid.*, p. 18.

NOTE TO §11 OF CHAPTER NINE

Some reference should perhaps be made in conclusion (virtually as a footnote to what has been said) to something that may well have sprung to mind in the course of reading the previous section. Some may deem it sufficient to say simply that a postulate as to the level of real wages (or alternatively the ratio of surplus to wages) is introduced 'from outside' as a sociological datum (dependent, *e.g.* on the state of class relations existing at a given time and place). Others, however, may feel some impatience with this, even to the point of regarding it as question-begging, and may sense a need to 'close the model' by introducing some more explicit explanation of the forces that determine the division of the total product between profit (or property-income) and wages. While it may have been legitimate at an early stage of capitalism to accept that wages were governed competitively by something akin to Marx's 'value of labour-power', and surplus accordingly treated as a residual, does not such an approach (which certainly had the merit of including labour-power, and hence wages, within the circle of value-relations) lose its relevance as soon as capitalism develops beyond its earlier competitive stage? Does it not lose both relevance and plausibility in a stage of monopoly-capitalism, with monopolistic (or oligopolistic) firms endowed with the power to pass on a wage-rise into prices and to enforce something like a minimum profit-margin or surplus-ratio? Some might feel inclined to maintain that in such circumstances real wages are determined as the residual rather than profits.

A complaint of this kind would seem to have inspired a recent statement by Dr Nuti about "the relation between the real wage rate and the profit rate uncovered by Sraffa and before him by the Russian economist Dmitriev". This, he observes, "provides scope for the concept of class struggle in the determination of relative shares". But he goes on to say: "unfortunately, however, there is no simple way of closing his system, *i.e.* of determining which point of the wage–profit relation is actually reached and how in any economy"; and this for two reasons. First, "the real wage-rate cannot be taken as exogenously determined as in the classical thought, fixed at a subsistence level in conditions of elastic labour supply". Secondly, "it cannot be determined *directly* by the class struggle . . . because after Keynes we have to recognise that wage bargaining determines *money* wages, while the real wage rate is determined by the behaviour of the price-level".* This latter is a cogent objection, and, in conjunction with the former, might incline one to think that under modern capitalism, with its high degree of concentration and monopoly, one may well need to look, in explaining distribution, towards factors that set a minimum to profit, rather than as formerly a minimum to wages. Otherwise (it may well be asked) do not critics of the orthodox theory of distribution place themselves in as vulnerable a position as those they criticise and seek to dethrone?

We have seen that Kalecki provided an explanation of distribution of this very type, and with the situation of modern capitalism evidently in mind. According to this the share of profits in (gross) output was determined by the degree of monopoly, which gave the firm or *entrepreneur* the *power* to exact a mark-up on prime cost by price-raising.† Whatever the level of money-wages, the ratio of prices to it (and hence the real-wage and profit-margin) will be dependent upon the price-raising power with which firms are endowed – something that varies in inverse relation to the amount of effective competition.

---

* D. M. Nuti, 'Vulgar Economy in the Theory of Income Distribution', *Science and Society* (New York) Vol. xxxv, No. 1, Spring 1971, p. 32 (being a paper presented to the first Conference of Socialist Economists in London in January 1970).

† If one could imagine all firms vertically integrated so as to include the production of all non-labour inputs, this would be equivalent to a mark-up on wage-cost. In so far as firms also possess a degree of monopoly in the labour market as buyers, they are able to exert a downward pressure on money-wages: to this extent the mark-up is not wholly accounted for by price-raising.

By such means, it would seem, capitalism has acquired the power to negate the growing influence of trade unionism over money-wages, and the ability to tolerate conditions in which the industrial reserve army can no longer play its former 'stabilising' rôle.

There are some formal difficulties about this theory as to how the degree of monopoly is to be appropriately defined. Kalecki himself interpreted this in terms of the inelasticity of the demand curve (and hence the ratio of average demand-price to marginal revenue and to marginal and average cost). But how is this to be transferred from the level of a particular product to the macroscopic level of the economy as a whole; and what real content does the notion have if the transfer can be satisfactorily achieved?* A more substantial difficulty is that by implication the mark-up would be zero under conditions of perfect competition. If surplus-value is *solely* the creation of monopoly, its emergence under the 'normal' competitive conditions envisaged by the classical economists and by Marx would seem to be denied. This objection would not be a serious one if the theory were clearly labelled as one appropriate to monopoly capitalism *per se*; an alternative explanation of surplus-value being admittedly appropriate to an earlier, competitive stage of the system, in conditions of a reserve of labour and elastic labour supply.†

Alternatively, and with a somewhat different emphasis, one might say that, while the classical Marxian explanation for the emergence of surplus-value continues to apply to

---

* Kalecki suggested that this could simply be done by taking a weighted average of the gross margins established in the several industries (by the inelasticity of their various demand-curves and by the state of oligopoly in them), "using as weights the respective value of sales" (*Studies in Economic Dynamics* (London, 1943) p. 11). A difficulty here is that when oligopoly is introduced, one has to deal with what has been called an 'imagined demand-curve'.

† Prof. Kalecki's own answer to this kind of objection was that 'perfect competition' constitutes "a most unrealistic assumption not only for the present phase of capitalism but even for the so called competitive capitalist economy of past centuries: surely this competition was always very imperfect. Perfect competition when its actual status as a handy model is forgotten becomes a dangerous myth" (*Selected Essays on the Dynamics of the Capitalist Economy* (Cambridge, 1971) p. 158).

modern capitalism, as to its earlier stage, the influence of monopoly enters in as an additive element in the stage of monopoly capitalism – an influence reminiscent of forms of exploitation characteristic of pre-capitalist stages of development.

An analogous difficulty applies to the post-Keynesian theory, according to which the share of profit in national income is dependent on the growth-rate of the economy together with the saving (or alternatively spending) propensity of capitalists. The implication of this would seem to be that in static conditions with zero-capital accumulation (Marx's 'simple reproduction') profits could be zero. This, however, could only be the case if capitalists persistently refused not only to invest but also to spend their (potential) incomes: surplus-value would then fail to accrue simply because it could not be 'realised', even though conditions favourable to its 'creation' were in existence. To this as a theory of income-distribution Dr Nuti has, again, raised the neat and persuasive objection that the postulated relationship "is a *necessary* relation that must *always* hold for macroeconomic equilibrium among *ex post* magnitudes. As such it cannot be disproved, and therefore, it does not provide a *theory* of the determination of the profit-rate and income shares, especially in the short run".* At any rate the theory when interpreted as a necessary relationship *ex post* bears little relation to *ex ante* magnitudes, to which reference is presumably made when 'propensities' are referred to as determinants.†

Yet another plausible hypothesis is that a minimum rate

---

* Nuti, *Science and Society*, p. 33. The version of Professor Kaldor's theory that appeared in 'Alternative Theories of Distribution' (*Review of Economic Studies*, 1955–6, No. 2) is, however, exempted from this criticism, since it contains a mechanism (namely appropriate adaptations of the price-level) whereby the adjustment of profit is achieved. But this implies that wage-earners are passive in face of a change in the price-level and that investment-plans are likewise unaffected.

† For one thing, a 'propensity to consume' when aggregated for a class implies a certain income and income-distribution; and these latter may well change between the initial situation (with its expectations on which propensities are based) and the final result (*i.e. ex post*).

of profit is somehow fixed by some kind of quasi-political
or institutional decision-mechanism. This is a plausible
interpretation, perhaps, of a tentative hint given by Mr
Sraffa when he suggests that in his system the rate of
profit, rather than the real-wage, could be postulated as
the independent variable: the former is "susceptible of
being determined from outside the system of production,
in particular by the level of the money rates of interest".*
The latter would presumably be fixed, in the main, by
the Central Bank, whether acting on its own initiative or
as an instrument of governmental monetary policy. If
one is inclined to view State policy as an instrument or
reflection of class interest, or of powerful pressure-groups
within the ruling class, one will tend to regard monetary
policy as a way of enforcing (more or less consciously),†
on behalf of capital-owners as a whole, such a profit-share
in the proceeds of production as existing circumstances
permit. True, they may at times decide to *lower*
interest-rates in pursuit of a 'cheap money policy', as in
time of war or of economic depression, or under the
influence of international economic relations.‡ (At times
of excess capacity, for example, it may well be in the
collective interest of profit-receivers to lower interest and
profit-rates if thereby investment-expenditure and hence
capacity-working can be augmented.) But the very fact
that the idea of a 'normal' long-term rate is so stubbornly
long-lived, apparently, even in disturbed times, lends support
to the notion that the conventional upshot of banking policy
is to set a substantial minimum to the profit share.§

Finally, before leaving such questions mention should no
doubt be made of a difficulty that some feel about
postulating real wages as an independent variable if this

* Sraffa, *Production of Commodities by Means of Commodities*, p. 33.
† To some extent, perhaps, *un*consciously and influenced by what has become
traditional.
‡ *E.g.*, excessive accumulation of reserves of gold or of foreign currencies.
§ As does also the apparent constancy of the share of profit in total income, on
which Kalecki especially laid stress in expounding his monopoly-theory.

is done (as by Marx) in value terms (*i.e.* of labour) or in terms of Sraffa's Standard Commodity. In the former case objection is made that wage-goods are not, in fact, bought by workers at their values but at their prices of production;* in the latter case it is objected that the actual consumption of workers will probably not consist of the Standard Commodity but of a quite different assortment of goods. In either case substantial content is lost from the postulate. This difficulty, however, would seem to be more apparent than real provided one is willing to accept the notion of a given standard of living as consisting of a variety of assortments of wage goods that are considered as equivalent by a typical worker's household, and to interpret 'a given level of real wages' in this sense. Then a definition in terms of one member of an equivalent set (whether in terms of labour necessary to produce it or of Standard Commodity) will retain its meaning when translated into another member of the same set of equivalents.

One can only conclude, at the time of writing, that such alternative explanations of distribution in our twentieth-century world are *sub judice* in current economic discussion, and that discussion (or even elaboration) of them has proceeded insufficiently far as yet to make final judgement possible, still less to speak of a *consensus*. Unsatisfactory this may be as a concluding note; nonetheless it would appear unavoidable. At least it may be an indication that political economy is not a closed text and that it remains open to the creative moulding of controversy with which its past is so richly endowed. Indeed, this is probably more true to-day than it was half a century ago when Keynes could write of "the general principles of thought which economists now apply to economic problems" as though these were an agreed corpus of theory.†

---

* *Cf.* Arghiri Emmanuel, *Unequal Exchange*, trans. from the French by Brian Pearce (London, 1972) App. v, esp. pp. 397, 407.

† In his Editor's Introduction to the early works in the Cambridge Economic Handbook Series – although he was to add that "even on matters of principle there is not yet complete unanimity of opinion".

INDEX

Abstinence, 104–5, 110, 129, 130, 170 n., 176

Abstraction
two main contrasted modes of, 25
degree of, appropriate to macroscopic scale of analysis, 150
different levels of, 210

Academy (1872)
Marshall's review of Jevons, 185

'Acceleration Principle', 226

Accumulation, of Capital
its effect on wages, 51
and profit, 73
does not invalidate labour principle of value (Ricardo), 78
results of, on society, 87–8
possibilities of improvement as a result of (Ricardo), 88
and 'gluts' (Malthus), 92 *seq.*
outstripping population, possibility of, 94–5
and Lauderdale, 95, 96–7
industry (and population) limited by, 132
and approach of stationary state (J. S. Mill), 135
and outrunning supply of labour-power (Marx), 158

Acta Œconomica, 15 n., 231 n.

Activity, social
and ideas, 17–18

'Adding-up Problem', 194 and n.

Advertising
effect of a. and selling expenditures, 212

Afanaseyev, V., 29 n.

Aggregation, illicit
of optimum condition applied to separate individuals into condition applied to society as a whole, 243–4

Allocation, 174, 177, 180

American Economic Review, 213 n., 228

Analysis (formal), *see* Economic A.

Anarchism, 139, 140 and n.

Approximation
Marx's Vol. I as, 147–8 and n.

Atomism, 168

Auspitz, Rudolf, 213

Austrian School
its chief figures, 167, 189 *seq.*
can its theory of value be reconciled with that of Ricardo and Marx?, 11 and n.
'imputation' as theory of distribution, 191
and derivation of distribution from exchange, 33–5, 170
preoccupation with criticism of socialist doctrine, 193
awareness of Marx, 167
theory of capital, 197 *seq.*
Wicksell defends, 200–1
Walras on similarity of to himself, 203 n.
'causal-genetic' approach of, 210
modern criticism of, 201–2, 247–8
preoccupation with dependence of distribution on demand-determined price-structure, 266
See: Menger, Böhm-Bawerk, Wieser

Aveling, Edward, *see* Moore and A.

Aveling, Eleanor, 147 n., 152 n.

Bagehot, Walter, 22, 121

Bailey, Samuel
on Ricardo's 'perversion of terms', 85–6 n.
attacks Malthus as well as Ricardo, 98 n.
his *Critical Dissertation*, attacking Ricardo on 'absolute value', 99–100, 101–2
on monopoly, 100–1
his part in 'the retreat from Ricardo', 111

Banking policy
Ricardo on, 22, 67